Security Management in Mobile Cloud Computing

Kashif Munir
University of Hafr Al-Batin, Saudi Arabia

A volume in the Advances in
Information Security, Privacy,
and Ethics (AISPE) Book Series

www.igi-global.com

Published in the United States of America by
   IGI Global
   Information Science Reference (an imprint of IGI Global)
   701 E. Chocolate Avenue
   Hershey PA 17033
   Tel: 717-533-8845
   Fax: 717-533-8661
   E-mail: cust@igi-global.com
   Web site: http://www.igi-global.com

                    Library of Congress Cataloging-in-Publication Data

Names: Munir, Kashif, 1976- editor.
Title: Security management in mobile cloud computing / Kashif Munir, editor.
Description: Hershey, PA : Information Science Reference, [2017] | Includes
   bibliographical references and index.
Identifiers: LCCN 2016017812| ISBN 9781522506027 (hardcover) | ISBN
   9781522506034 (ebook)
Subjects: LCSH: Cloud computing--Security measures. | Mobile
   computing--Security measures. | Computer networks--Security measures.
Classification: LCC QA76.585 .S444 2017 | DDC 005.8--dc23 LC record available at https://lccn.
loc.gov/2016017812

This book is published in the IGI Global book series Advances in Information Security, Privacy,
and Ethics (AISPE) (ISSN: 1948-9730; eISSN: 1948-9749)

British Cataloguing in Publication Data
A Cataloguing in Publication record for this book is available from the British Library.

Advances in Information Security, Privacy, and Ethics (AISPE) Book Series

ISSN: 1948-9730
EISSN: 1948-9749

MISSION

As digital technologies become more pervasive in everyday life and the Internet is utilized in ever increasing ways by both private and public entities, concern over digital threats becomes more prevalent.

The **Advances in Information Security, Privacy, & Ethics (AISPE) Book Series** provides cutting-edge research on the protection and misuse of information and technology across various industries and settings. Comprised of scholarly research on topics such as identity management, cryptography, system security, authentication, and data protection, this book series is ideal for reference by IT professionals, academicians, and upper-level students.

COVERAGE

- CIA Triad of Information Security
- Privacy Issues of Social Networking
- Global Privacy Concerns
- Tracking Cookies
- Internet Governance
- Device Fingerprinting
- Cyberethics
- Telecommunications Regulations
- Access Control
- Security Classifications

IGI Global is currently accepting manuscripts for publication within this series. To submit a proposal for a volume in this series, please contact our Acquisition Editors at Acquisitions@igi-global.com or visit: http://www.igi-global.com/publish/.

The Advances in Information Security, Privacy, and Ethics (AISPE) Book Series (ISSN 1948-9730) is published by IGI Global, 701 E. Chocolate Avenue, Hershey, PA 17033-1240, USA, www.igi-global.com. This series is composed of titles available for purchase individually; each title is edited to be contextually exclusive from any other title within the series. For pricing and ordering information please visit http://www.igi-global.com/book-series/advances-information-security-privacy-ethics/37157. Postmaster: Send all address changes to above address. Copyright © 2017 IGI Global. All rights, including translation in other languages reserved by the publisher. No part of this series may be reproduced or used in any form or by any means – graphics, electronic, or mechanical, including photocopying, recording, taping, or information and retrieval systems – without written permission from the publisher, except for non commercial, educational use, including classroom teaching purposes. The views expressed in this series are those of the authors, but not necessarily of IGI Global.

Titles in this Series

For a list of additional titles in this series, please visit: www.igi-global.com

Cryptographic Solutions for Secure Online Banking and Commerce
Kannan Balasubramanian (Mepco Schlenk Engineering College, India) K. Mala (Mepco Schlenk Engineering College, India) and M. Rajakani (Mepco Schlenk Engineering College, India)
Information Science Reference • copyright 2016 • 375pp • H/C (ISBN: 9781522502739) • US $200.00 (our price)

Handbook of Research on Modern Cryptographic Solutions for Computer and Cyber Security
Brij Gupta (National Institute of Technology Kurukshetra, India) Dharma P. Agrawal (University of Cincinnati, USA) and Shingo Yamaguchi (Yamaguchi University, Japan)
Information Science Reference • copyright 2016 • 589pp • H/C (ISBN: 9781522501053) • US $305.00 (our price)

Innovative Solutions for Access Control Management
Ahmad Kamran Malik (COMSATS Institute of Information Technology, Pakistan) Adeel Anjum (COMSATS Institute of Information Technology, Pakistan) and Basit Raza (COMSATS Institute of Information Technology, Pakistan)
Information Science Reference • copyright 2016 • 330pp • H/C (ISBN: 9781522504481) • US $195.00 (our price)

Network Security Attacks and Countermeasures
Dileep Kumar G. (Adama Science and Technology University, Ethiopia) Manoj Kumar Singh (Adama Science and Technology University, Ethiopia) and M.K. Jayanthi (King Khalid University, Saudi Arabia)
Information Science Reference • copyright 2016 • 357pp • H/C (ISBN: 9781466687615) • US $205.00 (our price)

Next Generation Wireless Network Security and Privacy
Kamaljit I. Lakhtaria (Gujarat University, India)
Information Science Reference • copyright 2015 • 372pp • H/C (ISBN: 9781466686878) • US $205.00 (our price)

Improving Information Security Practices through Computational Intelligence
Wasan Shaker Awad (Ahlia University, Bahrain) El Sayed M. El-Alfy (King Fahd University of Petroleum and Minerals, Saudi Arabia) and Yousif Al-Bastaki (University of Bahrain, Bahrain)
Information Science Reference • copyright 2016 • 327pp • H/C (ISBN: 9781466694262) • US $210.00 (our price)

www.igi-global.com

701 E. Chocolate Ave., Hershey, PA 17033
Order online at www.igi-global.com or call 717-533-8845 x100
To place a standing order for titles released in this series,
contact: cust@igi-global.com
Mon-Fri 8:00 am - 5:00 pm (est) or fax 24 hours a day 717-533-8661

Editorial Advisory Board

Table of Contents

Foreword xiii

Preface xv

Chapter 1
(SET) Smart Energy Management and Throughput Maximization: A New
Routing Protocol for WSNs 1
Hassan El Alami, INPT – Rabat, Morocco
Abdellah Najid, INPT – Rabat, Morocco

Chapter 2
A Cloud Intrusion Detection Based on Classification of Activities and Mobile
Agent...29
Nadya El Moussaid, Ibn Zohr University, Morocco
Ahmed Toumanari, Ibn Zohr University, Morocco

Chapter 3
Considering Middle Circles in Mobile Cloud Computing: Ethics and Risk
Governance 43
Mohammad Ali Shalan, University of Jordan, Jordan

Chapter 4
Managing Risk in Cloud Computing 73
Lawan Ahmed Mohammed, University of Hafr Albatin, Saudi Arabia

Chapter 5
On the Role of Game Theory in Modelling Incentives and Interactions in
Mobile Distributed Systems...92
Mohammed Onimisi Yahaya, University of Hafr Albatin, Saudi Arabia

Chapter 6

Security and Privacy Issues, Solutions, and Tools for MCC 121
  Darshan M. Tank, Gujarat Technological University, India

Chapter 7

Security Management in Mobile Cloud Computing: Security and Privacy
Issues and Solutions in Mobile Cloud Computing 148
  Basudeo Singh, R. V. College of Engineering, India
  Jasmine K.S., R. V. College of Engineering, India

Chapter 8

Security Model for Mobile Cloud Database as a Service (DBaaS) 169
  Kashif Munir, University of Hafr Al-Batin, Saudi Arabia

Related References 181

Compilation of References 223

About the Contributors 243

Index 246

Detailed Table of Contents

Foreword xiii

Preface xv

Chapter 1
(SET) Smart Energy Management and Throughput Maximization: A New
Routing Protocol for WSNs 1

Hassan El Alami, INPT – Rabat, Morocco
Abdellah Najid, INPT – Rabat, Morocco

Energy efficiency and throughput are critical factors in the design routing protocols of WSNs. Many routing protocols based on clustering algorithm have been proposed. Current clustering algorithms often use cluster head selection and cluster formation to reduce energy consumption and maximize throughput in WSNs. In this chapter, the authors present a new routing protocol based on smart energy management and throughput maximization for clustered WSNs. The main objective of this protocol is to solve the constraint of closest sensors to the base station which consume relatively more energy in sensed information traffics, and also decrease workload on CHs. This approach divides network field into free area which contains the closest sensors to the base station that communicate directly with, and clustered area which contains the sensors that transmit data to the base station through cluster head. So due to the sensors that communicate directly to the base station, the load on cluster heads is decreased. Thus, the cluster heads consume less energy causing the increase of network lifetime.

Chapter 2
A Cloud Intrusion Detection Based on Classification of Activities and Mobile
Agent 29

Nadya El Moussaid, Ibn Zohr University, Morocco
Ahmed Toumanari, Ibn Zohr University, Morocco

Cloud computing becomes the technology trend that attracts more and more both of the different forms of companies and attackers, for the reason that cloud computing provides a sharing pool of configured computing resources, such as servers, networks, applications, storage, and services, to end users. Therefore, securing sensitive data of companies from threats and attacks performed by internal or external attackers is a necessary requirement and exigency. For that purpose, in this paper presents an intrusion detection system that is based on mobile agent to collect and analysis gathered data from several virtual machines, in order to benefit from the advantages of mobile agents. The authors of this chapter propose to use C4.5 algorithm which is one of tree decision algorithms that classify data into normal and malicious one. The main purpose of our solution is creating a model of normal and abnormal behaviour.

Chapter 3
Considering Middle Circles in Mobile Cloud Computing: Ethics and Risk
Governance 43

Mohammad Ali Shalan, University of Jordan, Jordan

Mobile Cloud Computing (MCC) is increasingly asserted as the technology with the potential to change the way internet and information systems are being utilized into business enterprises. It is rapidly changing the landscape of technology, and ultimately turning the long-held promise of utility computing into a reality. Nevertheless, utilizing MCC is never a trivial task, thus calling for a special approach to get the benefits, reduce risks and control operations. The main objective of this chapter is to provide some specific guidelines to provide governance directions to align MCC into enterprise strategy and reduce risks resulted from utilizing middle circle providers; In this context, this chapter also promote and discuss some ethics that help client enterprises and MCC providers understand roles and obligations in an ever changing environment.

Chapter 4

Managing Risk in Cloud Computing 73
Lawan Ahmed Mohammed, University of Hafr Albatin, Saudi Arabia

Computer crime is now becoming a major international problem, with continual increases in incidents of cracking, hacking, viruses, worms, bacteria and the like having been reported in recent years. As a result of this massive vulnerabilities and new intrusion techniques, the rate of cybercrime has accelerated beyond imagination. In recent years, cloud computing have become ubiquitous, permeating every aspect of our personal and professional lives. Governments and enterprises are now adopting cloud technologies for numerous applications to increase their operational efficiency, improve their responsiveness and competitiveness. It is therefore vital to find ways of reducing and controlling the risk associated with such activities especially in cloud computing environment. However, there is no perfect-safe way to protect against all cyber attacks, hence, there is need for a proper recovery planning in the event of disaster resulting from these attacks. In this chapter, several means of limiting vulnerabilities and minimizing damages to information systems are discussed.

Chapter 5

On the Role of Game Theory in Modelling Incentives and Interactions in
Mobile Distributed Systems 92
Mohammed Onimisi Yahaya, University of Hafr Albatin, Saudi Arabia

Advances in wireless networking has led to a new paradigm of Mobile Distributed Systems (MDS), where data, devices and software are mobile. Peer-to-Peer (P2P) networks is a form of distributed system in which sharing of resources has some similarities to our traditional market in terms of goods and relationship. Game theory provides a mathematical framework for understanding the complexity of interdependent decision makers with similar or conflicting objectives. Games could be characterized by number of players who interact, possibly threaten each other and form coalitions, take actions under uncertain conditions. The players receive some reward or possibly some punishment or monetary loss. Our primary objective is to provide an insight into the role and suitability of game theory in the study of Economics of P2P systems. In order to achieve this objectives, we investigate different classes of game theory, review and analyze their use in the modelling of P2P system.

Chapter 6

Security and Privacy Issues, Solutions, and Tools for MCC 121
Darshan M. Tank, Gujarat Technological University, India

With the development of cloud computing and mobility, mobile cloud computing has emerged and become a focus of research. Mobile Cloud Computing (MCC) integrates mobile computing and cloud computing aiming to extend mobile devices capabilities. By the means of on-demand self-service and extendibility, it can offer the infrastructure, platform, and software services in a cloud to mobile users through the mobile network. There is huge market for mobile based e-Commerce applications across the globe. Security and privacy are the key issues for mobile cloud computing applications. The limited processing power and memory of a mobile device dependent on inherently unreliable wireless channel for communication and battery for power leaves little scope for a reliable security layer. Thus there is a need for a lightweight secure framework that provides security with minimum communication and processing overhead on mobile devices. The security and privacy protection services can be achieved with the help of secure mobile-cloud application services.

Chapter 7

Security Management in Mobile Cloud Computing: Security and Privacy Issues and Solutions in Mobile Cloud Computing 148
Basudeo Singh, R. V. College of Engineering, India
Jasmine K.S., R. V. College of Engineering, India

Mobile cloud computing is a technique or model in which mobile applications are built, powered and hosted using cloud computing technology. In Mobile Cloud computing we can store information regarding sender, data and receiver on cloud through mobile application. As we store more and more information on cloud by client, security issue will arise. This chapter presents a review on the mobile cloud computing concepts as well as security issues and vulnerabilities affecting Cloud Systems and the possible solutions available to such issues within the context of cloud computing. It also describes the pros and cons of the existing security strategy and also introduces the existing issues in cloud computing such as data integrity, data segregation, and security.

Chapter 8

Security Model for Mobile Cloud Database as a Service (DBaaS)................... 169
Kashif Munir, University of Hafr Al-Batin, Saudi Arabia

There's a big change happening in the world of databases. The industry is buzzing about Database-as-a-Service (DBaaS), a cloud offering that allows companies to rent access to these managed digital data warehouses. Database-as-a-service (DBaaS) is a cloud computing service model that provides users with some form of access to a database without the need for setting up physical hardware, installing software or configuring for performance. Since consumers host data on the Mobile Cloud, DBaaS providers should be able to guarantee data owners that their data would be protected from all potential security threats. Protecting application data for large-scale web and mobile apps can be complex; especially with distributed and NoSQL databases. Data centers are no longer confined to the enterprise perimeter. More and more enterprises take their data to the Mobile Cloud, but forget to adjust their security management practices when doing so. Unauthorized access to data resources, misuse of data stored on third party platform, data confidentiality, integrity and availability are some of the major security challenges that ail this nascent Cloud service model, which hinders the wide-scale adoption of DBaaS. In this chapter, I propose a security model for Mobile Cloud Database as a Service (DBaaS). A user can change his/her password, whenever demanded. Furthermore, security analysis realizes the feasibility of the proposed model for DBaaS and achieves efficiency. This will help Cloud community to get an insight into state-of-the-art progress in terms of secure strategies, their deficiencies and possible future directions.

Related References 181

Compilation of References 223

About the Contributors 243

Index 246

Foreword

The number of mobile device users and mobile apps available for these users are increasing dramatically. According to the International Telecommunication Union (ITU, 2016), by the end of 2015, there were more than 7 billion mobile cellular subscriptions, corresponding to a penetration rate of 97%, up from 738 million in 2000. Cisco (2016), reports that global mobile data traffic grew 74 percent in 2015 and has grown 4,000-fold over the past 10 years and almost 400-million-fold over the past 15 years. Most of these mobile device users and their mobile network operators are connected to cloud computing service providers to offer rich computational and Internet resources, which is Mobile Cloud Computing (MCC).

As we move from traditional desktop/laptop computing to mobile cloud computing, we also need to take into consideration the security management in mobile cloud computing. Mobile cloud computing uses wireless network technology for connectivity to the servers and cloud service providers, which is more vulnerable than wired networks. Almost all of the mobile device users data is stored with the cloud service providers server so that there is "always on" 24/7 access. Storage of an individual's data or a company's data with a third party always poses a security risk. Therefore, this book on Security Management in Mobile Cloud Computing is a timely publication for readers, academics, researchers and professionals to gain first-hand knowledge about the issues and challenges faced in managing security in Mobile Cloud Computing systems.

The number of variants of malicious software aimed at mobile devices has reportedly risen from about 14,000 to 40,000 or about 185% in less than a year, the United States Government Accountability Office stated (GAO, 2012). With the consumerisation of Information Technology, employees now bring their own devices (BYOD) and connect it to the corporate network. According to the Cloud Security Alliance (CSA, 2012), 69% of companies do not have a BYOD security policy and 64% of companies do not mandate or enforce mobile device security. Such ignorance might be due to lack of information about the risks and loss associated with such vulnerability. This book is aimed at informing the policy makers and practitioners on the different aspects of Security Management in Mobile Cloud Computing. It investigates the different protocols and architectures that can be used to design, create, and develop security mechanisms. It proposes innovative approaches and solutions to Mobile Cloud Computing security challenges.

Readers of this book will be enlightened on the following in regards to security management in mobile cloud computing: Chapter 2 presents an intrusion detection system to enhance security. Chapter 3 provides specific guidelines to reduce risks resulting from utilizing middle circle providers. Chapter 4 explores proper recovery planning in the event of disasters resulting from cyber-attacks. Chapter 6 proposes a framework that provides security with minimum processing overheads. Chapter 7 looks at security issues and vulnerabilities and the possible solutions to such issues. Chapter 8 discusses a security model for Mobile Cloud Database as a Service (DBaaS). In addition to the above, Chapter 1 presents a new routing protocol based on smart energy management and Chapter 5 looks at the Game Theory in modelling Peer-to-Peer network systems.

Sam Goundar
Victoria University of Wellington, New Zealand & KYS Business School, Malaysia

REFERENCES

Cisco. (2016). *Cisco visual networking index: Global mobile data traffic forecast update, 2015-2020*. Retrieved from: http://www.cisco.com/c/en/us/solutions/collateral/service-provider/visual-networking-index-vni/mobile-white-paper-c11-520862.html

CSA. (2012). *CSA identifies 17 key components for effective mobile device management of BYOD and company-owned devices*. Retrieved from: https://cloudsecurity-alliance.org/media/news/csa-publishes-mobile-device-management/

GAO U.S. Government Accountability Office. (2012). *Information security: Better implementation of controls for mobile devices should be encouraged*. Retrieved from: http://www.gao.gov/products/GAO-12-757

ITU Telecommunication Development Bureau. (2015). *ICT facts and figures*. Retrieved from: https://www.itu.int/en/ITU-D/Statistics/Documents/facts/ICTFacts-Figures2015.pdf

Preface

Mobile Cloud Computing (MCC) is gaining stream. According to the latest study from Juniper Research, the number of mobile cloud computing subscribers is expected to grow rapidly in the next five years. Considered as one of today's hottest new technology markets. MCC integrate different major technologies such as smart phones, tablets, services, big data and cloud computing in one platform provided to the end users. Many issues such as networking, cloud services, security, quality and the availability of services, user data management are still challenging to the rapid growth of MCC.

This book is essential for researchers, engineers, and professionals interested in exploring recent advances in Mobile Cloud Computing security. This book looks to discuss and address the difficulties and challenges faced in managing security in Mobile Cloud Computing Systems. This book chapters address different aspects of Security Management in MCC and investigates different protocols and architectures that can be used to design, create, and develop security mechanism by highlighting recent advances, trends, and contributions to the building blocks for solving security issues in MCC.

OBJECTIVES

The main objective of this book to provide opportunity to scientists, researchers, students, and practitioners to share their latest research results, ideas, and developments in the area of Mobile Cloud Computing. It provides an overview of the state of the art, latest techniques, studies, and approaches as well as future directions in this field.

TARGET AUDIENCE

Policy makers, academicians, researchers, advanced-level students, technology developers, and government officials will find this text useful in furthering their research exposure to pertinent topics in Mobile Cloud Computing and assisting in furthering their own research efforts in this field.

APPROACH

This book incorporates the concepts of security management in mobile cloud computing as well as design techniques, architecture and application areas. It also addresses advanced security issues such as digital forensic, big data, access control and fault tolerance etc. The chapters are organized as follows:

Chapter 1: (SET) Smart Energy Management and Throughput Maximization – A New Routing Protocol for WSNs

This chapter present a new routing protocol based on smart energy management and throughput maximization for clustered WSNs. The main objective of this protocol is to solve the constraint of closest sensors to the base station which consume relatively more energy in sensed information traffics, and also decrease workload on CHs.

Chapter 2: A Cloud Intrusion Detection Based on Classification of Activities and Mobile Agent

This paper presents an intrusion detection system that is based on mobile agent to collect and analysis gathered data from several virtual machines, in order to benefit from the advantages of mobile agents. This chapter propose to use C4.5 algorithm which is one of tree decision algorithms that classify data into normal and malicious one.

Chapter 3: Considering Middle Circles in Mobile Cloud

This chapter provides specific guidelines to provide governance directions to align MCC into enterprise strategy and reduce risks resulted from utilizing middle circle providers; In this context, this chapter also promote and discuss some ethics that help client enterprises and MCC providers understand roles and obligations in an ever changing environment.

Chapter 4: Managing Risk in Cloud Computing

This chapter explore proper recovery planning in the event of disaster resulting from cyber-attacks. In this chapter, several means of limiting vulnerabilities and minimizing damages to information systems are discussed.

Chapter 5: On the Role of Game Theory in Modelling Incentives and Interactions in Mobile Distributed Systems

This chapter explore the game theory which provides a mathematical framework for understanding the complexity of interdependent decision makers with similar or conflicting objectives. Chapter investigate different classes of game theory, review and analyse their use in the modelling of P2P system.

Chapter 6: Security and Privacy Issues, Solutions, and Tools for MCC

This chapter proposes lightweight secure framework that provides security with minimum communication and processing overhead on mobile devices. This chapter also discusses secure mobile-cloud application services.

Chapter 7: Security and Privacy Issues and Solutions in Mobile Cloud Computing

This chapter presents a review on the mobile cloud computing concepts as well as security issues and vulnerabilities affecting Cloud Systems and the possible solutions available to such issues within the context of cloud computing. It also describes the pros and cons of the existing security strategy and also introduces the existing issues in cloud computing such as data integrity, data segregation, and security.

Chapter 8: Security Model for Mobile Cloud Database as a Service (DBaaS)

This n chapter discusses a security model for Mobile Cloud Database as a Service (DBaaS). A user can change his/her password, whenever demanded. This chapter also presents security analysis to realize the feasibility of the proposed model for DBaaS.

Chapter 1
(SET) Smart Energy Management and Throughput Maximization:
A New Routing Protocol for WSNs

Hassan El Alami
INPT – Rabat, Morocco

Abdellah Najid
INPT – Rabat, Morocco

ABSTRACT

Energy efficiency and throughput are critical factors in the design routing protocols of WSNs. Many routing protocols based on clustering algorithm have been proposed. Current clustering algorithms often use cluster head selection and cluster formation to reduce energy consumption and maximize throughput in WSNs. In this chapter, the authors present a new routing protocol based on smart energy management and throughput maximization for clustered WSNs. The main objective of this protocol is to solve the constraint of closest sensors to the base station which consume relatively more energy in sensed information traffics, and also decrease workload on CHs. This approach divides network field into free area which contains the closest sensors to the base station that communicate directly with, and clustered area which contains the sensors that transmit data to the base station through cluster head. So due to the sensors that communicate directly to the base station, the load on cluster heads is decreased. Thus, the cluster heads consume less energy causing the increase of network lifetime.

DOI: 10.4018/978-1-5225-0602-7.ch001

INTRODUCTION

As it is known in recent years, impressive progress and extensive achievements in communication, computation, and surveillance fields have led to the development of WSNs technologies. Based on Akyildiz et al. (2002), WSNs have been used in many applications in several domains such as Healthcare applications, Environment monitoring applications, Agriculture applications, and Military applications. The energy constraint in WSNs is a very crucial issue, as sensors are usually functioned on limited and irreplaceable battery energy. Thus, the increasing network lifetime and throughput depends on efficient management of sensing sensor energy resources and topology of networks. Such disadvantages combined with a random distribution of large number of sensors and limited battery capacity of sensors, algorithms of routing in WSNs become more challenging compared to ad hoc networks refer Saleh et al. (2013). Thus, many routing protocols based on clustering algorithm have been proposed to reduce consumed energy in collecting and disseminating sensed data in WSNs. Clustering algorithm provides an effective way to extend the network lifetime of WSNs, the clustering operation is subdivided into two phases: setup phase and steady state phase. During the setup phase the cluster heads are selected and the clusters are organized. In steady state phase sensed data are transmitted from sensors to the base station through cluster heads which is already selected. Thus, the closest sensors to the base station consume more energy in information traffics and also workload on cluster heads relatively is increased, which leads to poor performance and decrease lifetime of clusters heads, so network lifetime of WSNs is decreased. To this end, energy in these sensor nodes is rare resource and must be managed in a smart manner. In this chapter the authors propose a new protocol based on smart energy management and throughput maximization for clustered WSNs, namely SET. The main goal of SET protocol is to maximize network lifetime and throughput by decreasing the workload on cluster heads in clustered WSNs which is decisive for application in various domains. After random deployment of sensors in network field, SET protocol forms two areas which are free area and clustered area. In free area where the base station is located the sensors (or closest sensors to the base station) send directly sensed data to the base station. Whereas in clustered area sensors are organized into clusters, each sensor is responsible to send data sensed to its respective cluster heads and cluster heads are responsible to forward the gathered sensed data to the base station. Therefore, in SET protocol the workload on cluster heads is decreased and number of packets successfully received at base station (throughput) is increased. SET routing protocol is employed for homogeneous and heterogeneous clustered WSNs. The sensors in SET are initially supplied with two energy levels. Thus, in this chapter the authors study impact of heterogeneity aware of sensors in terms of their energy level. In these network models there are three types of sensors called FNC (Free sensor, Normal sensor, cluster head), free sensors (or closest sensors to the base station) which are located in free area whereas the normal sensors and the cluster heads are distributed in clustered area. This chapter introduces related work in the second section. SET approach is presented in the third section. In the fourth section, simulation results of proposed protocol are discussed in terms of network lifetime, length of stable region for different value of heterogeneity, number of alive sensors per round and throughput maximization. Finally, the fifth section is the conclusion and future work of this chapter.

BACKGROUND

WSNs can be classified into homogeneous and heterogeneous networks. In homogeneous network, all the sensors have the same energy level whereas, in heterogeneous network, all the sensors are initially supplied with different energy levels. Thus, routing protocols are required when a source sensor cannot send its information directly to its sensor destination but has to forward on the intermediate sensors to rely these information on its behalf. Thus, the routing protocols are very important for managing communication among the sensors in WSNs. Generally, the routing protocols based on clustering algorithm have been proposed for managing the communication among sensors and also for decreasing the energy consumption in WSNs. The main objective of clustering algorithm based routing protocols is to distributed the energy consumption among the sensors in each cluster of network and maximize the lifetime of network. Heinzelman et al. (2000) proposed one of the famous routing protocols based on clustering algorithm which is low-energy adaptive clustering hierarchy (LEACH) which is clustering algorithm based hierarchical protocol for homogenous WSNs. The main aim of LEACH is to achieve the energy efficiency in the communication between sensors. The mechanism of operation of LEACH is dividing the network in clusters; each member cluster is responsible to communicate with its respective cluster head which is responsible to convey the gathered data sensed to the base station. Additionally, cluster heads in LEACH is randomly selected over time in order to balance the energy consumption of sensors. A given sensor n chooses random number between 0 and 1, and compares it with the following threshold value T(n):

$$T(n) = \begin{cases} \dfrac{p}{1 - p * (\mathrm{mod}\ (r, \frac{1}{p}))} & \text{if } n \in G \\ 0 & \text{otherwise} \end{cases} \tag{1}$$

3

Where r is the current round, p is the expected number of cluster heads in the round and n is the number of nodes in the network area. G is the set of nodes that have not been a cluster head in the last mod (r, 1/p) rounds. When T(n) is greater than random number, sensor is selected as cluster head for the current round. However, cluster heads are elected randomly that does not take into account distance between the sensors and base station, and the residual energy of each sensor. These disadvantages lead to minimize networks lifetime of WSNs.

The Threshold sensitive Energy Efficient sensor Network (TEEN) has been proposed by Manjeshwar and Agrawa (2001). This protocol is based on a clustering scheme where closer sensors form clusters and this process goes on the second level until the base station is reached. The objective of TEEN is to design for the conditions as sudden changes in the sensed attributes. The cluster heads election and communication between sensors of TEEN are similar to these of LEACH. The difference between TEEN and LEACH lies in the steady state phase. In LEACH, there is no control on the transmission of sensed data whereas in TEEN, when a sensor has sensed data to transmit, there are verifications of the hard threshold and the soft threshold. The hard threshold is a threshold value for the sensed attribute. It is the absolute value of the attribute beyond which, the sensor sensing this value must turn on its sender and report to its cluster head. The soft threshold is a small variation in the value of the sensed attribute which makes the sensor to turn on its sender and send. At the first moment, sensors send sensed data, when the value of the sensed attribute reaches its hard threshold. The transmissions in next moment occur, only when the current value of the sensed attribute is greater than the hard threshold and differs from soft threshold by an amount equal to or greater than the soft threshold. However, in some cases of TEEN protocol, inefficient CHs can be elected. This drawback leads to decrease network lifetime and unbalanced energy consumption in WSNs.

Lindsey and Raghavendra (2002) proposed the Power-Efficient Gathering in Sensor Information Systems (PEGASIS), this proposed is improved approach from LEACH protocol. The main idea of PEGASIS is that nodes are organized into a chain where each node receives from and sends to closest neighbor node only. The distance between sender and receiver is reduced as well as minimizing the amount of transmission energy. Figure 1 illustrates constructed chain using a greedy algorithm that starts from the farthest node from the base station. From Figure 2, the algorithm starts with node 0 that communicates to node 3. Then, node3 communicates to node 1 and node 1 communicates to node 2, which is the closest one to the base station. Because nodes already in the chain cannot be revisited, the neighbor distance will maximize gradually. When a node dies the chain will be reconstructed by repeating the same procedure to bypass the dead node.

Figure 1. Chain is constructed using the greedy algorithm

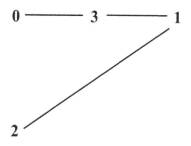

Figure 2. Token passing approach in PEGASIS

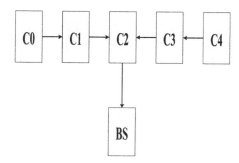

In one transmission round, a randomized node is appointed to be the leader to transmit sensed data to base station. If the base station stationed outside the field of this node, multi-hop transmission will be employed. The leader will be changed randomly in every round, so that overall energy dissipation is balanced out. For sending a sensed data in each round, a token is used for passing from one end of the chain to the other. Only node that has a token can transmit a sensed data to its intermediate node in the chain. When intermediate node receives sensed data from one neighbor along with a token, it aggregates the sensed data with its own packet and transmits a new packet to the next node in the chain. From Figure 2, C0 will pass its sensed data and token to C1. C1 aggregates a sensed data with its own packet and pass a new packet to the leader C2. C2 does not transmit a packet to the base station yet, but rather it passes a token to C4. When C2 receives a sensed data from C4 and C3, it aggregates and transmits the packet to base station.

While LEACH protocol assumes clustered homogeneous WSNs, Smaragdakis et al. (2004) proposed the Stable Election Protocol (SEP) for clustered heterogeneous WSNs. In this protocol, nodes are divided into normal and advanced nodes. Advanced nodes having a additional energy in comparison to normal nodes. E_0 is the initial energy of normal nodes and then

E_0 $(1+a)$ is the initial energy of advanced nodes. Thus, it is clear that advanced nodes have more chance to become a CH due to their significant probabilities. The probabilities for normal and advanced nodes are calculated as follows:

$$p_{nrm} = \frac{p}{(1 + \alpha * m)} \tag{2}$$

$$p_{adv} = \frac{p * (1 + \alpha)}{(1 + \alpha * m)} \tag{3}$$

Operation of SEP is divided into rounds as LEACH. However, the weak point of SEP is that each sensor always sends the sensed data to BS through cluster head even if distance between cluster head and base station greater than distance between sensor and base station. Thus, energy consumption is increased which causes decreasing network lifetime and throughput in WSNs.

In Qing et al. (2006), authors proposed a distributed energy efficient clustering (DEEC) for heterogeneous WSNs. In this protocol, nodes before the beginning of WSN operation are equipped with different energy levels. The cluster heads are selected by a residual energy based probability of a node to average energy of the network. This means that each node with higher residual energy has more chance to be CH for a current round. The cluster head selection process in DEEC is similar to that of LEACH. However, each node elects itself to be a CH with probability which is given by:

$$p_n = \frac{p_{opt} N (1 + a) E_n(r)}{(N + \sum_{n=1}^{N} a_n) \overline{E(r)}} \tag{4}$$

where p_{opt} is the expected number of cluster heads in the each round, N is the total number of nodes, $E_n(r)$ is residual energy of a node, and $E(r)$ is average energy of network. However, the clusters formed due to random selection of CHs are of different sizes and the cluster members transmit the sensed data to the cluster head even if these lie at shorter distance from the base station. Thus, these disadvantages leading to decrease energy level of the nodes and the cluster head in the clusters which lead to energy inefficient clusters.

Li and Han (2010) proposed an energy efficient cluster head election protocol for heterogeneous WSNs. The authors considered three types of sensor nodes. A certain number of the sensor nodes are equipped with the additional energy level than the other nodes. In this approach, all nodes are uniformly deployed. In this approach, the cluster head use time division multiple access (TDMA) schedule and transmit it to the cluster members. This schedule has been used to avoid the collisions among sent data, and also allows the radio components of each node members to be slept at all times except during time of transmission, thus decreasing the energy dissipated by the individual nodes. The goal of this approach is to decrease the energy dissipation of the cluster heads which are far away from the base station and balance the energy dissipation of the cluster heads which are close to the base station, a multi-hop routing protocol of cluster head has been presented, which introduces into the restriction factor of energy remainder when it selects the temporary nodes between cluster heads and base station, and also the minimum spanning tree algorithm has been included. In addition, this approach can also reduce the consumption of communication energy between node members and cluster heads. The deficiencies of proposed include; some cluster heads may be very close to each other and also may be very far from base station. These inefficient cluster heads could increase the energy consumption in WSNs.

Alla et al. (2012) authors proposed a Hierarchical Adaptive Balanced energy efficient Routing Protocol (HABRP) for heterogeneous WSNs. This proposed protocol is an extension of LEACH which enhances the stability period of clustering hierarchy and decrease probability of failure sensor nodes employing the characteristic parameters of heterogeneity. The goal of HABRP is to extend the stability period and network lifetime of WSNs. the operation in HABRP is divided into rounds; each round is divided into two phases, setup phase and steady phase. Each sensor knows when each round starts using a synchronized clock. During the set-up phase some high-energy nodes namely normal nodes, cluster head and gateway are elected as gateways, and other are choose as cluster heads. During the steady-state phase, sensed data are transmitted from the cluster members to the cluster head, cluster head aggregates sensed data and forward it to the base station through chosen gateway that requires the minimum communication energy to reduce the energy dissipation of cluster head and minimize probability of failure sensors. In addition, the process of CHs selection and clusters formation in HABRP are similar as in LEACH. However, randomly selected CHs and gateways are not optimal in number and also the CHs send the sensed data to gateway even if these lie at comparatively shorter distance from the base station.

Wang et al. (2013) propose Link aware Clustering Mechanism (LCM) routing protocol for WSNs. The main objective of this protocol is to establish a reliable way with balanced load. In order to do so, the cluster heads are elected on the bases of link condition and node status. Where, link condition indicates to quality and node status to energy level. This mechanism determines a clustering metric namely predicted transmission count. Thus, the cluster heads election based on priority and candidates with highest priority are selected as cluster heads. The drawbacks of this approach include unbalanced cluster size and not optimal in number of cluster heads which lead to decrease network lifetime of WSNs.

SET APPROACH

In order to minimize energy consumption in WSNs, many clustering algorithm based routing protocols have been proposed. However, these routing protocols suffer from many drawbacks such as: Firstly, cluster heads is elected randomly because these routing protocols depends on only a probabilistic model. So the selection criterion of these clustering routing based routing protocols can be enhanced in many techniques such as fuzzy logic based clustering approach and heuristic algorithms. Secondly, the number of cluster heads is not optimal thus; the sizes of clusters in network are different which leads to inefficiency energy in network. Thirdly, each sensor which belongs to a specific cluster transmits sensed data to the base station through cluster head even if its distance from the base station is less than that from the cluster head which leads to increase the workload on cluster heads. In order to overcome the mentioned challenges, clustering algorithm based a new routing protocol need to be proposed.

In this chapter authors describe SET protocol which is an extension of the clustering algorithm based routing protocols, which improves the stability period, network lifetime, throughput of WSNs, also decrease the workload on cluster heads. Operation of SET routing protocol is divided into rounds and each round is divided into the setup phase and the steady state phase. In this approach network area is divided into free area and clustered area. The sensors in free area send directly the data to the base station that decreases the workload on cluster heads which lead to reduce the energy consumption of cluster heads. Whereas clustered area is subdivided into clusters; each sensor which belongs to specific cluster, sends the data to the base station through cluster head. Additionally, in these network models, there are two types of sensors: free sensors (or closest sensors to the base station) and clustered sensors. Free sensors N_{NF} are distributed in free area whereas clustered sensors N_{CN} are distributed in clustered area. Additionally, the sensors in each area are divided into normal and advanced sensors.

Let m be the part of total sensors N_{NF} in free area which are equipped with α times more energy than others sensors. It notes that $(1-m)N_{FN}$ act as normal sensors with initial energy is E_0, and $m*N_{FN}$ act as advanced sensors. The number of free sensors and energy in free area is expressed by:

$$N_{FN} = N_{FN}m + N_{FN}(1-m) \tag{5}$$

$$E[N_{FN}] = E_0 N_{FN} m(1+\alpha) + E_0 N_{FN}(1-m) \tag{6}$$

In the clustered area, m is the part of total sensors N_{CN} which are equipped with α times more energy than others. $(1-m)N_{CN}$ is the number of normal sensors with initial energy is E_0, and $m*N_{CN}$ is number of advanced sensors. The number of clustered sensors and energy in clustered area is expressed by:

$$N_{CN} = N_{CN}m + N_{CN}(1-m) \tag{7}$$

$$E[N_{CN}] = E_0 N_{CN} m(1+\alpha) + E_0 N_{CN}(1-m) \tag{8}$$

The total energy in whole network is given by:

$$E_{total}[N] = E[N_{FN}] + E[N_{CN}] = NmE_0(1+\alpha) + NE_0(1-m) \tag{9}$$

Network Model

The basic network model of the protocol SET is illustrated in Figure 3. In free area, each sensor (or sensor closest to the base station) sends sensed data directly to the base station. Whereas, in clustered area each sensor sends the sensed data to its cluster head. The cluster head aggregates the collected sensed data and forwards it to the base station.

The operation of SET protocol is divided into rounds as shown in Figure 4. At every round each sensor which is located in free area directly sends data to the base

Figure 3. The SET network model

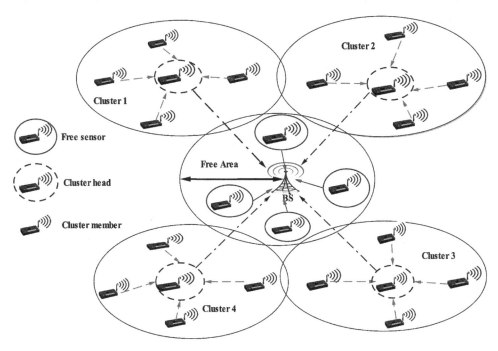

Figure 4. Time line showing SET operation

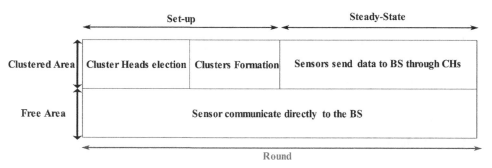

station. In clustered area round is divided into set-up phase and steady-state phase. During the set-up phase the cluster heads are selected and the clusters are organized. After the set-up phase, the steady-state phase begins when the sensed data are transmitted from the cluster members to the cluster heads to aggregate sensed data in single packet and transmit it to the base station.

Energy Model

For this chapter, four routing protocols, namely, LEACH, SEP, TEEN and SET (proposed protocol) had been analyzed based on according to the radio hardware energy consumption model shown in Figure 5, the expense of energy used by transmitting l bit message over a distance d to achieve an acceptable Signal-to-Noise Ratio (SNR)

In this work, the first order radio model shown in work of Rappaport and Theodore (1996) has been used to model the energy consumption. In order to transmit l bits of data over distance d, the energy consumed by the radio is given by equation (10), while the energy consumed for receiving l bits of data is given by equation (11).

$$E_{Tx}(l, d) = \begin{cases} l * E_{elec} + l * \varepsilon_{fs} * d^2 & \text{if } d < d_0 \\ l * E_{elec} + l * \varepsilon_{mp} * d^4 & \text{if } d \geq d_0 \end{cases} \tag{10}$$

$$E_{Rx}(l) = l * E_{elec} \tag{11}$$

E_{elec} is the energy dissipated per bit in the transmitter or receiver circuits. ε_{mp} and ε_{fs} are the energy dissipated factor of amplification for multipath fading and free space radio models, respectively. d_0 is he threshold distance ($d_0 = \sqrt{\dfrac{\mu_{fs}}{\mu_{mf}}}$).

Optimal Number of Cluster

Let N number of sensors are distributed randomly in the network field M*M with a centrally positioned BS. k is the number of clusters. In the network model of SET protocol, Network field is divided into free area and clustered area:

Figure 5. Radio energy dissipation model

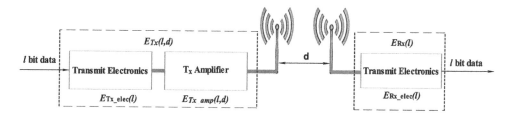

- The energy dissipated in free area:

There are N_{FN} free sensors distributed in free area, and transmit directly the packets to base station. Thus, the energy consumed by a free sensor per round is given by:

$$E_{FN} = lE_{elec} + l\varepsilon_{fs} d^2{}_{FN\_BS} \tag{12}$$

$$d^2{}_{FN\_BS} = \int\limits_0^{x_{max}} \int\limits_0^{y_{max}} (x^2 + y^2)\rho(x,y)dxdy = \rho \int\limits_0^R \int\limits_0^{2\pi} r^3 dr d\theta \tag{13}$$

In the SET protocol, the authors assume that the free sensors are distributed in the free area circle-shape which has the radius ($R = \sqrt{\dfrac{A}{\pi}}$) and $\rho(x,y)$ is constant for r and θ therefore, the density of nodes is uniform throughout the free area, then $\rho = \dfrac{1}{\pi R^2}$, (13) simplifies to:

$$d^2{}_{FN\_BS} = \frac{R^2}{2} \tag{14}$$

Therefore, in this case the expression for the total amount energy dissipated by free sensors is:

$$E_{FN}^{total} = lE_{elec} + l\varepsilon_{fs} \frac{R^2}{2} \tag{15}$$

- The energy dissipated in clustered area:

Let $\left(N_{CN} = N - N_{FN}\right)$ number of clustered sensors which are distributed randomly in clustered area $\left(M^2 - A^2\right)$. If there are k clusters, there are on average sensors $\dfrac{N - N_{FN}}{k}$ per cluster. The energy consumed by a cluster head per round is given by:

$$E_{CH} = lE_{elec}\left(\frac{N - N_{FN}}{k} - 1\right) + lE_{DA}\left(\frac{N - N_{FN}}{k}\right) + lE_{elec} + l\varepsilon_{mp}d^4_{CH\_BS} \qquad (16)$$

E_{DA} represents the amount of energy consumed by cluster heads for processing data aggregation and, $d^4_{CH\_BS}$ is average distance between cluster heads and base station is given by:

$$d^2_{CH\_BS} = \int\limits_0^{2\pi} d\theta \int\limits_0^{\sqrt{M^2 - \pi R^2}/\pi} \rho(r,\theta)r^3 dr \qquad (17)$$

In the clustered area we assume that the area occupied by each cluster is a circle with radius $R' = \sqrt{\dfrac{M^2 - \pi R^2}{\pi}}$ and $\rho(x, y)$ is constant for r and θ in $M^2 - \pi R^2$ then,

$$d^2_{CH\_BS} = \rho\int\limits_0^{2\pi} d\theta \int\limits_0^{\sqrt{M^2 - \pi R^2}/\pi} r^3 dr = \frac{\rho\left(M^2 - \pi R^2\right)}{2\pi}$$

If the density of nodes is uniform throughout the $M^2 - A^2$ then $\rho = \dfrac{1}{\left(M^2 - \pi R^2\right)}$ thus, the average distance of cluster head from the base station is given by:

$$d^4_{CH\_BS} = \left(\frac{M^2 - \pi R^2}{2\pi}\right)^2 \qquad (18)$$

The total energy dissipated in a clustered area per round could be obtained via:

$$E^{total}_{CN} = kE_{cluster} = \sum_{i=1}^{k}\left(E^i_{CH} + E^i_{non-CH}\left(\frac{N}{k} - n_i\right)\right) = kE_{CH} + E_{non-CH}\left(N - N_{FN}\right) \qquad (19)$$

where, $N_{FN} = \sum\limits_{i=1}^{k} n_i$ is the number of free sensors in free area.

13

In addition, the amount of energy consumed by the non-CH sensors is:

$$E_{non\_CH} = lE_{elec} + l\varepsilon_{fs}d^2_{n\_CH} \tag{20}$$

where $d^2_{n\_CH}$ is the distance between sensors and cluster head could be given via:

$$d^2_{n\_CH} = \int_0^{2\pi} d\theta \int_0^{\sqrt{M^2 - \pi R^2}/k\pi} \rho(r,\theta)r^3 dr = \frac{M^2 - \pi R^2}{2k\pi} \tag{21}$$

Finally, the total energy dissipated in the network per round is given by:

$$E_{total} = N_{FN}E_{FN} + \left(N - N_{FN}\right)E_{CN}^{total} = n\left(lE_{elec} + l\varepsilon_{fs}\frac{R^2}{2}\right) +$$

$$\left(N - N_{FN}\right)^2\left[2lE_{elec} + lE_{DA} + l\varepsilon_{fs}\left(\frac{M^2 + \pi R^2}{2k\pi}\right)\right] + \left(N - N_{FN}\right)kl\varepsilon_{mp}\left(\frac{M^2 - \pi R^2}{2\pi}\right)^2 \tag{22}$$

Optimal number of clusters per round has been found by setting the derivative of E_{total} with respect to k equating to zero according to Heinzelman et al. (2002):

$$k_{opt} = \sqrt{\frac{2\pi(N - N_{FN})}{M^2 - \pi R^2}}\sqrt{\frac{\varepsilon_{fs}}{\varepsilon_{mp}}} \tag{23}$$

Therefore, the optimal probability of sensor to become cluster head is given by equation 20:

$$P_{opt} = \frac{k_{opt}}{N - N_{FN}} \tag{24}$$

N_{FN} is the number of free sensor which communicate directly to base station.

The optimal probability for a sensor to become a cluster heads is very important. In their previous work of Heinzelman et al. (2000), the authors pointed that if the clusters are not formed in an optimal way, the total consumed energy of the WSN per round is increased exponentially either when the number of clusters that are established is greater or especially when the number of the formed clusters is less than the optimal number of clusters. Therefore, in the network model of SET protocol the probability of sensor which communicate directly to base station is given by:

$$P_{FN} = \frac{N_{FN}}{N} \qquad (25)$$

Cluster Heads Selection Algorithm

Once the sensors are deployed in the network area, each sensor located in clustered area elects itself with respect to its residual energy for election of cluster heads. The objective is to minimize the energy consumption and maximize the throughput of WSN and also to ensure sensed data is transmitted to BS. Each sensor in clustered area sends sensed data to the closest cluster head and cluster head makes sensed data aggregation. Let k_{opt} is the optimal number of clusters in each rounds. P_{opt} (equation 22) is the optimal probability of sensor to become cluster head. Each sensor must become cluster head once every $\dfrac{1}{P_{opt}}$ rounds.

For heterogeneous WSNs, SET protocol is to assign a weight to the optimal probability (equation 22). This weight must be equal to the initial energy of each sensor divided by the initial energy of the normal sensor. The weighted election probability for normal sensors define as P_{nrm}, and P_{adv} the weighted election probability for the advanced sensors. Smaragdakis et al. (2004) showed in their previous work that the number of nodes with energy equal the initial energy of normal node is defined as $N * (1 + \alpha * m)$. In order to conserve the minimum energy consumption in each round within an epoch, the average number of cluster heads per round per epoch must be constant and equal to optimal number of clusters per round k_{opt}. Therefore, the weighed probabilities for normal and advanced sensors are, respectively:

$$P_{nrm} = \frac{P_{opt}}{1 + \alpha * m} \qquad (26)$$

$$P_{adv} = \frac{P_{opt}}{1 + \alpha * m} (1 + \alpha) \qquad (27)$$

In Equation (1), it can replace by the weighted probabilities to obtain the threshold that is used to select the cluster head in each round.

In this network model there are threshold for normal sensors, and the threshold for advanced sensors. Thus, for normal sensors its threshold is given by:

$$
T\left(N_{nrm}\right) = \begin{cases} \dfrac{P_{nrm}}{1 - P_{nrm} * (\mathrm{mod}(r, \frac{1}{P_{nrm}}))} * \left(\dfrac{E_{residual}\left(N_{nrm}\right)}{E_{initial}\left(N_{nrm}\right)}\right) & \text{if } \mathrm{N}_{nrm} \in G_{nrm} \\ 0 & \text{otherwise} \end{cases}
$$

(28)

where r is the current round and N_{nrm} is the number of normal sensors in the clustered area. The value r is the round number. G_{nrm} is the set of sensors that have not been a cluster head in the last $\dfrac{1}{P}$ rounds. $\dfrac{E_{residual}\left(N_{nrm}\right)}{E_{initial}\left(N_{nrm}\right)}$ is the metric of residual energy, which means the bigger residual energy a normal sensor has, the bigger probability it will have to become a cluster head.

Similarly, the threshold for advanced sensors is given by:

$$
T\left(N_{adv}\right) = \begin{cases} \dfrac{P_{adv}}{1 - P_{adv} * (\mathrm{mod}(r, \frac{1}{P_{adv}}))} * \left(\dfrac{E_{residual}\left(N_{adv}\right)}{E_{initial}\left(N_{adv}\right)}\right) & \text{if } \mathrm{N}_{adv} \in G_{adv} \\ 0 & \text{otherwise} \end{cases}
$$

(29)

where r is the current round and N_{adv} is the number of normal sensors in the clustered area. The value r is the round number. G_{adv} is the set of sensors that have not been a cluster head in the last $\dfrac{1}{P_{nrm}}$ rounds. $\dfrac{E_{residual}\left(N_{adv}\right)}{E_{initial}\left(N_{adv}\right)}$ is the metric of residual energy, which means the bigger residual energy an advanced sensor has, the bigger probability it will have to become a cluster head.

Throughput Maximization in WSN

The throughput maximization constraint is a joint routing protocol and scheduling constraint, it need to transport each flow and schedule the wireless links so that flows can be practicably accommodated subject to the battery level and interference problems. In this approach the authors define throughput as the number of packets successfully received at the base station. Thus, the free sensors which are located in free area transmit directly the data to the base station that means the number of packet which is sent to the base station is increased, and in clustered area, clustered sensors send the packets to base station thorough cluster heads which are already selected, so the workload on cluster heads is decreased due to free sensors thus, the number of packets is increased to the base station. In addition, when sensed data travel from source (sensor) to destination (base station) across a wireless link, some of them fail to reach destination (base station) due to the bad status of wireless link, as a definition in many technical language, it is referred to as dropped packets. In order to compensate for packets dropped, in this chapter authors use Random Uniformed Model which is used by Zhou, et al. (2009) according to this model the dropped packets is related to the status of wireless link. If a given wireless link is in good status, packets are successfully received at destination (base station) otherwise it is dropped due to bad status of wireless link. Additionally, the computer sub_code of wireless link status has been implemented in SET protocol, the authors fix the optimal probability of wireless link to be in bad status (dropped packets) as 30%, as cited by Zhou, et al. (2009); random number between 0 and 1 has been generated to determine if the packets are successfully received at the base station. From this SET approach, throughput can be maximized by maximizing the network lifetime which is in turn fulfilled by efficient utilization of the energy.

Computer Code (sub_code of wireless link status for SET protocol)

```
P_opt= Optimum probability of wireless link to be in bad sta-
tus;
Rnd= Randomly number(0,1);
For j=1 to number of packet send to base station (BS)
        If(Rnd<P_opt)
            wireless_link_status='bad';
        Else
            wireless_link_status='good';
        End If
End For
```

Summary of SET Protocol

SET is a self-organizing, clustering protocol that uses randomization to distribute the energy load evenly among the sensors in the wireless network. This proposed approach makes two types of sensors: free sensors (in free area) and clustered sensors (in clustered area). The free sensors communicate directly to the base station whereas; the clustered sensors transmit the sensed data to the base station through cluster head. The flow diagram of the SET protocol is described as Figure 6.

In the clustered area, each clustered sensor elects itself to become cluster head at the starting of each round with a certain probability which is defined initially. These CH_sensors broadcast their status to other clustered sensors using advertisement message (CHs_ADV). The non CH_sensors wait the advertisement message (CHs_ADV) from all CH_sensors. Each clustered sensor determines to which cluster it wants to belong by picking the cluster head that requires the minimum communication energy, and reply the join request (Join_REQ) message to picked cluster heads, and the CH_sensors wait for join request message form clustered sensors. Once all the clustered sensors are organized into clusters in the clustered area, each CH_sensor creates allocate Time Division Multiple Access (TDMA)

Figure 6. The SET protocol: flow diagram

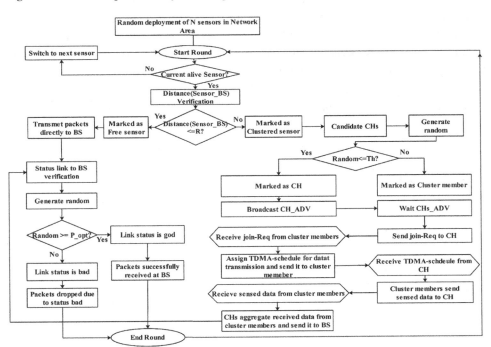

schedule and broadcasts it to the cluster members. This allows the radio components of each non CH_sensor to be turned off at all times except for its send time, thus reducing the energy consumed in the individual clustered sensors. Once the cluster heads received all the sensed data from the cluster members, the CH_sensors aggregates the sensed data and transmit it to the base station, whereas, in free area, the free sensors transmit the sensed data directly to the base station. During the operation of SET protocol, the base station receives directly sensed packets from the selected CH_sensors and from the free sensors. In this chapter, throughput is defined as the number of packets received successfully at the base station. In addition, when the packets travel from the CH_sensors or from the free sensors to the base station across a wireless link, some of packets have been dropped. According to the work of Zhou, et al. (2009), the random number between 0 and 1 has been generated to check link status and compares it with an optimal probability P_{opt} which is set predefined. If the random number is less than optimal probability, the status link is bad, packet which is sent to the base station is dropped, and otherwise packet is received successfully at the base station. The main objective of SET protocol is to decrease the workload on cluster heads and also to solve the problem of closest sensors to the base station which consume relatively more energy in data sensed traffics, so more number of packets successfully received at the base station for the current round. Briefly, the sensor sends the sensed data:

- To the chosen cluster head if:

$$E_{sensor\_BS} > E_{sensor\_CH} + E_{CH-BS} \tag{30}$$

These sensed data are transmitted to the base station using *Sensor-CH-BS* routing.

- To the base station directly if:

$$E_{sensor\_BS} <= E_{sensor\_CH} + E_{CH-BS} \tag{31}$$

Where E_{sensor_BS} is total energy dissipated for send data from free sensor to the base station and E_{sensor_CH} is total energy dissipated for send data from sensor to the cluster head and E_{CH-BS} is total energy dissipated for send data from cluster head to the base station, Figure 7 shows the transmitting of sensed data to base station.

Figure 7. Transmitting of sensed data to base station

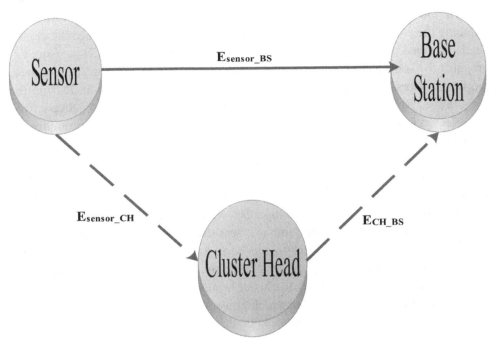

SIMULATION RESULTS AND DISCUSSION

The objective of this approach in conducting simulations is to analyze the performance of SET protocol by comparing it with three well known clustering algorithm based routing protocols like LEACH, TEEN and SEP. this routing proposed is designed for clustered WSNs that have static sensors. The 100 sensors are randomly distributed in the network area of 100m². The base station installed at a point (50, 50). Average results shown in this section are obtained after running the simulation 3 times. Moreover, the values used in the first order radio model in this simulation are described in Table 1.

In order to evaluate SET protocol, the following performance metrics are used:

- **Network Lifetime:** It is the time interval from the start of WSN operation until the death of the last alive sensor.
- **Stability Period:** It is the time interval from the start of WSN operation until the first sensor dies.
- **Energy Residual:** It is the difference between the initial energy and consumed energy of sensor.

Table 1. Configuration parameters

Type of Parameter	Value
Transmitter/Receiver Electronics	50nJ/bit
Transmit Amplifier (if d to BS <=do)	10pJ/bit/m2
Transmit Amplifier (if d to BS >do)	0.0013pJ/bit/m4
Data Aggregation	5nJ/bit/message
Packet size	400bit

- **Number of Dropped Packets:** Dropped Packets due to bad status of wireless link.
- **Throughput:** Number of packets successfully received at the base station.
- **Node Density:** The number of sensors in a given network field.

In the upcoming subsections, the authors implement SET protocol in the selected simulation environments.

1. Implementation of SET Protocol in Homogeneous WSN

LEACH, SEP, TEEN, and SET are a homogeneity-aware routing protocols for WSNs. The sensors in LEACH, SEP, TEEN and SET are initially supplied with one level of energy. Here, according to the work of Smaragdakis et al.(2004) $\alpha = 0$ for homogenous WSN. Therefore, in work of Manjeshwar and Agrawa (2001)the value of soft threshold is set at 2F and that hard threshold at 100F.

Based on stability period and the network lifetime LEACH, SEP, TEEN and SET is compared in Figure 8 which show the stability period of LEACH and SEP protocols is limited to 892 rounds and the TEEN protocol is also limited to 1257, whereas the stability period of SET extents up to 1956 rounds in homogeneous WSNs. On the other hand, Figure 9 showed that more the number of packets received at base station in SET protocol relative to LEACH, SEP and TEEN protocols. Moreover, SET protocol extends the stability period further due to direct communication of free sensors to base station.

As the probability of packet drops is directly related to the number of packets successfully received at the base station that is why SET protocol performs the least in comparison to LEACH, SEP and TEEN routing protocols. Due to free sensors network lifetime is increased as well as the rate at which packets successfully received at base station (Throughput). Additionally, the nature of adopted number of dropped packets (Figure 10) model supposes that greater packet transmitting rate is directly related to the rate at which packets are dropped.

Figure 8. Number of alive sensor per round

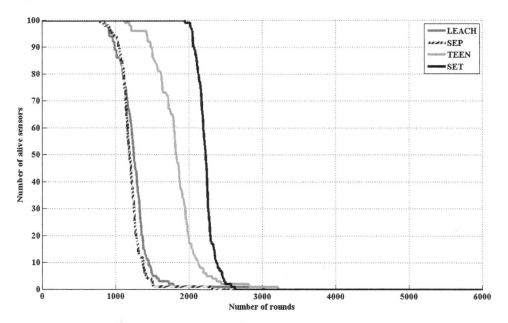

Figure 9. Number of packets received to base station (throughput) per round

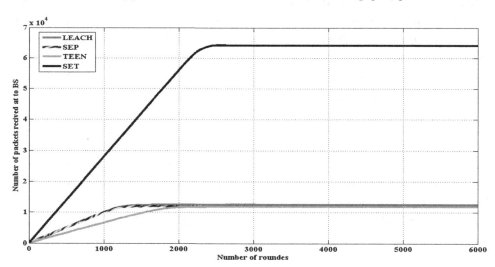

Figure 10. Number of packets dropped per round

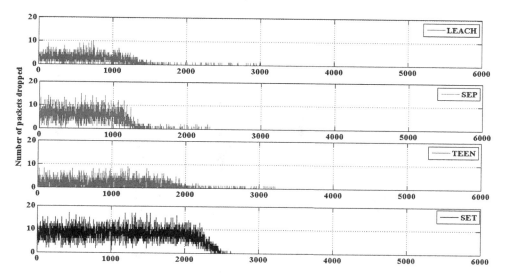

Figure 11 shows the number of rounds for 1%, 25%, 50%, and 75% of sensor death is observed for SET, TEEN, SEP and LEACH. Results in Figure 8 clearly illustrate the positive impact of the proposed SET protocol for decreasing number of dead sensors while the protocol rounds proceed, and hence, increasing the network lifetime of homogeneous WSNs. It is clear SET protocol has longer network lifetime precisely the stability period than LEACH, SEP and TEEN.

The performance of SET protocol is compared with that of the original TEEN, SEP, and LEACH routing protocols in terms of residual energy has been shown in Figure 12. With use of free sensors (node closest to the base station) for transmitting directly sensed data to the base station. It is clear that proposed protocol SET performs superior to TEEN, SEP and LEACH. This is due to the gain of the energy consumed by free sensors to the base station. Moreover, in the case of SET protocol energy of the network becomes further conserved. This means that the cluster heads now forward relatively less data sensed to the base station.

Figure 13 shows the impact of varying density of sensor nodes on network lifetime in LEACH, SEP, TEEN and newly SET protocol. Clearly, the network lifetime first maximizes and then minimizes whenever the number of sensors in TEEN, SEP, and LEACH are varied. Initially, it is observed that network lifetime of TEEN, SEP and LEACH is increasing from the 40 to 100 sensors due to the small size of the cluster. As a result the workload on CHs is decreased and the distance between source and destination can be shorter. Whereas from the 100 to 200 sensors the network lifetime of TEEN, SEP and LEACH is decreasing, so as the energy con-

Figure 11. Sensor death percentage per number of rounds

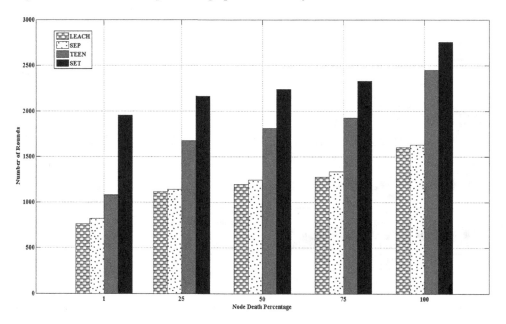

Figure 12. Energy analysis comparison of SET, TEEN, SEP, and LEACH for homogeneous WSN

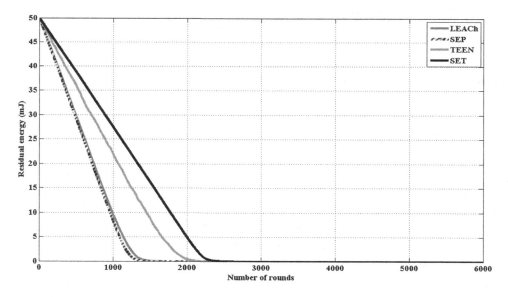

sumption of sensors precisely of cluster heads increases due to the workload on cluster heads. Whereas that network lifetime of proposed protocol SET is relatively more stable even if the number of sensors is increased; it is evident that some sensors (free sensors) communicate directly with the sink that decreases the workload on CHs.

2. Implementation of SET Protocol in Heterogeneous WSN (Impact of Heterogeneity Degree)

Figure 14 shows the length stable region of SET, TEEN, SEP and LEACH protocols for different values of percentage of energy heterogeneity, it is clear that if the number of advanced sensor is increased with $a=1$ (Smaragdakis et al. 2004) the stability period of SET, TEEN, SEP and LEACH is extended. In addition, due to some advanced nodes (advanced free nodes) located in free area the proposed protocol SET improves the stability period compared to TEEN, SEP and LEACH protocols.

CONCLUSION AND FUTURE WORK

While the energy efficiency and throughput maximization are major critical factors in designing algorithm of routing protocols for wireless sensor networks, many cluster-

Figure 13. Sensor density analysis comparison of SET, TEEN, SEP, and LEACH for homogeneous WSN

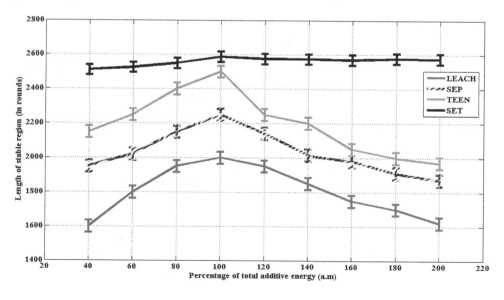

Figure 14. Length of stable region for different values of energy heterogeneity with a=1

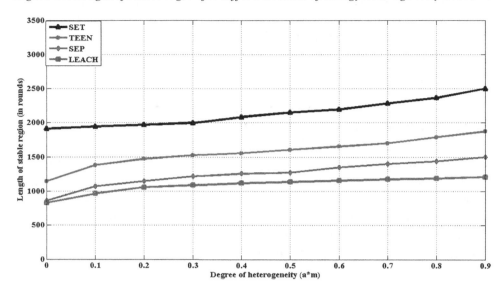

ing algorithm based routing protocols have been proposed to achieve these critical factors. However, clustering algorithm based routing protocols are applicable under specific constraints. Such as in some cases, inefficient cluster heads can be elected. Because many clustering algorithm based routing protocols depend on probability to select cluster heads, and also some cluster heads can be located in the edge of network area. Thus, unbalanced size of clusters leads to increase workload on cluster heads and closest sensors to the base station consume relatively more energy in sensed information traffics which means that the network lifetime is minimized. This chapter proposed smart energy management and throughput maximization based a new protocol for clustered WSNs, namely SET protocol. Algorithm of SET protocol divide network field into free area which contains the free sensors (or closest sensors to the base station) that communicates directly with base station, and clustered area which contains the sensors that transmit sensed data to base station through cluster heads which are already selected. Thus, the workload on cluster heads is relatively decreased and also the constraint of the closest sensors to the base station which consume more energy in information traffics is relatively solved. Moreover, this routing approach reduces overall energy consumption in WSNs. Simulation results demonstrate the effectiveness of the new routing approach with regards to enhancement of the network lifetime, stability period and throughput of homogeneous and heterogeneous clustered WSNs in all of the selected sensor densities and network lifetimes. This protocol is more efficient energy and is more powerful in prolonging the network lifetime and particularly the stability period compared to LEACH, SEP, and TEEN protocols in both homogeneous and heterogeneous clustered WSNs. As a future work, it can be maximized for handling mobile base station. Also, a further direction of this proposed protocol will be to implement its algorithm in well-known routing protocols such as LEACH, SEP, TEEN, DEEC to enhance network lifetime and throughput of homogeneous and heterogeneous environments.

REFERENCES

Akyildiz, I. F., Su, W., Sankarasubramaniam, Y., & Cayirci, E. (2002). A survey on sensor networks. *Communications Magazine, IEEE, 40*(8), 102-114.

Alla, S. B., Ezzati, A., & Mohsen, A. (2012). *Hierarchical Adaptive Balanced Routing Protocol for Energy Efficiency in Heterogeneous Wireless Sensor Networks.* INTECH Open Access Publisher.

Heinzelman, W. B., Chandrakasan, A. P., & Balakrishnan, H. (2002). An application-specific protocol architecture for wireless microsensor networks. *IEEE Transactions on Wireless Communications*, *1*(4), 660–670. doi:10.1109/TWC.2002.804190

Heinzelman, W. R., Chandrakasan, A., & Balakrishnan, H. (2000, January). Energy-efficient communication protocol for wireless microsensor networks. In *System sciences, 2000. Proceedings of the 33rd annual Hawaii international conference on*. IEEE. doi:10.1109/HICSS.2000.926982

Li, H. (2010, October). An energy efficient routing algorithm for heterogeneous wireless sensor networks. In *Computer Application and System Modeling (ICCASM), 2010 International Conference on* (Vol. 3, pp. V3-612). IEEE.

Lindsey, S., & Raghavendra, C. S. (2002). PEGASIS: Power-efficient gathering in sensor information systems. In *Aerospace conference proceedings, 2002. IEEE* (Vol. 3, pp. 3-1125). IEEE.

Manjeshwar, A., & Agrawal, D. P. (2001, April). TEEN: a routing protocol for enhanced efficiency in wireless sensor networks. In *Null* (p. 30189a). IEEE. doi:10.1109/IPDPS.2001.925197

Qing, L., Zhu, Q., & Wang, M. (2006). Design of a distributed energy-efficient clustering algorithm for heterogeneous wireless sensor networks. *Computer Communications*, *29*(12), 2230–2237. doi:10.1016/j.comcom.2006.02.017

Rappaport, T. S. (1996). *Wireless communications: principles and practice* (vol. 2). Prentice Hall PTR.

Saleh, S., Ahmed, M., Ali, B. M., Rasid, M. F. A., & Ismail, A. (2014). A survey on energy awareness mechanisms in routing protocols for wireless sensor networks using optimization methods. *Transactions on Emerging Telecommunications Technologies*, *25*(12), 1184–1207. doi:10.1002/ett.2679

Smaragdakis, G., Matta, I., & Bestavros, A. (2004, August). SEP: A stable election protocol for clustered heterogeneous wireless sensor networks. In *Second international workshop on sensor and actor network protocols and applications (SANPA 2004)* (pp. 1-11).

Wang, S. S., & Chen, Z. P. (2013). LCM: A link-aware clustering mechanism for energy-efficient routing in wireless sensor networks. *Sensors Journal, IEEE*, *13*(2), 728–736. doi:10.1109/JSEN.2012.2225423

Zhou, Q., Cao, X., Chen, S., & Lin, G. (2009, December). A solution to error and loss in wireless network transfer. In *Wireless Networks and Information Systems, 2009. WNIS'09. International Conference on* (pp. 312-315). IEEE. doi:10.1109/WNIS.2009.103

Chapter 2
A Cloud Intrusion Detection Based on Classification of Activities and Mobile Agent

Nadya El Moussaid
Ibn Zohr University, Morocco

Ahmed Toumanari
Ibn Zohr University, Morocco

ABSTRACT

Cloud computing becomes the technology trend that attracts more and more both of the different forms of companies and attackers, for the reason that cloud computing provides a sharing pool of configured computing resources, such as servers, networks, applications, storage, and services, to end users. Therefore, securing sensitive data of companies from threats and attacks performed by internal or external attackers is a necessary requirement and exigency. For that purpose, in this paper presents an intrusion detection system that is based on mobile agent to collect and analysis gathered data from several virtual machines, in order to benefit from the advantages of mobile agents. The authors of this chapter propose to use C4.5 algorithm which is one of tree decision algorithms that classify data into normal and malicious one. The main purpose of our solution is creating a model of normal and abnormal behaviour.

DOI: 10.4018/978-1-5225-0602-7.ch002

INTRODUCTION TO INTRUSION DETECTION SYSTEMS

Information systems are vulnerable, and remain as long as users have the liberty to use internet and access secure or unsecure areas on the web, also as long as attackers keep on their malicious activities against systems and applications that contains sensitive data. Therefore, installing firewalls, sitting passwords and access control policies, to secure these systems, remains inadequate and not one hundred present efficient to protect those systems and the sensitive information within it from attackers. In order to detect computer attacks and react in case of any violation the intrusion detection systems came to existence. The first concept of intrusion detection system in general (IDS) was introduced by James Anderson in 1980, he introduced that audit trails contain important information that may be useful in tracking misuse or understanding the behaviour of the user, this work was the beginning of host-based intrusion detection system (HIDS). Later in 1987, Denning published a model of intrusion detection (1987). In the earlier stage of the IDS's development, the analysis of audit trails wasn't in real time, that's due to slow analysis. Therefore, intrusions were detected after they occurred. Herblein et al (1990) had developed Network Security Monitor that analysis, network traffic that provide a massive amount of information in real time, which in turn enables responses and react in real time. Then researches led to introducing Distributed Intrusion Detection System (DIDS) (1991) that combines distributed monitoring and data reduction with centralized data analysis to monitor a heterogeneous network of computers.

In general intrusion IDSs can be classified into two main categories depending on the type of analysed data: Host-based intrusion detection system (HIDS) and Network-based intrusion detection system (NIDS). HIDSs are characterized by the analysis of events and traces generated by the System, while NIDS analyse the data crossing the network. The performance of intrusion detection system, including its method of analysis, is related to two important concepts that assess its performance such as false negative and false positive.

According to the analysis method, IDS are classified into two classes: 1/ anomaly-based IDS and 2/ Signature-based IDS.

Anomaly-Based IDS

This approach proposed by Anderson (1980) and extended by Denning (1987), from a Simple finding that the exploitation of vulnerability in a system, or an intrusion attempt, involves behaviour modification in a service, an application, or a user.

This approach based on comparing the behaviour of users to a reference called a profile. Therefore, any activity or behaviour of a monitored entity (user, service, different, etc...) different from the normal behaviour or profile is an intrusion. Anomaly detection approach comprises two phases which are: first one is the construction of a normal profile; second one is evaluating any deviation of the observed behaviour with respect to the normal profile. The profile comprises a set of measurements corresponding to a "normal" behaviour that may characterize a user, service, application or system. The construction of this profile is the result of a learning phase, during which the system is "observed" to gather information from the "normal" or "abnormal" use of this system. This information is then used to generate a typical usage pattern. This profile is a set of parameters that can be of different natures:

- **The Statistical:** The profile is made up from statistical data characterizing the evolution over time of an application, user or system.
- **Logical Inference Rule:** A set of logical rules of inference defines the normal profile of a user from its previous activities. These rules can be set manually or automatically generated from observations.
- **Machine Learning**: Machine learning is used in the abnormality detection approach in order to learn a profile corresponding to the normal behaviour of a user. The learning phase uses a set of observations of a user or the system to generate this profile. The profile can be, for example, represented by a neural network which has as an input a set of parameters to be observed (processor's usage time available memory, size and type of package, etc.).
- **Data Mining**: Applied anomaly detection, Data Mining aims to extract observations characteristics data that represents the user's profile, application or system.

Signature-Based IDS

This approach detect intrusions by using a base of knowledge, known by "signature of attacks database" and a pattern matching method for recognizing defined signatures. The scenarios or base of attack signatures can be of different nature:

- **Pattern:** A Pattern Can express a sequence of system calls, a sequence of user commands or even a set of network packets of a specific attack.
- **Logical Inference Rule:** The signature database can be representing a set of logical rules of inference intended as input to an expert system. The rules are defined manually. These rules reflect the expertise of a safety operator and are written in language that can be specific to intrusion detection.
- **Automaton:** An attack scenario can also be represented using automata and finite machine's state. An automaton is the sequence of actions needed to

achieve the attack (Eckmann, 2002). This approach allows expressing complex signatures with several possibilities of steps in the automaton to achieve the same state.

These techniques and methods have been used in different environments such as single machine or networks, in small scale or in large scale such as cloud computing. Researches in intrusion detection systems combine several methods (Moorthy et al, 2012; Ektefa et al, 2010; Mingqiang et al, 2012; Prabakar Muniyandi et al, 2011; Guan et al, 2003) in order to increase its performance in term of false negative and false positive rates, also the rate of detection and to overcome the drawbacks of traditional techniques (Moorthy et al., 2012)

This chapter presents an intrusion detection system based on mobile agents to gather and analyse collected information and machine learning algorithm to create a model that will be used in the analysis phases in a cloud computing environment. The introduction presents a history of intrusion detection; the rest of this chapter is as follow: next section describes the attacks in cloud computing. Then related work in third section. Fourth section presents the proposed work with results obtained during our experiments, finally the conclusion.

ATTACKS IN CLOUD COMPUTING

Cloud computing contains three service models, according to the National Institute of Science and technology (NIST), which are infrastructure as a service (IaaS), platforms as service (PaaS) and software as services (SaaS), through these services cloud computing is characterized by a shared pool of configured computing resources that attract attackers in order to gain access privileges to sensitive data or exploiting the shared resources to perform attacks against other services. Therefore cloud computing suffers from various security issues (Jaydip et al., 2014; Hamlen et al., 2010) related to security standards such as any misconfiguration in the security policy or lack of auditing, those two points are the main vulnerabilities, in cloud computing, exploited by attackers to gain unauthorized access to the information. Also the network misconfiguration and the internet protocol vulnerabilities can lead to serious issues. Attackers exploit any weakness related to the authentication mechanism or insecure trust. In general, cloud computing issues are related to security standards, network, access control, data and cloud services. These issues lead to attacks that are categorized into four major categories namely Availability, Data Security, Network Security and Identity Management (Gruschka et al., 2010), that affect the availability, confidentiality and integrity of data. The non-cloud and traditional attacks still remain in the cloud computing environment (Khalil et al., 2013). This section describes the attacks most used against cloud computing:

Denial of Service (DoS)

DoS is aimed to make a service unavailable, to prevent legitimate users of a service from using it. It's one of the famous attacks performed on cloud computing, and can be performed from inside and outside of the network (Gruschka et al, 2010; Karnwal et al, 2012; Gul, 2010; Rashmi et al, 2015).

DoS fall into four types which are:

- Distributed denial of service (DDoS),
- HTTP based DdoS,
- XML-based DdoS,
- Representational State Transfer-based DoS attacks (REST-based DoS).

Theft of Service

This type of attack, the attacker tries to gain access to some cloud services or to use some services for a longer period by exploiting the scheduler Vulnerabilities in hypervisor scheduler (Gruschka et al., 2010; Gul et al., 2010).

Injection Attack

This attack attempts to inject malware services or virtual machine in the cloud, in order to gain privileges, access to unauthorized cloud resources or users data, to perform credential information leakage (Khalil, 2013; Apecechea, 2014).

Cross VM Side-Channel

The cross VM side channel is an attack, where the attacker uses a virtual machine (VM) attempt to extract information from a victim VM in the cloud (Zhang et al., 2012; Irazoqui et al.,2014).

VM Rollback

The virtualization is one of the main vulnerabilities of cloud computing, where the attacker uses snapshots of virtual machines (Szefer et al, 2012; Ali et al,2015).

Targeted Shared Memory

This attack consists on exploiting the vulnerability of shared memory of virtual and physical machines, to perform other attacks such as cited above (Khalil et al., 2013).

RELATED WORK

Intrusion detection systems based on traditional paradigm are limited in detecting new and unknown attacks listed by Moorthy et al. (2012). Thus, researchers are oriented to use machine learning and data mining algorithms in order to increase the rate of detection and decrease the rate of false negative and false positive such as support vector machines and classification tree (Ektefa et al., 2010), Neural networks and genetic Algorithms (Moorthy et al, 2012) and clustering (Mingqiang et al, 2012; Muniyandi et al, 2011; Guan et al, 2003) .

In cloud computing, Roschke et al. (2009) have proposed an IDS management architecture that contains several distributed sensors and a central management unit that correlate and analyse different alerts provided by multiple sensors. A sensor can be represented by any HIDS or NIDS namely Snort, Samhain, F-secure Linux security, etc... The role of each sensor is detecting and reporting any captured malicious behaviour in VMs. During the interoperability between different IDS approaches, Debar et al (2004) have proposed an Intrusion Detection Message Exchange Format (IDMEF). Gul et al (2010) have presented a distributed cloud IDS (DCIDS) based on multi-threading technique. To detect malicious packets Gul et al proposed sensors that monitor network (ICMP/ TCP/ IP/ UDP packets). DCIDS contains three modules: first one is capture and queuing model, second one analysis and processing model and the third one is reporting module which is the responsible for informing the cloud users, and the provider of cloud computing services in case of attack or any misconfiguration.

Kannan et l. (2012) proposed intrusion detection system (IDS) based on fuzzy SVM classifier audit data and featured selection based on genetic algorithm to select useful features. Dastjerdi et al. (2009) have proposed Mobile agent based IDS which can be applied by Cloud clients. This IDS contains a static agent and a mobile agent, agency and the IDS control Centre (IDSCC). Where static agents are implemented in every virtual machine, their roles is generating alerts in case of the detection of any suspicious activity in the monitored VM, then save that information in a log file and send alerts ID to the DISCO. The IDCC sends mobile agent to each VMs that have the same alert in order to investigate, collect information, correlate and send or move back the result of investigation to IDS control Centre. Next the IDSCC analyse those results in order to detect any intrusion by comparing results with intrusion patterns, then saves the information in IDSCC database. Each IDS agency in VMs sends a status as heart beat (HB) to IDSCC in regular time interval, in case of non-receiving of the HB, the VM is considered as compromised and possibility of intrusion.

Sathya et al (2013) proposed multi-level IDS in cloud computing based on C4.5 algorithm in order to analyse Tcpdump data and classify it into normal and abnormal traffics. Where, the first level classifies the network records to normal or attack. While, the second level identifies the four classes and categories. The third level, the attack type of each class is identified. And the security level is divided into three levels, high, medium and low. VM is assigned to a user according to the security level defined by Sathya et al. The anomaly level of a user is defined by its behaviour during the running of cloud services.

Doelitzscher et al. (2011) proposed a cloud incident detection system Security Audit as a Service (SAaaS) based on autonomous and intelligent agents to define normal behaviour and detect abnormal behaviour from normal one. The SAaaS architecture component is divided into three layers: Input, processing and output layer.

Intrusion detection systems can be compromised in case of attacking the monitored host, where it's implemented. Intrusion detection systems can be compromised in case of attacking the monitored host, where it's implemented. Thence, this chapter presents distributed IDS which contain various mobile agents to gather and analyse information using machine learning algorithms and a centre that manages the mobile agent in the network, also the triggered detected intrusions. Mobile agent characterized by its ability to adapt to any changes in the environment, since cloud computing is not a stable environment.

PROPOSED WORK

The proposed intrusion detection system contains a mobile agent is charged to collect data and analyse collected data using C4.5 algorithm. KDD dataset has been used in experiments.

Architecture

The architecture of the proposed IDS consists of collector mobile agent, analyzer mobile agent and IDS centers that manage all mobile agents.

The Collector Mobile Agent

The mobile agent collector collects the network activities using JpCap library based on Java. JpCap collects real-time packets and stored in a file in Order to be analysed by the mobile agent analysis.

The Analyser Mobile Agent

This mobile agent is responsible for analysing received data from collectors using machine learning algorithms. Network activities are analysed and classified into normal and malicious activities using C4.5 algorithm that provides a high level of detection for DOS, DdoS, U2R and probe. U2R and R2L are two types of attack that are hard to detect. However U2R is detected with 0,83%.

Once the intrusion is detected, analyser mobile agent sends the information about it to DIDS centre, in order to update the intrusions data base and informs other analyser mobile agent.

IDS Centre

Is the manager of our IDS, which manages the mobile agents of the proposed system, IDS centre contains 1/ A platform that create, kill and host mobile agents, 2/ A data base that contains the detected intrusions, 3/ A service to authenticate each mobile agent in the network, in order to detect any malicious mobile agent. The DIDS centre sends collector and analyser mobile agents to activate VM (Figure 1).

KDD Dataset

The used dataset consists of 10% of the original KDD dataset that is almost 500000 connection vectors, where each vector contains 41 features and labelled with "normal" or "attack" type label. The used protocols are TCP, UDP and ICMP.

Table 1 cites the 41 features:

Attacks are categorized into four types; Table 2 describes different attacks of each category.

Pre-Processing Phase

The pre-processing phase is one of the important phases in machine learning, performed on data vectors in order to extract features (i.e. extracting significant features), remove noise from data, and normalization. Table 3 describes the extracted features from 41 features:

Figure 1. A general architecture of proposed IDS

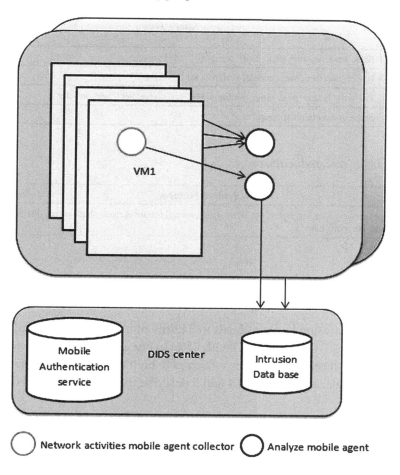

Table 1. List of 41 features

Type	Attack Type
Real	Duration, src_bytes, dst_bytes, wrong_fragment, urgent, hot num_failed_logins, logged_in, num_compromised, root_shell, su_attempted, num_root, num_ file_creations, num_shells, num_access_files, num_outbound_cmds, is_host_login, is_guest_ login, count, srv_count, serror_rate, srv_serror_rate, rerror_rate, srv_rerror_rate, same_srv_rate, diff_srv_rate, srv_diff_host_rate, dst_host_count, dst_host_srv_count, dst_host_same_srv_rate, dst_host_diff_srv_rate, dst_host_same_src_port_ rate, dst_host_srv_diff_host_rate, dst_host_serror_rate, dst_host_srv_serror_rate, dst_host_ rerror_rate, dst_host_srv_rerror_rate
String	protocol_type, service, flag, land,

Table 2. List of different types of attack for each category

Attack Category	Attack Type
DoS	Back, land, neptune, pod, smurf, teardrop
U2R	Buffer_overflow, load module, Perl, root kit
R2L	Ftp_write, guess_pwd, imap, multihop, phf, spy, warezclient, warezmaster
prob	Satan, ipsweep, nmap, portsweep

Table 3. List of selected features

Selected Features
Protocol_type, service, flag, src_bytes, dst_bytes, land, wrong_fragment, root_shell, count, diff_srv_rate, dst_host_same_src_port_rate

Results

The classification using k-means leads to 34.90% of incorrectly clustered instance, while NaiveBayes 7.61% and SMO with 25%. In our experiments, we have applied C4.5 algorithm on selected features, which give high detection of abnormal traffic and low rate of false alerts. Tables 4 and 5 describe the results obtained during our experiments.

Table 4 shows the results of traffic classification obtained, where the correctly classified instance is 99.9723% and the mean absolute error is 0.0004. In Figure 2, the traffic is classified into two clusters, one for the normal traffic and other for abnormal traffic.

Table 5 describes the results obtained during experiments for each type of attacks.

As it mentioned in Table 5, C4.5 detects most of attacks with a rate of 0.99 using the extracted features that represent the efficient features with a strong correlation. Figure 3 represents the rate of detection of all attacks.

Table 4. Rate of detection of normal and abnormal traffic

Class	TP Rate	FP Rate	Precision	F-Mesure
Normal	1	0.002	1	0,998
Abnormal	0.998	0	1	1

Table 5. Rate of detection of each attack type

Class	TP Rate	FP Rate	Precision	F-Mesure
Normal	1	0	0.999	0,999
DoS	0.97	0	0.97	0.97
U2R	0.828	0	0.60	0.45
R2L	0.485	0	0.703	0.56
Probe	0.70	0	0.77	0.73

Figure 2. Classification of traffic into normal and abnormal

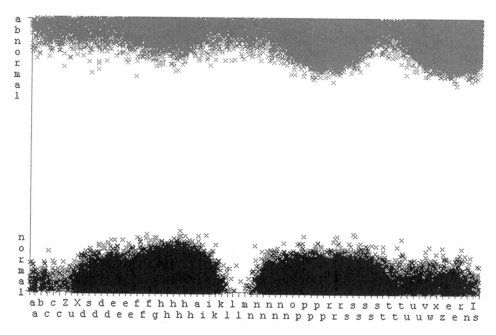

Figure 3. The rate of classification of each attack

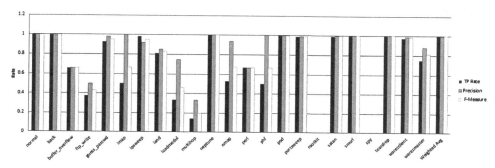

CONCLUSION

Cloud computing represents the trend of several structures and companies to save them from consuming energy, money and resources on building their own IT infrastructure. This cloud computing contains various benefits for businesses and end users. However, even the existence of all these benefits, cloud computing, suffers from security issues and threats. Where is considered attractive for attackers because it contains powerful infrastructure and the most important sensitive data of users. For that purpose, we proposed the distributed intrusion detection system based on the combination between mobile agents and machine learning algorithms, in order to detect a high rate of attacks and threats. For further work, the proposed distributed intrusion detection system will be ameliorated regarding the rate of detection of R2L. Also adapted for all types of cloud (private, public and hybrid).

REFERENCES

Ali, M., Samee, U. K., & Athanasios, V. V. (2015). Security in cloud computing: Opportunities and challenges. *Information Sciences*, *305*, 357–383. doi:10.1016/j.ins.2015.01.025

Anderson James, P. (1980). *Computer Security Threat Monitoring and Surveillance*. Fort Washington.

Dastjerdi, A. V., & Bakar, K. A. (2009). Distributed Intrusion Detection in Clouds Using Mobile Agents. *Third International Conference on Advanced Engineering Computing and Applications in Sciences* (pp.175 – 180). Sliema. doi:10.1109/ADVCOMP.2009.34

Debar, H., Curry, D., & Feinstein, B. (2004). *The Intrusion Detection Message Exchange Format, Internet Draft Technical Report*. IETF Intrusion Detection Exchange Format Working Group.

Denning, D. E. (1987). An intrusion-detection model. *IEEE Transactions on Software Engineering*, *SE-13*(2), 222–232. doi:10.1109/TSE.1987.232894

Doelitzscher, F., Reich, C., Knahl, M., & Clarke, N. (2011). An autonomous agent based incident detection system for cloud environments. *Third IEEE International Conference on Cloud Computing Technology and Science* (pp. 197 – 204). doi:10.1109/CloudCom.2011.35

Eckmann, S., Vigna, G., & Kemmerer, R. (2002). Statl: An attack language for state-based intrusion detection. *Journal of Computer Security*, *10*(1-2), 71–103.

Ektefa M. & Memar S. & Memar F. & Suriani Affendey L. (2010). Intrusion Detection Using Data Mining Techniques. *Information Retrieval & Knowledge Management*, 200-203.

Gruschka, N., & Jensen, M. (2010). Attack Surfaces: A Taxonomy for Attacks on Cloud Services. *IEEE 3rd International Conference on Cloud Computing*, (pp. 276 – 279).

Guan, Y., Ghorbani, A., & Belacel, N. (2003). Y-Means: A clustering method for intrusion detection. CCECE 2003 CCGEI 2003, (pp. 1083- 1086).

Gul, I., & Hussain, M. (2011). Distributed Cloud Intrusion Detection Model. *International Journal of Advanced Science and Technology*, 71-82.

Hamlen, Kantarcioglu, Khan, & Thuraisingham. (2010). Security Issues for Cloud Computing. *International Journal of Information Security and Privacy*, 36–48.

Heberlein, L. (1990). A Network Security Monitor, *Proceedings of the IEEE Computer Society Symposium, Research in Security and Privacy*, (pp. 296-303).

Irazoqui, G., Inci, M. S., Eisenbarth, T., & Sunar, B. (2014). Fine grain Cross-VM Attacks on Xen and VMware are possible!*IEEE Fourth International Conference on Big Data and Cloud Computing (BdCloud)*, (pp. 3-5).

Kannan, A., Maguire, G. Q., Sharma, A., & Schoo, P. (2012). Genetic Algorithm based Feature Selection Algorithm for Effective Intrusion Detection in Cloud Networks. *IEEE 12th International Conference on Data Mining Workshops*, (pp. 416 – 423).

Karnwal, T., Sivakumar, T., & Aghila, G. (2012). A comber approach to protect cloud computing against XML DDoS and HTTP DDoS attack. *IEEE Students Conference on Electrical, Electronics and Computer Science (SCEECS)*, (pp. 1 - 5). doi:10.1109/SCEECS.2012.6184829

Khalil, M., Khreishah, A., Bouktif, S., & Ahmad, A. (2013). Security Concerns in Cloud Computing. *10th International Conference on Information Technology: New Generations* (pp. 411 – 416).

Mingqiang, Z., Hui, H., & Qian, W. (2012). A Graph-based Clustering Algorithm for Anomaly Intrusion Detection. *The 7th International Conference on Computer Science & Education (ICCSE)*, (pp. 1311- 1314).

Moorthy, M., & Sathiyabama, S. (2012). A Study of Intrusion Detection using Data Mining. *IEEE-International Conference On Advances In Engineering, Science And Management (ICAESM)*, (pp. 8-15).

Prabakar Muniyandi, A., Rajeswari, R., & Rajaram, R. (2011). Network Anomaly Detection by Cascading K-Means Clustering and C4.5 Decision Tree algorithm. *International Conference on Communication Technology and System Design*, (pp. 176 – 182).

Rashmi, V. D., & Kailas, K. D. (2015). Understanding DDoS Attack & its Effect in Cloud Environment. *Proceedings of 4th International Conference on Advances in Computing, Communication and Control (ICAC3'15)*, (pp 202–210).

Roschke, S., Cheng, F., & Meinel, C. (2009). Intrusion Detection in the Cloud. *Eighth IEEE International Conference on Dependable, Autonomic and Secure Computing*, (pp. 729 – 734).

Sathya, G., & Vasanthraj, K. (2013). Network Activity Classification Schema in IDS and Log Audit for Cloud Computing. *International Conference on Information Communication and Embedded Systems (ICICES)*, (pp. 502 – 506). doi:10.1109/ICICES.2013.6508322

Sen, J. (2014). *Security and Privacy Issues in Cloud Computing. In Architectures and Protocols for Secure Information Technology Infrastructures* (pp. 1–45). IGI Global. doi:10.4018/978-1-4666-4514-1.ch001

Snapp, Brentano, Dias, Goan, Heberlein, Ho, ... Mansur. (1991). DIDS (Distributed Intrusion Detection System) – Motivation, Architecture, and An Early Prototype. In *Proceeding of the14th National Computer Security Conference.*

Szefer, J., & Lee, R. B. (2012). Architectural support for hypervisor-secure virtualization. *The Seventeenth International Conference on Architectural Support for Programming Languages and Operating Systems*, (pp. 437-450).

Zhang, Juels, Reiter, & Ristenpart. (2012). Cross-VM Side Channels and Their Use to Extract Private Keys. *ACM Conference on Computer and Communications Security*, (pp. 305-316).

Chapter 3
Considering Middle Circles in Mobile Cloud Computing:
Ethics and Risk Governance

Mohammad Ali Shalan
University of Jordan, Jordan

ABSTRACT

Mobile Cloud Computing (MCC) is increasingly asserted as the technology with the potential to change the way internet and information systems are being utilized into business enterprises. It is rapidly changing the landscape of technology, and ultimately turning the long-held promise of utility computing into a reality. Nevertheless, utilizing MCC is never a trivial task, thus calling for a special approach to get the benefits, reduce risks and control operations. The main objective of this chapter is to provide some specific guidelines to provide governance directions to align MCC into enterprise strategy and reduce risks resulted from utilizing middle circle providers; In this context, this chapter also promote and discuss some ethics that help client enterprises and MCC providers understand roles and obligations in an ever changing environment.

INTRODUCTION

Mobile Cloud Computing (MCC) among, other technologies, has emerged as a growing trend of scalable, flexible and powerful computing, capable of introducing a paradigm shift in how technology is delivering value to the business, with signifi-

DOI: 10.4018/978-1-5225-0602-7.ch003

cant global investments, MCC is showing the power to completely revolutionize the business mindset, and promotes new working styles.

However, several risks and issues are surrounding the mobile cloud utilization, where the concept of secure surrounding perimeter has been vanished with users getting more mobile while introducing internal or external service providers considered as middle circles, in addition to the substantially considerable effects for moving company's key applications, and corporate information to be processed in multiple devices that are not owned by the client enterprise. More challenge raised because the adoption of mobile cloud computing applications might begin outside the technology organization, causing plenty of loose activities and associations.

This chapter aims to portray a picture for risk structures associated with the MCC shifts, and to introduce governance and ethics mechanisms to orchestrate such a heterogeneous environment; aiming to maximize the value generated from MCC platforms that is not yet mature enough to provide risk-optimized benefits with a combined performance management tools, risk governance has a unique value in such situations.

The chapter insight is putting risk, governance and ethics in the heart, while providing highly valuable experience to those looking for guidance while utilizing more middle circles in their mobile cloud journey, it aims to increase navigation clarity through the fear, uncertainty and doubt, and to provide answers of questions related to improving organizational readiness for cloud adoption in a structured and systematic approach. This chapter characterizes MCC middle circles and correlate responsibilities required for service decomposition and duties segregation.

A main objective of this chapter is to define the risk governance transformations necessary to understand the concatenated middle circles that provide altogether the MCC services, projections and effects in the real-world, additionally, this chapter aims to help enterprises manage the ethics surrounding MCC transformation projects and contracts in a smooth and efficient manner.

BACKGROUND

Mobile and Cloud Computing represents the network of business platforms (Baya, Mathaisel, & Parker, 2010) as a new way to conceptualize and manage the integration between business and technology, actually there is no universal way to measure business technology alignment in literature (HBR, 2011; De Haes & Grembergen, 2009), however risk and governance are gaining more space to reshape the cloud era. Major associated dimensions can be identified in literature, these being technology, governance, risk management, social, mobile and cloud computing, all are evolving with plenty of research dedicated to each topic individually or bi-combined with another (Aven, 2008; Ackermann, 2012; Goranson, 1999). "Digital transformation occurs when the physical and digital works, join forces" (Shelton, 2013), nowadays more research are correlating these topics.

"The miniature nature and resources limitations of smart mobile devices, crave for lightweight efficient distributed application framework with minimum possible resource consumption and maximum possible throughput" (Kant & Ruchi, 2014) this promotes the move into utility model of computing where "an application can start small and grow to be enormous overnight. This democratization of computing means that any application has the potential to scale, and that even the smallest seed planted in the cloud may be a giant." (Sosinsky, 2011). Today "The whole concept of enterprise mobility is one that concerns employees and consumers at every level." (Campagna, Lyer, & Krishnan, 2013).

Such scenarios promote the talks about technology risks rather that information technology risks, where "cloud computing and technology transformations have reshaped significantly the business domains" (Menken & Blokdijk, 2008). Usually we used to say that technology must support business strategy, nowadays, "there are times when technology will lead us into the next realm of the previously unthinkable" (Vice, 2015). This is obvious today with "many enterprises establishing technology in the core of their operations" (Turban, Leidner, McLean & Wetherbe, 2008). That is why board members are being directly accountable for technology and requiring strong governance in analogy to their responsibility for enterprise objectives and key assets (Hardy, 2006; Shawish & Salama, 2014).

The governance concept has developed over the past few years, today cloud computing practitioners are trying to take a more structured approach to the art of governing, and turn it, as much as possible, into a science that can define a paradigm for cloud governance while considering the cloud architecture design that is comparative in convolution to the business logic complexity (Jayaswal, Kallakurchi, Houde, & Shah, 2014; Brown & Laird & Gee & Mitra, 2008). Value proposition and maturity considerations require some tailoring to fit the cloud era and increase MCC scalability and elasticity.

Risk Management is the process which enables the enterprise to set the risk tolerance, identify potential risks and prioritize them based on the enterprise's business objectives in association with internal controls (AAIRM, 2002). The mobile cloud computing paradigm is set to drive technology over the next decade and integrate the resources availability through the 3As (Anywhere, Anything, Anytime) (Mastorakis, Mavromoustakis, & Pallis, 2015), thus a broader and more inclusive risk process means that opportunities and risks will be sought proactively (Hillson, 2008; Brotby, 2006; Davis, Schiller, & Wheeler, 2006; Schlarman, 2009).

Plenty of articles are trying to understand MCC large-scale network architecture in which computing power, software, storage services, and platforms are delivered on demand to end users (Rodrigues, Lin, & Lioret, 2013) and where "some applications are designed as mobile-cloud applications right from the start" (Soyata, 2015) with associated fragmentation remains one of the major drawbacks of different mobile operating systems (Chandrasekaran, 2011; Stantchev & Stantcheva, 2013). We among others are trying to clarify how governance define the key benefits and provide measures that help an enterprise determining when intended goals are met (COSO,2012).

In summary, it can be argued that recent progress in MCC and technology environments has promoted research on risk management, governance, technology uplifting and ethics associated to middle circle providers (Abram, 2009; Marks, 2015; Segal, 2011). The main differentiator of this chapter is to jointly address all related topics trying to orchestrate the wide spectrum elements in a manner that help practitioners and researches understanding correlations and planning necessary enhancements.

RISK AND GOVERNANCE DEFINITIONS

"Risk is the possibility that an event will occur and adversely affect the achievement of objectives" (COSO, 2012), either in a positive or negative manner. Risk Management is the act of aligning risk exposure and capability to handle technology according to the stakeholders' risk tolerance, thus it acts as a primary means for decision support upon resources that are designed to protect the confidentiality, integrity, and availability of technology assets. To be effective, an enterprise must establish clear chains of responsibility to empower people, measurements to gauge effectiveness, policies to guide the enterprise meeting its goals, control mechanisms to ensure compliance, and communication to keep all stakeholders informed.

Governance is a strategic lesson learned the hard way over the past decade, that need to be revisited in the mobile and cloud era to handle challenges and hurdles. Risk and governance practices are passing deep transformations.

This section is meant to keep practitioners abreast of evolving transformations and informed on effective approaches, it includes in-depth discussion of the challenges and activities that can be helpful while utilizing MCC services.

Enterprise Risk Management

Due to the progressive nature of challenges, a risk management program is necessary to provide enterprises with required flexibility to move ahead, however implementation still requires a tremendous amount of effort. "Risk Management is the process which enables the enterprise to set the risk tolerance, identify potential risks and prioritize them based on the enterprise's business objectives in association with internal controls" (Crouhy, Galai & Mark, 2006). Enterprise Risk Management (ERM) includes the methods and processes utilized to manage risks and size opportunities to achieve the enterprise objectives.

Risks have a changing nature, also risk tolerance and appetite changes over the time responding various changes, thus it will be a must to conduct risk assessments periodically to identify areas that are high priority to the enterprise, and to engage relevant stakeholders up to the board level who should be aware of major risk affecting the business, as it is necessary to get business stakeholders—department managers, team leads, and senior executives—to think about risks as a part of a business strategy conversation.

Risk changes might affect four major elements including likelihood rating that indicates the probability that a risk may occur, impact to evaluate the consequences of risk events if they are materialized, risk tolerance which is the specific maximum risk that an enterprise is willing to take regarding each relevant risk and risk appetite to determine the amount and type of risk an enterprise is willing to accept in pursuit of its business objectives in a comfortable manner with an acceptable degree of uncertainty to handle. Other terms are less popular such as risk capacity and risk threshold to determine the enterprise ability to support risk, monitor actual risk exposure not to deviate too much and to establish triggers for management action when necessary. With dynamic and fluid risk parameters changing over time, the assessment plan and risk profile indicates the enterprise's risk acceptance level at a point in time, before being changed at later stage.

Risk management requires buy-in from the top-down so that support exist for new initiatives and processes. Management need to select a risk response strategy for every risk that is identified or analyzed, such as avoidance of exiting activities giving rise to risk, mitigation by taking action to reduce the risk likelihood or impact, sharing or insurance is utilized to transfer a portion of the risk or considering risk acceptance based on cost/benefit decision thus no action to be taken.

Governance Pillars

Governance, as the term connotes, is the set of processes, customs, policies, laws, and institutions affecting the way an enterprise is directed, administered or controlled, it also includes the relationship among the many stakeholders involved and the enterprise goals.

Principles of good governance include transparency, effectiveness and efficiency, accountability, strategic focus, sustainability, equity, fairness and respect of law where any chosen solution should be operationally and legally feasible as well as ethically acceptable. Among these principles of good governance there exist four major pillars; Accountability obligation to report, explain and be answerable for the consequences of decisions it has made on behalf of the stakeholders. Transparency to enable stakeholders understanding the decision-making process and follow the related rule of law in consistency to achieve justice. Governance is responsive serving the entire stakeholders needs in a responsible manner while balancing competing interests in a timely and appropriate way, it is also effective and efficient to implement decisions and follow processes that make the best use of the available people, resources and time to ensure the best possible results in equity and fairness. Audit is sometimes considered as the fifth governance pillar.

Good governance is based on the acceptance of the rights of shareholders, as the true owners of the enterprise, and the role of senior management as trustees. Actually, there are many models of governance which follow similar basic principles in relation to auditing behaviors and processes, management structures, corporate responsibility and compliance, transparency and information disclosure; leading to "establishing chains of responsibility, authority, and communication to empower people carry out their roles and responsibilities while establishing measurement, policy, and control mechanisms" (Brown, Moore, & Tegan, 2006), clarifying the ownership structure and the exercise of control rights.

In its participatory form, governance is the job of every stakeholder, particularly the most vulnerable, who should have opportunities to participate in the processes that affects their decisions, however the board of directors are playing a main role in technology governance under the corporate governance umbrella, as part of its responsibility in approving the company's strategy, setting its policies, and attracting high-level executives, as well as ensuring the company's credibility to its shareholders and to the official bodies.

Governance is almost voluntary with vast Implementation, analysis, performance and operational issues that must be part of sufficiently flexible policies and practices to embrace both incumbent and new resources equally, and in a way that is sufficiently consistent and comprehensive to satisfy key business needs and goals.

Governance must be executed with formality, rigor and transparency; to become part of the enterprise fabric with a defined, documented, communicated and repeatable processes. With such approach, enterprises can develop and maintain policies that address the current governance needs and have enough flexibility to address evolving conditions.

RISK GOVERNANCE FOR MOBILE CLOUD COMPUTING

ISACA defined IT risk as "the business risk associated with the use, ownership, operation, involvement, influence and adoption of IT within an enterprise. IT risk consists of IT-related events that could potentially impact the business." (ISACA, 2013), however "Business Technology Risk" seems to be more accurate, where IT is no longer the sole domain of technology that is utilized within enterprises, as most of the business units have owned specialized technologies, sometimes without the need for IT support. Actually, "The inclusion of risk management into external vendors' operation will lead to an improvement in achieving its business-level objectives" (Fit´O & Guitart, 2014).

"This distinction occurs because what matters is the effect of a potential risk on the achievement of organizational objectives – not the effect on the IT function's objectives" (Marks, 2015). The bottom line is that technology risks need to be sized by technical staff, then considered within the context of business objectives to check its maturity to the board review, as the board cannot afford to consider every risk based on the silos assessment, sometimes a sort of specialization is required to classify the risks and mitigate them across the board (Vice, 2015).

Risk accompanies change, it is a permanent and important part of life where the willingness and capacity to take risk is crucial for achieving economic development and introducing new technologies. MCC is part of a major technology shift, thus plenty of risks are arising from emerging technologies but are being accompanied by potential benefits and opportunities. To maximize benefits, such changes should be surrounded by a constitution to enable cross functional analysis and comprehensive risk assessment in directed dynamic measurement methods, enabled ownership and accountability, while ensuring the ability to respond quickly with meaningful response mechanisms. Risk governance acts as the constitution that directs the decision making processes, criteria and policies involved in the planning, architecture, acquisition, deployment, operation and management of a MCC capabilities.

Defining Risk Governance

Risk governance applies the principles of good governance to the identification, assessment, management and communication of risks in a broad context. It is concerned with how relevant risk information is collected, analyzed and communicated, and how management decisions are taken. Risk governance approach offers a broad view of risk across the enterprise, and standardizes risk management rather than isolating it to individual regulatory or operational silos. Enterprises gain not only greater insight into risk within business units, but also can evaluate the interactions of risks and processes across the enterprise and more easily identify emerging challenges before they become critical to the entire enterprise.

Risk governance goes beyond traditional risk analysis to include the involvement and participation of various stakeholders as well as considerations of the broader legal, political, economic and social contexts in which a risk is evaluated and managed. Risk governance refers to the constitutions, rules conventions, processes and mechanisms by which decisions about risks are taken and implemented. It can be both normative and positive, because it analyses and formulates risk management strategies to avoid and/or reduce the human and economic costs caused by risks. Board members should subsequently become conscious about the importance of risk governance communications to meet the stakeholders' expectations.

Concepts and tools for evidence-based risk governance, addresses some key questions such as: What is the role of technology in risk governance? Do enterprises and people understand the risk and its consequences? Do stakeholders have the capacity to manage the risk and the resilience to deal with unavoidable consequences? What are the secondary impacts of a risk and how it is managed? What organizational and economic values affect our willingness to accept the risk? To what extent should a precautionary approach be used to address uncertainty and ambiguity? and how best should one balance an inclusive approach to decision-making with the need to reach a decision?

Analysis suggests that the patterned adoption of risk governance across some enterprises is related to how entrenched governance norms and accountability demands can handle both the identification and acceptance of adverse governance outcomes within the stakeholders. This analysis not only questions assumptions about the universality of, and convergence towards, risk governance across enterprise settings, but also potentially offers an important insight into the institutional logics that underlie the concept of "risk governance" itself.

Developing Risk Governance for MCC

The fundamental issues of risk governance in Mobile Cloud Computing concern the identification and implementation of the appropriate organizational structures, processes, and controls to maintain effective rollout and operation, while assuring reasonable technology usage and information flow across the enterprise and supply chain, encompassing providers and customers of services and their supporting third party vendors. The scope of risk governance in the MCC encompasses the enterprise architecture, old and new technologies, contracts, finance, service categorization, analytics and many others. Well-developed risk governance result in technology enabled programs that are scalable with the business, repeatable across the enterprise, measurable, sustainable, defensible, continually improving, and cost-effective on an ongoing basis.

Risk-based approaches have become popular in many industries and enterprises, likewise, risk governance has become a central idea for the mobile cloud computing due to the fact that MCC roadmap is not totally clear, thus attention is required to both the probability and impact of potential adverse outcomes to help enterprises exploring assessment platforms, create risk profiles and partner with third-party providers to improve regulatory management and compliance strategies. Much attention should be paid to the normative rationales and to challenge institutionally embedded expectations of different stakeholders including various business units.

Enterprises should work to identify and describe the causes of the most commonly occurring deficits utilizing a risk governance approach and aiming to help stakeholders to better understand how these deficits occur and how they can be minimized. Developing such a risk governance is important for dealing with new risks and, in most cases, this can lead to revising approaches to existing risks, also it responds to deficits operation at various stages of the risk handling process, from the early warnings of possible risk to the formal stages of assessment, management and communication. Risk governance should look into the deficit categories, related to the assessment or understanding of risks, in addition to risk management.

HANDLING MCC MIDDLE CIRCLES

The National Institute of Standards and Technology (NIST) defines cloud computing as: "A model for enabling ubiquitous, convenient, on-demand network access to a shared pool of configurable computing resources (e.g. networks, servers, storage, applications, and services) that can be rapidly provisioned and released with minimal management effort or service provider interaction" (Mell & Grace, 2011).

The above definition aimed towards a mature setup, which is not the actual situation as of today where cloud means various things to different practitioners; and the situation is even worse when Mobile Cloud Computing is considered with the existence of multiple contractors and suppliers in the middle of the loop sometimes without clear contracts and responsibilities.

The relative immaturity of MCC business technology, chain providers and service scenarios still challenges success criteria. However, leveraging adjacent technologies like cloud and mobile provide a strong platform with the additional long term investment protection and reach capabilities, required to meet investment criteria and business objectives as business matures. The availability of various partners and deployment options flexibly extend the network value proposition, enhance mobile strategies and enable new forms of participation.

Potential consequences of risks and deficits in MCC environment may include lost opportunities; costs incurred owing to inefficient regulations; loss of public or customers' trust; inequitable distribution of risks and benefits between business units, enterprises and vendors; excessive focus on high profile risks, to the neglect of higher probability but lower profile risks; failure to move from 'business as usual' and trigger action.

This section is listing key areas in MCC where middle circles affect the MCC architecture, performance roadmap and introduce plenty of risks, also the risk based assessment is discussed.

Service Decomposition and Segregation of Duties

The technology shifts created by mobile and cloud are drastically changing the business landscape where successful businesses must find ways to extend and connect their existing infrastructures to the billions of mobile devices that exist today and the massive amount of data that is being generated, much of which will be stored in the cloud.

Technology and business leaders alike are under increasing pressure to tailor service access for the demands of mobile workforces or clients, and to the requirements of business development opportunities. At the same time, IT has anchored existing security and business policies in existing web services, technology investments and proven business workflows, controls, and visibility.

The MCC era has divided technology management into two categories; one is managed by middle circles' contractors while the other technology is controlled by the enterprise employees; both technologies can store or transmit confidential electronic information, however this might be partially accurate as enterprise staff can acquire external consultancy or acquire embedded services such as webmail or online data storage.

Because MCC is evolving continuously, senior executives and their counterparts should move from a compliance-based approach of technology towards a risk-based approach, this shift requires senior management to think differently about risk and stop handling compliance as a checklist but as a one factor in the risk profile. This will enable enterprises to comply with industry's regulatory pressure, while utilizing the risk governance directions to ensure they have the controls and processes in place to meet requirements outlined by risk-based frameworks.

Usually we used to say that technology must support business strategy, nowadays, there are times when technology will lead us into the next realm of the previously unthinkable. Board members need to be aware and prepared to evaluate MCC trends and how they impact current – and future – business plans. This is increasingly important as "practice has shown that information and technology risks are often not well understood by the enterprise's key stakeholders, including board members and executive management". (Shalan, 2010)

Good orchestration allows enterprises to maintain existing technology investments while rapidly deploying cloud platforms that allows enterprises at any stage of mobility to begin fueling business development, affiliate programs, and cross-organizational and external innovation via partners, developers, or employees.

Outsourcing or Contracting (Man in the Middle)

MCC among other innovations are converging to change modern enterprises dramatically as well its central technology shops, affecting enterprise information, technology and application development. These forces are forming a nexus, a connected group of phenomena, which is highly disruptive. MCC is promising a major change without full-time data scientists or massive racks of servers, that is capable to provide paramount services with increased flexibility utilizing the interconnectedness, social networking, and fast-paced technological change. However, this is introducing multiple middle circles which is creating a potential to increase vulnerabilities and to create new risks with impacts on a much larger scale, and sometimes over a longer time span.

The providers of MCC adds a layer of risk between the enterprise and its or client's information because most of the physical, technical, and administrative safeguards are managed by the cloud service provider, however enterprises can use cloud computing services if the enterprise uses reasonable efforts to adequately address the potential risks associated with it.

MCC is not yet mature or perfect, thus deficits might exist leading to failure in the identification, framing, assessment, management and communication of risk issues that is being introduced by several middle contractors, additional concern exist about how defects are being addressed. This leads to plenty of risks and challenges that are overseen throughout the risk handling process limiting its effectiveness and forming an actual and potential shortcoming that should be remedied or mitigated.

MCC providers are acting as mediators that can help to correlate the Small/Medium and Large Enterprise levels of requirements, which was far away from each other prior to the cloud era. Today the gap is decreasing while SMEs are increasingly acquiring more public cloud services from the wide portfolio of infrastructure and software offerings, thus including specialized solutions to handle the right mix of themes around the globe including compliance and regulations in various countries in cost effectiveness and reasonable support.

Identity and Access Management (IAM)

Segregation of duties accompanied by IAM is required to avoid accidental disclosure of data through utilization of sufficient checks and processes. The upfront signaling of value systems can reduce the occurrence of certain classes of risks such as unauthorized and malicious leak of information by disgruntled employees or middle circle contractors. Typically, insiders are exponentially more of a threat than outsiders and managing the control is not managing a risk, this is more exposed in MCC where more insiders or middle circles are being introduced making the ability to respond quickly and effectively more critical.

Identity, credential and access management becomes essential when multiple cloud offerings are integrated and applications coordinated. Corporate and customer sensitive information must be kept private, and access to protected applications must be controlled in a different manner than traditional computing models.

The utilization of cloud identity and access management practice for authentication, authorization, and audit of the users accessing mobile and cloud services is having three different paths to manage data flow between enterprise and clouds comprising identity management to, from and within the cloud, however the adoption of identity management services is climbing among enterprise organizations, where it supports specific business activities, and maturing several related industry standards and protocols to provide well federated identity solutions.

Risk-Based Assessment

Technology in general, and cloud computing in particular are promoting the shift to risk based approaches rather than compliance approaches, this has been brewing for some time and is crucial because MCC doesn't have clear compliance checks that are capable of covering its entire spectrum neither the regulations can perform this task, thus business heads have to start thinking in terms of acceptable risk levels versus compliance requirements to mark off a checklist, where it is difficult for enterprises to properly assess risk beforehand; frequent conversations promotes awareness across all lines of business. MCC governance calls exhaustive discussion and changes in language, trying to reach the truth moment for the entire enterprise when everyone understands the difference and reach an agreement on risk approaches.

The correlation of enterprise architecture with the cloud initiate the "client-cloud" architecture, in analogy to the earlier shift to "client-server" computing, which is reshaping the mission of technology that is likely to come under serious scrutiny while moving to MCC. Thus the cloud becomes the control point for what lives down in the client, complex applications will not be necessarily required to gain efficiencies, thus enterprises need to look to platforms that are more efficient to replace, and look at the available options.

Metrics and standards for measuring performance and effectiveness of technology management should be established prior to moving into the cloud. At a minimum, enterprises should understand and document their current metrics and how they will change when operations are moved into the cloud, where a provider may use different or incompatible metrics. MCC decision matrix is describing the key decision domains for principles, architecture, infrastructure, business applications, and funding prioritization to remove any ambiguity and ensures that technology decisions are optimized to return the maximum benefits.

At a different plane, complete elimination of the risk of data loss can be employed by bringing in data redundancy measures such where service levels, uptime and business continuity can be improved by bringing in a rule based risk management environment as the category of preventable risks is the most understood risk management category. Risk governance approach, insists that everything should start with risk assessment, to manage an assessed risk, not perceived risk and to understand inherent versus residual risk while involving any middle stakeholder and prepare for the response plan.

MIDDLE CIRCLE GOVERNANCE

Because MCC, as well, cloud computing is a relatively new industry, it is unregulated, considering the influx of services providers who are willing to enter this industry, there is a need to offer ethics and governance guidelines to help all stakeholders. Client enterprises are conflating few terms, for instance there should be a difference between enterprise use of technologies that would be unethical and enterprises use that would not be unethical but might be ill-advised. Governance is very important to control the enterprises behaviors towards cloud and MCC providers among other service providers.

Usually there may be a gap between technology-related service measures that are ethically required and measures that are merely consistent with best practices, governance usually flatten the roadmap for best practices. For example, it may be consistent with technology governance and best practices to install sophisticated firewalls and various protections against malware, but enterprises who install a basic level of protection are not necessarily engaged in unethical conduct. Similarly, it might be inadvisable to use a provider who does not comply with industry standards regarding encryption, but it is not necessarily unethical if an enterprise decides to do so.

Middle Circle Characterization

Many entities cooperate together to provide a competent cloud service, which includes Cloud Service Provider (CSP), Mobile Cloud Computing Provider (MCCP), Mobile Carrier (MC), cloud consumer, end users in addition to cloud auditors or regulators and government agencies.

Plenty of MCC providers today are niche players, who are just appeared on the yard, complete information about the service provider including contact details should be well verified and documented as part of MCCP corporate identity that presents its enduring symbol to show how the MCCP view itself in accordance with business objectives, also how it wishes to be viewed by others, to be recognized and remembered.

MCCP Character should be investigated including its history, length in business, funding, policies, and procedures among a long queue combining security measures, recovery plans, back up policies and its disaster plans. MCCP character also includes the number, location and tier classification of the data centers. Geographical Diversity is a typical characteristic to indicate if a service provider is likely to provide services from multiple locations to achieve service resiliency when adverse events affect one of the locations.

It is also important to understand the locations in which the MCCP provides their services from, even the locations that carry out their business activities, as this may indicate the legal jurisdictions that are relevant to their services, in certain cases necessary disclosures should be made to identify the distance between service locations, stating both onshore and offshore locations, listing all countries where the service is provided or even offices are located. Regions' specific disclosures can affect ethical behaviors that differ from country to another, thus it is important to list the countries to which variation from policy may be applied, and a comparison of country-specific disclosures should be communicated.

Infrastructure ownership is a differentiator where some MCCP providers don't own their cloud servers and instead use Amazon or Microsoft cloud servers for storing data and backing it up, such a case creates an issue if the provider defaults on a payment to servers' owner who might immediately cut off access to data and may not be able to return it to you if it goes out of business, in addition to the fact that terms and conditions may differ between provider and servers' owner. Application ownership including the source code for the applications may not be available to license on client systems outside of MCCP service provision; thus it might not be possible to use client data downloaded from MCCP systems in its native form outside of MCCP service, thus it is important to state details of how the application can be run outside of the MCCP systems.

Ethical Obligations

Ethics are usually built around reasonable care, which may include considerations to investigate the MCCP security measures, policies, recoverability methods, and other procedures to determine if they are adequate and employing available technology to guard against reasonably foreseeable attempts to infiltrate the data. Client enterprises should investigate the provider's ability according to different scenarios such as, to purge and wipe any copies of the data and to move the data to a different host if the client becomes dissatisfied or otherwise wants to change providers.

When using new technologies, reasonable precautions should be taken to increase the level of security, confidentiality and operability, it is the executive team responsibility to perform a trusted technology assessment considering number of factors prioritized according to its significance to the strategy roadmap. One consideration will be how this new technology help the business goals? how the particular technology differs from other media use? how to control the usage? who is permitted to monitor usage, to what extent and on which grounds.

As a new technology MCC implicate several ethical obligations, where MCCPs have a duty to provide competent services to client enterprises, which arguably requires MCCPs to deploy appropriate technology in their practices. Client enterprise should make reasonable efforts to ensure that MCCP contractors complies with the same professional obligations when handling their account, similarly, any ethical rules should be propagated and cascaded to ensure that a third party employed by an MCCP is pursuant to client enterprise ethical rules, and both are subject to the same ethical nondisclosure obligations. MCCP must acknowledge and accept such obligations.

Client enterprises should usually allocate time slots to continuously negotiating specific contract terms to consider the update of contract timing, warranties, indemnification, governing law and jurisdiction. Client enterprises should also include specific terms in the contract concerning the provider's obligation to maintain client confidentiality as a fundamental aspect of the such relationship, including how the MCCP will handle confidential information. Additionally, enterprise want to negotiate a price policy for as long as possible so the provider can't raise monthly fees at his sole discretion.

Terms of service policy should also be considered since some MCCPs offer premium support packages that are additional to their standard service offering and can be directed for a certain customer. It should be clear what sets of the standard support mechanisms and service level agreements (SLAs) apply to the services, comprising standard support hours and the timing clock. The issue reporting, communicating mechanism and the response time for support requests should be defined and classified into reasonable scenarios such as major incidents, unscheduled outage, or normal incident, for which the MCCP should define the communication details and the expected resolution times, in addition to the expected details level that will be provided to client enterprise following each incident report. If an MCCP intention is to shut down or isolate any service offering that is impacting, or will impact, service level agreements, MCCP obligations should be clear if specific tools should be required to enable safe shutdown, including the operation methods and service based mechanisms.

Customer engagement scenarios should be clear to client enterprise, as some MCCPs do not allow the auditing of its services by customers, similarly an MCCP may have an acceptable use policy that is applicable to specific services. Additional "plain language" statements may be requested to include any clarification of the MCCP position with regard to contract and service provisions contained in client enterprise contracts.

Business Continuity Concerns

While utilizing an MCCP services, plenty of eggs will be in his basket, thus MCCP should disclose his own business continuity preparations including any upstream provider's redundancy, failover and other service agreements. To achieve business continuity, it is important to ensure adequate security measures, where it is necessary to review the security and privacy policies of an MCCP before using his cloud for handling the client enterprise information or files. This piece of advice is almost universally ignored and its importance is not stressed enough.

Many reasonable security precautions, are free or inexpensive and easily implemented, such as data encryption which is a basic step that should be implemented to ensure the confidentiality, especially when using public wireless connections with enabled firewalls, another basic step is to activate password protection features on mobile devices to help protecting data access if the device is lost, stolen or left unattended. It is important that an MCCP mandate and keep up with such precautions without losing focus or continuous relaxation.

MCCPs and client enterprises should have an action plan for every problem scenario; including information about who gets notified and what steps are taken and by whom in case of provider outages or internet interruption, also they should have a plan in place for termination; whether the client enterprise cease the contract or the provider goes out of business, this should stress the importance to keep a copy of data locally, and setup methods for the client enterprise to retrieve the data in an accessible format, also to control how long the MCCP can retain enterprise's data after termination of the relationship. If an application can't be available for licensing on client systems, then data usage in its native format outside of MCCP service should be considered.

An MCCP should back up data adequately, these backups are not limited to customer data, but they should also include any data or configuration items which form the service being provided by the MCCP, such as configuration settings, files, documents, operating systems, applications and permissions. Understanding the backup procedures of an MCCP and its maintenance policies allows the customer to make decisions on what further steps may be added to ensure sufficient data backup. These procedures should include backups frequency either immediate, hourly, daily, weekly or monthly; backup contents such as system data, client data, statistical data and operating system data; backup storage location if being stored onsite, offsite, offshore and the relative location and distance from the location of the data being backed up.

The backup and subsequent restoration capabilities should be comprehensive enough to enable the MCCP to fully restore-to-operation the service and any customer data. The frequency and methodology of data restoration and associated backup testing should be mentioned including how often the tests are conducted and the state of how restoration is verified, if being sample tests, full restore, comparison or else. Access to backup data or archived data should be clearly articulated including the method it is available through and the management of restoration requests for customer data including the timeframe that it will be commenced within, and the backup data retention period. The permission of client audits of backup data. Regular maintenance program is also required to ensure the reliability and stability of MCCP cloud resources and service offerings. If any service is paid the expected costs should be mentioned

Data Management

To ensure the understanding of information usability rights, the ownership of data supplied by the client enterprise to the service provider need to be clearly disclosed, as unclear policies regarding ownership of stored data may lead to multiple conflicts. MCCP or CSP should clearly identify if they claim ownership of any data or information uploaded to their service, even when the data and information are being traverse or stored on the upstream provider's networks or systems. In these instances, that provider is expected to consider the data and information that client enterprise use or transmit as owned by client enterprise not by CSP, MCCP or upstream provider. Even the ownership of metadata and other statistical information, such as anonymized data generated as a result of the use of CSP service, should be considered with the purposes it may be used for.

Service providers may host data on a number of servers, located locally or offshore, knowing where hosted data is located can help client enterprises assess any risks or benefits for their business. It is important to note that any legal jurisdictions over data and information may change depending on the location. Thus storage of information on servers in countries with fewer legal protections may harm the electronically stored information.

Data access by others should be detailed in an MCCP or CSP ethics when the provider is approached by various parties and law enforcement agencies, it should be clear if a provider does or doesn't provide access to customer data to third parties including the law enforcement agencies. It is expected that the provider will notify the client enterprise if a third-party requests production of the data, where some cloud providers may produce decrypted files pursuant to a court order, when those providers hold the decryption key. However, client enterprises can add its own encryption before storing files and other client information with cloud providers, thus even if those providers produce files, they will still be encrypted and unreadable. Alternatively, enterprises can search for cloud providers that do not hold the decryption key to stored data.

Data Transportability should clarify how customers' data can be accessed both during and after a service has been provided, with the right provisions. During the service period, data access should be described in contract terms, including how data can be downloaded from service during the service provision period via certain formats. At the cessation of service to client, data should be accessible via certain methods, at no additional charges. Data access by MCCP or CSP should be stopped through a deletion of all customer data at the cessation of service in an acceptable time frame and notification mechanism, with such data should not be used in any business functions, or other purposes, or to generate revenue other than through provision of the service. Policies for data destruction is important, when a client enterprise no longer wants the relevant data available or transferring the data if a client switches service providers.

Data format may consider the portability and interoperability data features that the service provider may have, where all client data should be exported to multiple standardized format at any stage of the service delivery, such as CSV and XML with all associated relationships. Application Programming Interface (API) usage to access data should also be clarified during service provisioning and consumption, or if an API is not relevant to the service offered. Provider should clearly identify any API operations that require data to be transmitted in specific formats. Data encryption responsibilities should be completely understood by the client enterprise if the provider encrypts confidential data, including who can determine the encryption sufficiency and how it should be used in all data transportability scenarios.

MCCP is expected to take precautions to protect data and guard against unauthorized attempts to access data, such as data breaches representing unauthorized access to confidential client information by a vendor's employees, sub-contractors or by outside parties like hackers via the Internet, also there should be policies for notifying customers of security breaches and understanding what will happen when there is a data breach or if a client discover that his data has been lost or compromised. Service providers should always notify the client enterprise as soon as practicable in a specified means, unless that notification would compromise a criminal investigation into the breach, notification parameters and conditions should be clear. When a CSP or an MCCP is in possession of evidence of criminal activity associated with the breach, such as an evidence of hacker activity, the provider should always notify appropriate law enforcement agencies with a pre-specified parameters and conditions.

Code of Conduct

A fundamental code of conduct need to be put together as a voluntary framework to help evaluating MCCPs and CSPs, such code will not be prescriptive but proactive to answer vendors and consumer's needs who can adopt or understand it easily.

Adherence to an agreed code of conduct can empower the professional service providers to demonstrate and benchmark their ethics, processes, and practices to build a trust relationship with potential customers. The code of conduct also help client enterprises to create informed decisions through the disclosure of MCCPs and CSPs practices, thereby empowering them to gain confidence on the providers' ability to meet their requirements.

Code of conduct also demonstrates trust in the mobile and could computing service industry by offering a format which can be dependent on both customers and suppliers. However, MCCPs and CSPs have the option to increase their compliance level over the code by undertaking extra compliance modules or certifications which can offer a higher compliance level in areas of jurisdictions, data formats, human resources procedures, business continuity, service dependencies, data transportability, and security among other modules.

The code of conduct is expected to take care of MCCPs and CSPs, who provide services that are remotely hosted, whether within a certain countries or from them, but meeting the cloud computing definition. However, it doesn't provide legal obligations for any party if adhering to it, and if a provider is found to be falsifying information then they will have to be punished under local or international laws.

The code of conduct must include information that should be disclosed to clients, both prospective and current to improve mobile and cloud computing service standards, set up disclosure standard and create impartiality between customers and suppliers with regards to privacy, sovereignty, and data protection. As an overall it strengthens mobile and cloud computing's integrity locally and internationally.

One unique code of conduct was put by the Institute of IT Professionals (IITP, 2013) in New Zealand which was based on applied core principles and banking on existing work in computing, cloud and mobile practice at local, regional and international levels, while filtering and comprising established works rather than creating a new one or reinventing the wheel. The IITP code is consistent with global structure and practice; where it considers established approaches to resolve core issues in cloud computing, so that the results can be applied everywhere in consistency with other technology' practices. The IITP code of conduct was developed based on arbitrary approach to establish demonstrable good decisions and practices, that was facilitated in consultation with a wide range of stakeholders whose consensus was considered with the intention to obtain a broad support. A steering committee ensured that process and principles all adhere to considerable evidences, necessary compliance process and afterwards activities to maintain the integrity of the code of conduct.

FUTURE RESEARCH DIRECTIONS

Risk accompanies change, it is an inherited component of life and the willingness to take and accept risk is crucial for development and progress. Risk governance is setting the roles to enable stakeholders to benefit from changes while minimizing the negative consequences. Technology is now everywhere, mobile and cloud computing is extending the reach and stretching the services that can be used without significant capital expenditure. Actually it is the time to move into risk based analysis and utility based computing with the existence of multiple middle circles of service providers who will need special governance and ethics.

Mobile and cloud computing and associated technologies opens a wide research terrain and opportunities presenting large margins of research both in theories and in their application to real life case studies. Risk governance is very important to handle a lot of challenges and "men-in-the-middle", provide self-standing services that can be utilized from everywhere, also to standardize the business transformation approaches. This opens a wide discussion about ethics, contracting and outsourcing in addition to fundamental changes in programming structure that lead to mini-services and associated phenomena.

MCCP and SCP are utilizing optimization and acceleration techniques in a wide spectrum to orchestrate various components to minimize risk association and increase harmony. The relation between client enterprises and service providers is rephrased leading to a wide change in mentality and collaboration of both teams. Actually all the above topics will require plenty of research which might be considered as part of the SMAC (Social, Mobile, Analytic and Cloud) arena where there exists a lot of dependencies and correlations.

The development of an effective and acceptable risk governance frameworks for mobile cloud computing and code of conduct are challenges that requires the participation of a very wide range of stakeholders. This effort, in order to be successful, should be benefited from existing efforts to create common frameworks of understanding and practice.

CONCLUSION

Mobile and cloud computing among other technologies are reshaping the future, plenty of benefits are justifying the acceptance of such technologies from technical and management perspectives, however it is important to invest in the ongoing assessments and optimization for MCC governance; to ensure requirements are continuously met, the benefits are measured, and the accepted challenges are rewarded in a dynamic transformation.

Practice has shown that risk associated with mobile and cloud technologies are often not well understood by the enterprise's key stakeholders, including board members and executive management, however without a clear understanding, senior executives have no point of reference for prioritizing and managing enterprise risks and objectives. Risk governance approach offers a broad view of risk across the enterprise, and standardizes risk management to gain greater insight and evaluate the interactions of risks and processes across the enterprise and more easily identify emerging challenges before they become critical to the entire enterprise.

The mobile and cloud computing phenomena has trigged a major dependency on middle circle service providers or "men-in-the-middle" phenomena, which creates new dimensions into the enterprise governance structure, processes, and controls. As part of their due diligence client enterprises should assess these providers for sufficiency, maturity, and consistency with the client enterprise's governance and ethics, also they should manage the associated contracts and service agreements, such activities should also be cascaded to carriers and sub-contractors of the main service provider. MCCP and CSP ethics should be agreed and documented in a code of conduct that is clarifying responsibilities, practices and data handling.

Rollout of mobile and cloud computing projects are unique, where it should utilize the best enterprise architecture and follow agile methodologies, to move with sure steps to satisfy the integration and isolation rules, manage various providers and orchestrate services to regenerate the enterprise specific processes that fit all business areas.

Risk Governance has to achieve the seemingly impossible; to open and protect the enterprise processes and information effectively and balance risks with opportunities. This chapter attempts to present such an effort and aspires to ignite fruitful discussion that will eventually lead to an increased number of research studies in the field of mobile and cloud computing governance and risk maturity, paving the way for a smooth and fruitful relationship between service providers and client enterprises.

REFERENCES

Abram, T. (2009). The hidden values of it risk management. *Information Systems Audit and Control Association Journal, 2009*(2), 40-45.

Ackermann, T. (2012). *IT Security Risk Management: Perceived IT Security Risks in the Context of Cloud Computing*. Berlin, Germany: Springer-Gabler.

Aven, T. (2008). *Risk analysis: Assessing uncertainties beyond expected values and probabilities*. West Sussex, UK: John Wiely and Sons, Ltd. doi:10.1002/9780470694435

Baya, V., Mathaisel, B., & Parker, B. (2010). The cloud you don't know: An engine for new business growth. PWC Journal of Technology Forecast, 1(4), 4-16.

Brotby, W. (2006). *Information security governance: Guidance for boards of directors and executive management*. Rolling Meadows, IL: IT Governance Institute.

Brown, W. A., Moore, G., & Tegan, W. (2006). *SOA governance—IBM's approach*. Somers, NY: IBM Corporation.

Brown, W., Laird, R., Gee, C., & Mitra, T. (2008). *SOA Governance: Achieving and Sustaining Business and IT Agility*. Indianapolis, IN: IBM Press.

Campagna, R., Lyer, S., & Krishnan, A. (2013). *Mobile Device Security for Dummies*. Hoboken, NJ: John Wiley & Sons.

Chandrasekaran, I. (Ed.). (2011). Mobile Computing with Cloud. In Advances in Parallel Distributed Computing (pp. 513-522). Berlin: Springer-Verlag GmbH. doi :doi:10.1007/978-3-642-24037-9_51 doi:10.1007/978-3-642-24037-9_51

COSO. (2012). Enterprise Risk Management for Cloud Computing. Durham, NC: The Committee of Sponsoring Organizations of the Treadway Commission (COSO).

Crouhy, M., Galai, D., & Mark, R. (2006). *The essentials of risk management*. New York: McGraw-Hill Inc.

CSA (The Cloud Security Alliance). (2011). *Security guidance for critical areas of focus in cloud computing v3.0*. Retrieved September 09, 2015, from https://downloads.cloudsecurityalliance.org/initiatives/guidance/csaguide.v3.0.pdf

Davis, C., Schiller, M., & Wheeler, K. (2006). *IT auditing: Using controls to protect information assets*. Emeryville, CA: McGraw-Hill Osborne Media.

De Haes, S., & Grembergen, W. (2009). *Enterprise governance of information technology: Achieving strategic alignment and value*. New York: Springer. doi:10.1007/978-0-387-84882-2

Fit'o, J., & Guitart, J. (2014). Introducing Risk Management into Cloud. *Journal of Future Generation Computer Systems*, *32*(1), 41–53.

Goranson, H. (1999). *The agile virtual enterprise: Cases, metrics, tools*. New York: Quorum Books.

Hardy, G. (2006). New roles for board members on IT. *Governance Journal*, *13*(151), 11–14.

HBR (Harvard Business Review). (2011). *Harvard Business Review on Aligning Technology with Strategy*. Boston: Harvard Business School Publishing.

Hillson, D. (2008). Why risk includes opportunity. *The Risk Register Journal of PMI's Risk Management Special Interest Group*, *10*(4), 1–3.

IITP. (2013). Cloud computing code of practice version 2. Wellington, New Zealand: Institute of IT Professionals (IITP).

ISACA. (2013). COBIT5 for Risk. Rolling Meadows, IL: Information Systems Audit and Control Association (ISACA).

Jayaswal, K., Kallakurchi, K., Houde, D., & Shah, D. (2014). *Cloud Computing Black Book*. New Delhi, India: Dreamtech Press.

Kant, H., & Ruchi, D. (2014). *The Proliferation of Smart Devices on Mobile Cloud Computing. Haroldstr*. Düsseldorf, Germany: LAP Lambert Academic Publishing.

Marks, N. (2015). *The myth of IT risk*. Retrieved September 09, 2015, from https://normanmarks.wordpress.com/2015/08/28/the-myth-of-it-risk/

Mastorakis, G., Mavromoustakis, C., & Pallis, E. (2015). *Resource Management of Mobile Cloud Computing Networks and Environments*. Hershey, PA: IGI Global. doi:10.4018/978-1-4666-8225-2

Mell, P., & Grace, T. (2011). The NIST Definition of Cloud Computing. Gaithersburg, MD: National Institute of Standards and Technology (NIST). doi:doi:10.6028/NIST.SP.800-145 doi:10.6028/NIST.SP.800-145

Menken, I., & Blokdijk, G. (2008). *Virtualization: The complete cornerstone guide to virtualization best practices*. Brisbane, Australia: Emereo Pty Ltd.

Rodrigues, J., Lin, K., & Lioret, J. (2013). *Mobile Networks and Cloud Computing Convergence for Progressive Services and Applications*. Hershey, PA: IGI Global.

Schlarman, S. (2009). IT risk exploration: The IT risk management taxonomy and evolution. *Information Systems Audit and Control Association Journal, 2009*(3), 27-30.

Segal, S. (2011). *Corporate Value of Enterprise Risk Management: The Next Step in Business Management*. Hoboken, NJ: John Wiley & Sons.

Shalan, M. A. (2010). Managing IT Risks in Virtual Enterprise Networks: A Proposed Governance Framework. In S. Panios (Ed.), *Managing Risk in Virtual Enterprise Networks: Implementing Supply Chain Principles* (pp. 115–136). Hershey, PA: IGI Global. doi:10.4018/978-1-61520-607-0.ch006

Shawish, A., & Salama, M. (2014). Cloud Computing: Paradigms and Technologies. In F. Xhafa & N. Bessis (Eds.), *Inter-cooperative Collective Intelligence: Techniques and Applications* (pp. 39–67). Berlin, Germany: Springer-Verlag. doi:10.1007/978-3-642-35016-0_2

Shelton, T. (2013). *Business Models for the Social Mobile Cloud: Transform Your Business Using Social Media, Mobile Internet, and Cloud Computing*. Indianapolis, IN: John Wiley & Sons. doi:10.1002/9781118555910

Shinder, D. (2013). *Selecting a Cloud Provider*. Retrieved September 09, 2015, from http://www.cloudcomputingadmin.com/articles-tutorials/architecture-design/selecting-cloud-provider-part1.html

Sosinsky, B. (2011). *Cloud Computing Bible*. Hoboken, NJ: Wiley Publishing, Inc.

Soyata, T. (2015). *Enabling Real-Time Mobile Cloud Computing through Emerging Technologies*. Hershey, PA: IGI Global. doi:10.4018/978-1-4666-8662-5

Stantchev, V., & Stantcheva, L. (2013). Applying IT-Governance Frameworks for SOA and Cloud Governance. In M. D. Lytras, D. Ruan, R. D. Tennyson, P. Ordonez De Pablos, F. J. García Peñalvo, & L. Rusu (Eds.), *Information Systems, E-learning, and Knowledge Management Research* (pp. 398–407). Berlin, Germany: Springer-Verlag. doi:10.1007/978-3-642-35879-1_48

Turban, E., Leidner, D., McLean, E., & Wetherbe, J. (2008). *Information technology for management: Transforming organizations in the digital economy*. John Wiley and Sons Inc.

Vice, P. (2015). *Taking risk management from the silo across the enterprise.* Retrieved September 09, 2015, from http://www.aciworldwide.com/-/media/files/collateral/aci_taking_risk_mgmt_from_silo_across_enterprise_tl_us_0211_4572.pdf

Vice, P. (2015). *Should IT Risks Be Part of Corporate Governance?* Retrieved September 09, 2015, from http://insurance-canada.ca/blog/2015/08/30/should-it-risks-be-part-of-corporate-governance/

ADDITIONAL READING

AAIRM. (2002). *A risk management standard.* London UK: The Institute of Risk Management, the National Forum for Risk Management in the Public Sector and the Association of Insurance and Risk Managers.

Aljawarneh, S. (Ed.). (2012). *Cloud Computing Advancements in Design, Implementation, and Technologies.* Hershey, PA, USA: IGI Global.

Alnuem, M., Alrumaih, H., & Al-Alshaikh, H. (2015). *Enterprise risk management from boardroom to shop floor.* Paper presented in The Sixth International Conference on Cloud Computing, GRIDs, and Virtualization, Nice, France.

Antonopoulos, N., & Gillam, L. (Eds.). (2010). *Cloud Computing: Principles, Systems and Applications.* London, UK: Springer-Verlag. doi:10.1007/978-1-84996-241-4

Ben Halpert, B. (2011). *Auditing Cloud Computing: A Security and Privacy Guide.* Hoboken, NJ, USA: John Wiley & Sons. doi:10.1002/9781118269091

Bento, A., & Aggarwal, A. (Eds.). (2013). *Cloud Computing Service and Deployment Models: Layers and Management.* Hershey, PA, USA: IGI Global. doi:10.4018/978-1-4666-2187-9

Biske, T. (2008). *SOA governance.* Birmingham, United Kingdom: Packt Publishing.

Booker, S., Gardner, J., Steelhammer, L., & Zumbakyte, L. (2004). What is your risk appetite? The risk-it model. *Information Systems Audit and Control Association (ISACA). Journal, 35*(2), 38–43.

Bostrom, A. (Ed.). French, S. (Ed.), & Gottlieb, S. (Ed.). (2008). Risk assessment, modeling and decision support: Strategic directions. Heidelberg, Germany: Springer-Verlag

Braithwaite, J., Coglianese, C., & Levi-Faur, D. (2007). Can Regulation and Governance Make a Difference? *Regulation and Governance Journal. Wiley Publishing Asia Pty Ltd, 1*(1), 1–7.

Broder, J. (2006). *Risk analysis and the security survey*. Burlington, Massachusetts, USA: Butterworth-Heinemann Elsevier.

Busby, J., & Zhang, H. (2008). How the subjectivity of risk analysis impacts project success? *Project Management Journal, 39*(3), 86–96. doi:10.1002/pmj.20070

Buyya, R., Broberg, J., & Goscinski, A. (Eds.). (2010). *Cloud Computing: Principles and Paradigms*. Hoboken, NJ, USA: John Wiley & Sons.

Chao, L. (Ed.). (2012). *Cloud Computing for Teaching and Learning: Strategies for Design and Implementation*. Hershey, PA, USA: IGI Global. doi:10.4018/978-1-4666-0957-0

Daecher, A., & Galizia, T. (2015). *Ambient computing. Deloitte Journal of Tech Trends 2015, 6 (1)* (pp. 34–49). United Kingdom: Deloitte University Press.

Dallas, G. (Ed.). (2004). Governance and risk. New York, USA: McGraw-Hill companies Inc.

Drucker, P. (1999). *Management challenges for the 21st century*. New York City, New York, USA: HarperCollins Publishers Inc.

Dutta, A., Peng, G. C., & Choudhary, A. (2013). Risks in enterprise cloud computing: The perspective of IT experts. *Journal of Computer Information Systems, 53*(4), 39–48. doi:10.1080/08874417.2013.11645649

Easwar, K. L. (2014). *Segmentation of Risk Factors associated with Cloud Computing*. Paper presented at 2nd International Conference on Cloud Security Management [ICCSM], Reading, UK.

Furht, B., & Escalante, A. (Eds.). (2010). *Handbook of Cloud Computing*. Berlin, Germany: Springer Science & Business Media. doi:10.1007/978-1-4419-6524-0

Grembergen, W. (Ed.). (2003). *Strategies for information technology governance*. Hershy, Pennsylvania, USA: Idea Group Publishing.

Hoogervorst, J. (2009). *Enterprise governance and enterprise engineering*. Diemen, Netherlands: Springer. doi:10.1007/978-3-540-92671-9

Hubbard, D. (2009). *The Failure of Risk Management: Why It's Broken and How to Fix It*. Hoboken, NJ, USA: John Wiley & Sons.

Information Resources Management Association (Ed.). (2015). Cloud Technology: Concepts, Methodologies, Tools, and Applications (Vols. 1–4). Hershey, PA, USA: IGI Global.

Jamsa, K. (2012). *Cloud Computing*. Burlington, MA, USA: Jones & Bartlett Publishers.

Jordan, E., & Silcock, L. (2005). *Beating IT risks*. West Sussex, England: John Wiely and Sons, Ltd.

Kaplan, R., & Mikes, A. (2012). Managing Risks: A new framework. *Harvard Business Review, 90*(6), 48–63.

Kark, K., & Vanderslice, P. (2015). CIO as Chief Integration Officer. Deloitte Journal of Tech Trends 2015, 6 (1), pp. 04-19, Deloitte University Press, United Kingdom.

Kunreuther, H. (2006). Risk and reaction: Dealing with interdependencies. *Harvard International Review: Global Catastrophe, 28*(3), 17–23.

Kunreuther, H. (2008). *The weakest link: Risk management strategies for dealing with interdependencies* (Working Paper # 2008-10-13). Philadelphia, Pennsylvania, USA: University of Pennsylvania, the Wharton School.

Kwak, Y. (2003). *Perception and practice of project risk management*. Paper presented in the Project Management Institute Global Congress North America, Baltimore, Maryland USA.

Lientz, B., & Larssen, L. (2006). *Risk management for IT projects*. Oxford, United Kingdom: Butterworth-Heinemann.

McDonald, K. (2010). *Above the Clouds: Managing Risk in the World of Cloud Computing, Cambridge shire*. United Kingdom: IT Governance Ltd.

Moeller, R. (2008). *Enterprise risk management and the project manager*. Paper presented at Project Summit & Business Analyst World, Philadelphia, USA.

Moran, A. (2014). *Agile Risk Management*. New York, USA: Springer. doi:10.1007/978-3-319-05008-9

Moran, A. (2015). *Managing Agile: Strategy, Implementation, Organization and People*. Berlin, Germany: Springer. doi:10.1007/978-3-319-16262-1

Newman, M. (2004). Firewalls: Keeping the big, bad world out of your firm. *San Fernando Valley Business Journal, 9*(18), 21–22.

Niemann, K. (2008). *From Enterprise architecture to IT governance: Elements of effective IT management*. Wiesbaden, Germany: Springer-Verlag.

NIST (National Institute of Standards and Technology). (2015). *cloud computing service metrics description* Retrieved September 09, 2015, from http://www.nist.gov/itl/cloud/upload/RATAX-CloudServiceMetricsDescription-DRAFT-20141111.pdf

Peltier, R. (2005). *Information security risk analysis*. Boca Raton, Florida, USA: Taylor and Francis.

PMI. (2008). *A Guide to project management body of knowledge*. Newtown square, Pennsylvania, USA: Project Management Institute.

Raj, B. (2012). Cloud Enterprise Architecture, Poca Raton, FL, USA: CRC Press: Taylor & Francis Group. doi:doi:10.1201/b13088 doi:10.1201/b13088

Ramirez, D. (2008). IT risk management standards: The bigger picture. *Information Systems Audit and Control Association (ISACA) Journal, 2008*(4), 35-39.

Renn, O. (2008). *Risk governance: Coping with uncertainty in a complex world*. London, United Kingdom: Earthscan Publications Ltd.

Rittinghouse, J., & Ransome, J. (2009). Cloud Computing: Implementation, Management, and Security, Poca Raton, FL, USA: CRC Press: Taylor & Francis Group.

Rothstein, H., Borraz, O., & Huber, M. (2013). Risk and the Limits of Governance. Exploring varied patterns of risk-based governance across Europe. *Regulation and Governance Journal. Wiley Publishing Asia Pty Ltd, 7*(2), 215–235.

Sawyer, S., & Tapia, A. (2005). The sociotechnical nature of mobile computing work: Evidence from a study of policing in the United States. *International Journal of Technology and Human Interaction, 1*(3), 1–14. doi:10.4018/jthi.2005070101

Schekkerman, J. (2006). *How to survive in the jungle of enterprise architecture frameworks*. Victoria, BC, Canada: Trafford Publishing.

Sosinsky, B. (2011). *Cloud Computing Bible*. Indianapolis, IN, USA: John Wiley & Sons.

Tarkoma, S. (2012). *Publish / Subscribe Systems: Design and Principles*. Hoboken, NJ, USA: John Wiley & Sons. doi:10.1002/9781118354261

Thuraisingham, B. (2013). Developing and Securing the Cloud, Poca Raton, FL, USA: CRC Press: Taylor & Francis Group. doi:doi:10.1201/b15433 doi:10.1201/b15433

Tiwari, A., Sharma, V., & Mahrishi, M. (2014). Service Adaptive Broking Mechanism Using MROSP Algorithm. In *Proceedings Advanced Computing, Networking and Informatics-: Wireless Networks and Security Proceedings of the Second International Conference on Advanced Computing, Networking and Informatics (ICACNI-2014)* (vol. 2, pp. 383-392). Springer, PA, USA doi:doi:10.1007/978-3-319-07350-7_43 doi:10.1007/978-3-319-07350-7_43

Türke, R. (2008). *Governance: Systemic foundation and framework*. Heidelberg, Germany: Springer-Verlag. doi:10.1007/978-3-7908-2080-5

Udoh, E. (Ed.). (2011). *Cloud, Grid and High Performance Computing: Emerging Applications*. Hershey, PA, USA: IGI Global. doi:10.4018/978-1-60960-603-9

Vose, D. (2008). *Risk analysis: A quantitative guide*. West Sussex, England: John Wiley and Sons, Ltd.

Walewski, J., & Gibson, G. (2003). *International project risk assessment: methods, procedures, and critical factor (Research. Rep. No. 31)*. Austin, Texas: The University of Texas at Austin, Construction Industry Studies Centre.

Warrier, S., & Shandrashekhar, P. (2006). A Comparison Study of Information Security Risk Management Frameworks in. Paper presented in the Asia Pacific Risk and Insurance conference, Tokyo, Japan.

Westerman, G., & Hunter, R. (2007). *IT risk: Turning business threats into competitive advantage*. Boston, Massachusetts, USA: Harvard Business School Publishing.

Zhao, F. (Ed.). (2006). *Maximize business profits through e-partnerships*. Hershey, PA: IRM Press. doi:10.4018/978-1-59140-788-1

KEY TERMS AND DEFINITIONS

Cloud Service Provider (CSP): An entity that provides computing services based on their existing platforms and apply certain rules for these services.

Code of Conduct: A voluntary framework to start screening service providers in a proactive manner to answer stakeholders needs who can adopt or understand it easily.

Ethics: Consideration to investigate measures, policies, and other procedures to determine if they are adequate and employing available guards against reasonably foreseeable attempts.

Governance: A set of processes, customs, policies, laws, and institutions affecting the way an enterprise is directed, administered or controlled.

Middle Circle (MC): A middle service provider who can be external or internal to an enterprise and working to enable certain cloud service in the loop.

Mobile Cloud Computing (MCC): A platform that is utilizing mobile devices and cloud computing architecture to provide various computing services.

Mobile Cloud Computing Provider (MCCP): An entity that provides mobile computing services based on their existing platforms and apply certain rules for these services.

Risk Governance: An approach that offers a broad view of risk across the enterprise, and standardizes risk management rather than isolating it to individual regulatory or operational silos.

Risk Management: The act of aligning exposure to risk and capability to handle information and technology with the stakeholders' risk tolerance.

Chapter 4
Managing Risk in Cloud Computing

Lawan Ahmed Mohammed
University of Hafr Albatin, Saudi Arabia

ABSTRACT

Computer crime is now becoming a major international problem, with continual increases in incidents of cracking, hacking, viruses, worms, bacteria and the like having been reported in recent years. As a result of this massive vulnerabilities and new intrusion techniques, the rate of cybercrime has accelerated beyond imagination. In recent years, cloud computing have become ubiquitous, permeating every aspect of our personal and professional lives. Governments and enterprises are now adopting cloud technologies for numerous applications to increase their operational efficiency, improve their responsiveness and competitiveness. It is therefore vital to find ways of reducing and controlling the risk associated with such activities especially in cloud computing environment. However, there is no perfect-safe way to protect against all cyber attacks, hence, there is need for a proper recovery planning in the event of disaster resulting from these attacks. In this chapter, several means of limiting vulnerabilities and minimizing damages to information systems are discussed.

INTRODUCTION

Cloud computing typically refers to resources such as infrastructure, platforms and/ or software provided as a service over the Internet: In many countries, these services are used to control, manage, and operate systems. Transportation, banking, power system, health services, telecommunication, and the like are highly automated and

DOI: 10.4018/978-1-5225-0602-7.ch004

computerized. These systems, in addition to defense, government, and education form part of a society's critical information infrastructure.

According to International Data Corporation (IDC), cloud has changed the fundamental nature of computing and how business gets done and it will continue to do so through 2020 (IDC, 2015). In fact, IDC predicts that by 2020 clouds will stop being referred to as "public" and "private" and ultimately they will stop being called clouds altogether. It is simply the new way business is done and IT is provisioned.

As SearchCIO.com Features Writer Karen Goulart wrote "Cloud Disaster Recovery (Cloud DR) is a fast-growing area of disaster preparedness". Cloud for DR is not a single-point solution, but it must now be considered part of any plan. Though, there are more use of cloud disaster recovery on a personal level, but there is need for improvement of cloud DR on a business level. The need for such requirements are due to some of the reasons mentioned below:

- The increase adoption of cloud computing, and growing demand for managed security services are playing a major role in shaping the future of cloud-based security services. Even though there are various on-premise solutions available for all types of security, cloud security has become the prime importance for business who want to support growing number of remote work force.
- According to the *Global Technology Adoption Index 2015* Report by Dell (www.dell.com/GTAI), more than any other reason named. Security is also most frequently the top risk of adopting public cloud (44%) and SaaS (38%).
- Also according to the same Index Report, 54% of midmarket companies' security budgets are invested in security plans versus reacting to threats.
- According to the 2015 International Business Resilience Survey, conducted by Marsh and Disaster Recovery Institute International (DRI), firms consider cyber and IT-related risks to be the most likely to occur and have the greatest potential impact on their operations.
- 54% of an organization's security budget is invested in security plans versus reacting to threats. Dell & TNS Research discovered that midmarket organizations both in North America and Western Europe are relying on security to enable new devices or drive competitive advantage. In North America, taking a more strategic approach to security has increased from 25% in 2014 to 35% today. In Western Europe, the percentage of companies taking a more strategic view of security has increased from 26% in 2014 to 30% this year.

This chapter examines some the threats associated with cloud computing and attempts to highlights various methods of limiting their impact. The rest of the chapter is organized as follows; the next section looks into the security challenges and risk associated with cloud computing. Section three deals with counter measures or plan of action not only based on security attack but also in the event of disaster. The section covers areas such as disaster planning and risk management and assessment. Finally, conclusion is given in section four.

SECURITY CHALLENGES AND RISK IN CLOUD COMPUTING

According to (LLP, Chan, Leung & Pili, 2012), "Risk is the possibility that an event will occur and adversely affect the achievement of objectives". The types of risks (e.g., security, integrity, availability, and performance) are the same with systems in the cloud as they are with non-cloud technology solutions. An organization's level of risk and risk profile will in most cases change if cloud solutions are adopted (depending on how and for what purpose the cloud solutions are used). This is due to the increase or decrease in likelihood and impact with respect to the risk events (inherent and residual) associated with the CSP that has been engaged for services. Some of the typical risks associated with cloud computing are:

Disruptive Force

When an industry member adopts cloud solutions, other organizations in the industry could be forced to follow suit and adopt cloud computing (LLP, Chan, Leung & Pili, 2012).

Security and Compliance Concerns

Depending on the processes cloud computing is supporting, security and retention issues can arise with respect to complying with regulations and laws such as the *Sarbanes-Oxley Act of 2002* (Pincus, & Rego, 2008), the *Health Insurance Portability and Accountability Act of 1996* (HIPAA), and the various data privacy and protection regulations like *USA PATRIOT Act*, the EU Data Protection Directive, Malaysia's *Personal Data Protection Act 2010*, and India's *IT Amendments Act* are enacted in different countries. In the cloud, data is located on outside of the organization's direct control. Depending on the cloud solution used (SaaS, PaaS, or IaaS), a cloud customer organization may be unable to obtain and review network operations or security incident logs because they are in the possession of the CSP. The CSP may be under no obligation to reveal this information or might be unable to do so without violating the confidentiality of the other tenants sharing the cloud infrastructure (LLP, Chan, Leung & Pili, 2012). Others as mentioned by the authors include:

- **Cyber-Attack:** The consolidation of multiple organizations operating on a CSP's infrastructure presents a more attractive target than a single organization, thus increasing the likelihood of attacks. Consequently, the inherent risk levels of a CSP solution in most cases are higher with respect to confidentiality and data integrity.
- **Data Leakage:** A multi-tenant cloud environment in which user organizations and applications share resources presents a risk of data leakage that does not exist when dedicated servers and resources are used exclusively by an organization. This risk of data leakage presents an additional point of consideration with respect to meeting data privacy and confidentiality requirements.

Attack Surface

A hypervisor or virtual machine monitor is an additional layer of software between an operating system and hardware platform, needed to operate multi-tenant VMs and applications hosted thereupon. Besides virtualized resources, the hypervisor normally supports other programming interfaces to conduct administrative operations, such as launching, migrating, and terminating VM instances. Compared with a non-virtualized implementation, the addition of a hypervisor causes an increase in the attack surface (Jansen & Grance, 2011). The complexity in VM environments can also be more challenging than their traditional counterpart, giving rise to conditions that undermine security (Kalpana, 2012). For example, paging, check pointing, and migration of VMs can leak sensitive data to persistent storage, subverting protection mechanisms in the hosted operating system. The hypervisor itself can also be compromised. A zero-day exploit in the HyperVM virtualization application purportedly led to the destruction of approximately 100,000 virtual server based Websites hosted at Vaserv.com (Garfinkel & Rosenblum, 2005).

Virtual Network Protection

Most virtualization platforms have the ability to create software-based switches and network configurations as part of the virtual environment to allow VMs on the same host to communicate more directly and efficiently. For example, the VMware virtual networking architecture supports same-host networking in which a private subnet is created for VMs requiring no external network access. Traffic over such networks is not visible to the security protection devices on the physical network, such as network-based intrusion detection and prevention systems (Vieira, Alexandre, Carlos Westphall & Carla Westphall, 2009). To avoid a loss of visibility and protection against intra-host attacks, duplication of the physical network protections may be required on the virtual network

Authentication

A growing number of cloud service providers support the SAML standard and use it to administer users and authenticate them before providing access to applications and data. SAML provides a means to exchange information, such as assertions related to a subject or authentication information, between cooperating domains. SAML request and response messages are typically mapped over the Simple Object Access Protocol (SOAP), which relies on XML for its format. With Amazon Web Services, for example, once a user has established a public key certificate, it is used to sign SOAP requests to the EC2 to interact with it. SOAP message security validation is complicated and must be carried out carefully to prevent attacks. XML wrapping attacks involving the manipulation of SOAP messages have been successfully demonstrated against Amazon's EC2 services (Gajek, Jensen, Liao & Schwenk, 2009 and Gruschka &Iacono, 2009). A new element (i.e., the wrapper) is introduced into the SOAP Security header; the original message body is then moved under the wrapper and replaced by a bogus body containing an operation defined by the attacker. The original body can still be referenced and its signature verified, but the operation in the replacement body is executed instead.

Denial of Service

A denial of service attack involves saturating the target with bogus requests to prevent it from responding to legitimate requests in a timely manner. An attacker typically uses multiple computers or a botnet to launch an assault. Even an unsuccessful distributed denial of service attack can quickly consume a large amount of resources to defend against and cause charges to soar. The dynamic provisioning of a cloud in some ways simplifies the work of an attacker to cause harm. While the resources of a cloud are significant, with enough attacking computers they can become saturated (Jensen, Schwenk, Gruschka & Iacono, 2009). For example, a denial of service attack against Bit Bucket, a code hosting site, caused an outage of over 19 hours of downtime during an apparent denial of service attack on the underlying Amazon cloud infrastructure it uses (Brooks, 2009 and Metz, 2009). Besides publicly available services, denial of service attacks can occur against private services, such as those used in cloud management. For example, a denial of service attack occurred against the cloud management programming interface of the Amazon Cloud Services involved machine instances replicating themselves exponentially (Slaviero, 2009). Internally assigned no routable addresses, used to manage resources within the service provider's network, and may also be used as an attack vector. A worst-case possibility that exists is for elements of one cloud to attack those of another or to attack some of its own elements (Leavitt, 2009).

Abuse of Cloud Services

Many Infrastructure as a Service (IaaS) providers make it easy to take advantage of their services. All you need to register and start using their cloud services is a credit card. Cybercriminals actively target cloud services providers, partially because of this relatively weak registration system that helps obscure identities, and because many providers have limited fraud-detection capabilities. Stringent initial registration and validation processes, credit card fraud monitoring, and subsequent authentication are ways to remediate this type of threat.

Shared Technology Issues

Public clouds deliver scalable services that provide computing power for multiple tenants, who many not necessarily belong to the same organization. Dense virtualization can lead to multiple tenant data co-residing in the same hardware subsystems, from CPU subsystems to memory and storage. Even with a virtualization hypervisor to mediate access between guest operating systems and physical resources, there is concern that attackers can gain unauthorized access and control of your underlying platform with software-only isolation mechanisms. This is a key issue faced by most IT organizations in achieving their virtualization goals—and subsequently in moving workloads to the cloud.

Data Loss

Protecting data can be a headache because of the number of ways it can be compromised. Some data—customer, employee, or financial data, for example—should be protected from unauthorized users. But data can also be maliciously deleted, altered, or unlinked from its larger context. Loss of data can damage your company's brand and reputation, affect customer and employee trust, and have regulatory compliance or competitive consequences. In 2011, for example, 174 million records were compromised, costing organizations an average of $5.5 million—or $194 per compromised record.

Hijacking of Accounts or Services

Attacks such as phishing and fraud continue to be an ongoing threat. With stolen credentials, hackers can access critical areas of your cloud and potentially eavesdrop on transactions, manipulate or falsify data, and redirect your clients to illegitimate sites. IT organizations can fight back with strong identity and access management, including two-factor authentication where possible, strong password requirements, and proactive monitoring for unauthorized activity.

Just to illustrate hackers alone, in one three-month period alone:

- A hacker penetrated LinkedIn's website security and published a list of *6.5 million* hashed passwords, and then used cutting-edge hardware and software to decode many of the passwords (LinkedIn, 2012a; Ars Technica, 2012).
- Dropbox revealed that usernames and passwords stolen from other websites were used to sign into a number of its customer accounts (Drobox, 2012).
- A 19-year-old hacker used a few easily obtainable pieces of personal information to convince Apple customer service that he was a prominent reporter, reset the reporter's Apple password, and used the information from the reporter's Apple account to access his iCloud, Amazon, Gmail and Twitter accounts (Wired, 2012a, 2012b).

Once a hacker or for that matter an insider such as a disgruntled systems administrator or anyone with access privileges obtains the credentials of a legitimate user, he or she can access, decrypt, change, re-encrypt and save files. Server-side file encryption would provide no indication that the files had been tampered with.

A very similar scenario could play out if a hacker or an insider at a cloud service provider obtained access to the keys used to encrypt the data. The bad actor might be able to decrypt, change and replace stored files without anyone knowing what had happened. Another challenge that companies face is proving that they have not altered their own records. Neither client-side nor server-side encryption solves this problem, as the owner of the record scan always decrypt data, alter it, and finally re-encrypt it.

Loss of Control

When services are fully managed and delivered by a third party, an organization loses control over how it secures its environments. Organizations that use cloud computing for critical business functions such as credit card processing, online banking, etc. need to find an answer to ho users are concern with the following:

1. Is your data safe in the cloud and at the provider?
2. Is your data kept private in the cloud and at the provider?
3. Can other clients of the provider access your data?
4. Is your data backed up and retained for enough time?

To answer the above question, a simple survey was conducted to understand the user's perception about risk in using cloud computing as indicated in Figure 1.

Based on the above mentioned points, the key risks associated with the use of cloud computing are depicted in Figure 2.

Recently, a report by Holger Schulze (2015) listed the some major trends in cloud security as follows:

- Security is still the biggest perceived barrier to further cloud adoption. Nine out of ten organizations are very or moderately concerned about public cloud security.
- The dominant cloud security concerns involve unauthorized access, hijacking of accounts, and malicious insiders. Almost 80% of managers are concerned about personal cloud storage services operated by employees or visitors.
- The most popular method to close the cloud security gap is the ability to set and enforce consistent cloud security policies. Encryption for data at rest and in motion top the list of most effective security controls for data protection in the cloud.
- Is cloud computing delivering on the hype? Yes on flexibility, availability and cost reductions. But security and compliance remain the biggest concerns.
- Despite SaaS providers making massive investments in security, 36% of respondents believe that major cloud apps such as Salesforce and Office 365 are less secure than on-premise applications.

Figure 1. User's perception: risk in using cloud computing

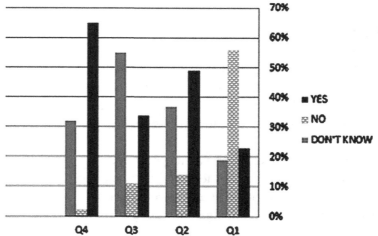

Figure 2. Security risks in cloud

The report is the result of comprehensive research in cooperation with the 250,000+ member Information Security Community on LinkedIn to explore the specific drivers and risk factors of cloud infrastructure, how organizations are using the cloud, whether the promise of the cloud is living up to the hype, and how organizations are responding to the security threats in these environments. The biggest security threats are shown in Figure 3.

Figure 3. Biggest security threats

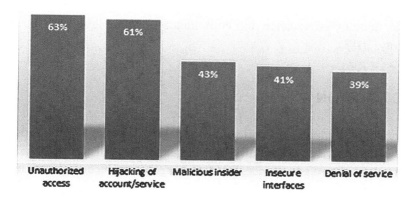

A similar survey by Marsh and DRI International stated that among 10 suggested risk scenarios, the top risks in terms of impact and likelihood are: reputational damage from a sensitive data breach (impact 79% - likelihood 79%); the failure in a main IT data center (59% - 77%); and online services being unavailable due to a cyber attack (58% - 77%). The risks with the lowest potential impact originate from a product recall event (15% - 21%). https://www.drii.org/newsdetails.php?newsid=72.

TRENDS AFFECTING CLOUD SECURITY

To manage cloud security in today's world, you need a solution that helps you address threats to your data and infrastructure, as well as the major challenges of cloud computing. These include:

- **Changing Attackers and Threats:** Attacks aren't coming just from isolated hackers now. More and more, organized crime is driving well-resourced, sophisticated, targeted attacks for financial gain.
- **Evolving Architecture Technologies:** With the growth of virtualization and rise in cloud adoption, perimeters and their controls within the data center are in flux, and data is no longer easily constrained or physically isolated and protected.
- **Consumerization of IT:** As mobile devices and technologies continue to become more common, employees want to use personally owned devices to access enterprise applications, data, and cloud services.
- **Dynamic and Challenging Regulatory Environment:** Organizations and their IT departments face ongoing burdens of legal and regulatory compliance with increasingly prescriptive demands and high penalties for noncompliance or breaches. 90% of IT professionals are concerned about an inability to monitor governance and compliance (Technology-Cloud Computing Survey, 2013).

PLAN OF ACTION

As the amount of computer networks users and the number of machines on the net dealing with sensitive/confidential issues increases, so will the potential for the crackers/hackers. As a consequence, it is necessary to introduce very strict measures which will seek to prevent them. However, it is necessary to be aware that there are a number of factors which make this hard:

1. There are a large number of sophisticated users with the ability to intercept and/ or modify any information that a sender sends to a receiver (or vice versa). In addition, they can introduce their own traffic on to the network in an attempt to fool the receivers that they are legitimate senders (or vice versa).

2. The scale of the problem is not widely recognised, and many system administrators do not understand the nature of the threats they face, have little idea of what constitutes a reasonable security policy, and know little of the remedies which they can take. Instead, they rely solely on software, which is demonstrably inadequate.

3. Security policies are often seen by employees as either time-consuming and unacceptable or as an indication that they are not trusted. As a result, they are often ignored or subverted, leaving huge holes for potential attackers.

4. There are, generally restrictive, regulations about the dissemination and use of encryption technology. For example, the export of encryption technology from US is illegal without a license, and the importation and use of encryption is practically illegal in France.

5. Although operating fraudulently is a global problem, in view of the fact that the computer networking is a presently a global resource, it is unclear under whose legal jurisdiction a crime has been committed when one defrauds an institution or individual in another country.

In view of the above, security solutions must consider various factors instead of focusing on boarder security alone, as the intruder can even be an insider. Moreover, tools such as firewalls, virus scanners, and intrusion detection systems are rapidly maturing, but rapid technology advances, a plethora of nonsecure products, and the growing complexity of corporate networks diminish their effectiveness. To appropriately respond to their increased vulnerability, corporations must focus on building a layered defense to secure the information assets (Mike, 2002). As a guide, Figure 4 shows three steps of an in-depth plan.

The first step (boarder security) is the *Network Layer Security* which consists of; virus scanning, firewalls, intrusion detection, virtual private networking, denial-of-service protection etc. The second step (authentication) is the *Proof of Identity* which involves; username/password, password synchronization, public key, tokens, biometrics, single sign-on etc. The third step (authorization) is the *Permission Based on Identity*, it consists of; user/group permission, enterprise directories, enterprises user administration, rules-based access control etc.

Furthermore, it is always essential to have a proper backup of valuable data. Back up is a method of protecting data (recovering) in case of lost, integrity, and confidentiality. Today, with the low cost of computer discs it easy to have a reliable backup systems based on centralized and individualize bases. For instance, it is easy

Figure 4. A layered defense

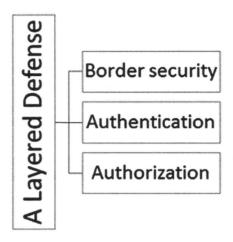

and inexpensive for companies or organization to issue smart cards to their customers/users that may contains customer's data as a backup copy under possession of the customers in addition to the centralized backup system of the company. With back up system companies can automatically protect their data on a daily basis to ensure continuity.

Planning for Disaster

Disaster recovery planning (DRP) has taken on a new sense of urgency in recent years. Emerging issues like terrorism, hackers, viruses, worms, an increased reliance on computers, and the increasing occurrence of emergencies and disasters have all led to increase in paying more attention to DRP. For instance it is estimated that the total economic impact of *Code Red* was $2.6 billion, while *Sircam* cost another $1.3 billion. In comparison, most experts estimate that 9/11 attacks will cost around $15.8 billion to restore IT and communication capabilities (Allen, 2002).

Disaster recovery planning is not just about computer system availability. While this was the original concept, today, the definition of disaster recovery has been broadened to mean: "The ability to respond to an interruption in services by implementing a disaster recovery plan to restore an organization's critical business functions. It should be noted that disaster recovery for computer systems and services is only one component of an effective business continuity plan. It is perhaps appropriate at this juncture to clarify the term disaster recovery planning, also known as contingency planning. Hardy (1992) proposed that all events that occur at an organization could be described in the dimensions of predictable/unpredictable and controllable/uncontrollable as shown in Figure 5. He offered the following grid to categorize the events and the organizational response to those events.

Contingency planning, then, is planning for those events that are both unpredictable and uncontrollable. The Federal Emergency Management Agency (FEMA) in the US uses the term "emergency" to describe these unpredictable, uncontrollable events. It defines emergency as: "Any unplanned event that can cause death or significant injuries to employees, customers or the public; or that can shut down businesses, disrupt operations, cause physical or environmental damage, or threaten the facility's financial standing or public image" (FEMA, 1996). Contingency Plan team should consider the following: Risk of failure, Risk of contingency planning, Desire outcomes, and the Potential impact among others.

Recovery Process

The first step in the disaster recovery process is to perform a business impact analysis that considers all of the potential impacts from each type of disaster. As a guide disaster recovery plans should consider how to deal with these possible events:

- Natural Disasters (Earthquake, Fire, Flood, Storms)
- Terrorist Acts
- Power Disruptions, Power Failure
- Computer Software or Hardware Failures

Figure 5. Contingency planning framework

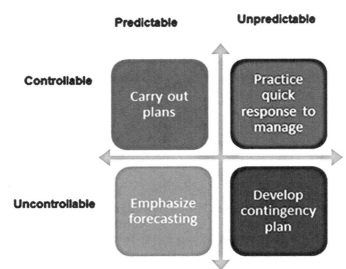

- Computer attacks due to Hackers, Worms, Viruses, etc.
- Processing Shutdowns
- Labor Strife (Walkouts, Shutdowns)

Having determined the potential events we must next look at the impacts of each event and the magnitude of the resulting disruptions. This critical activity will determine which scenarios are most likely to occur and what recovery processes are needed.

Risk Analysis

Organizations and companies should take a careful approach when creating and managing information security. A comprehensive security risk assessment is needed to help organizations understand their vulnerabilities and establish a security baseline. In view of this need, risk information and communication has become a very active field of research and application in recent years. There are several journals (e.g. *Risk Analysis, Journal of Risk Research, Australasian journal of Disaster and Trauma Studies etc*), as well as professional societies in Europe, USA and Japan, annual congresses and a large number of web sites, all indicative of the high relevance of risk issues.

A cyclic, holistic approach to information assurance maintains an organization's security posture in parity with changing threats and vulnerabilities (Mike, 2002). This approach is depicted in Figure 6.

Figure 6. Risk management lifecycle

Finally, interdisciplinary co-operation across different scientific disciplines as well as between researchers and public authorities seems the best way to enhance further the validity and usefulness of risk information and communication efforts.

Risk Assessment

In general, risks are assessed by evaluating preferences, estimating consequences of undesirable events, predicting the likelihood of such events, and weighing the merits of different courses of action. In this context, risk is formally defined as a set of ordered pairs of outcomes (O) and their associated likelihoods of occurrence.

Quantitative Risk Analysis Calculations

The key variables and equations used for conducting a quantitative risk analysis are shown below:

First, we need to determine the probability of loss caused by identified threat. This is known as the *exposure value* (EV). The value ranges from 0% to 100%.

Second, we need to determine a potential monetary loss factor for a single incident. This is known as the *single loss expectancy* (SLE).

Single Loss Expectancy (SLE) = Asset Value x Exposure Value. For instance, if the asset value is $10,000,000 and the probability of EV is 0.2, then;

SLE = 10,000,000 x 20% likelihood = $2,000,000

Third, we need to determine the annualized rate of occurrence (ARO). This is the estimated frequency a threat will occur within a year and is characterized on an annual basis. A threat occurring once in 10 years has an ARO of 0.1; a threat occurring 10 times in a year has an ARO of 10.

Finally, we need to determine how many times we could expect this loss to occur over a full year. This is known as the annualized loss expectancy (ALE). The formula to calculate ALE then is SLE x ARO. The summation of ALE can be defined as follows:

$$ALE = \sum_{k=1}^{n} I(O_k)F_k$$

where;

$\{O_1 \ldots\ldots O_n\}$ = Set of harmful outcomes

$I(O_k)$ = Impact of outcomes k in currency

F_k = Frequency of outcomes k

Assuming that based on a current system, cloud violations occur 10 times per year, then ALE is shown to be;

$2,000,000 x 10 = $20,000,000 ALE

The safeguard cost/benefit analysis or simply cost benefit analysis (CBA) = (ALE before implementing safeguard) – (ALE after implementing safeguard) – (annual cost of safeguard) = value of safeguard to the company.
Assuming that violations occur 1 times in 10 years; then ALE is shown to be;

$2,000,000 x 0.1 = $200,000 ALE

If the annual cost of the security solution/safeguard is $10,000, then

CBA = $20,000,000 – ($200,000 +$10,000) = $19,790,000

Therefore, the company stands to save, or avoid, about $20 million per year in potential losses by enforcing a security solution. Though, this does not mean that the company will have $20 million as a profit line in the revenue report. However, it clearly makes sense to spend the $10,000 to avoid the potential $20 million annual loss

Regulatory and Legal Issues

The need to prove that data and files are authentic is always important, but that requirement is particularly compelling when organizations must show compliance with laws and regulations. This includes situations related to:

- **Regulated Industries:** Where companies need to document, for example, how they comply with HIPAA rules for protecting personally identifiable health information, SEC 17a-4 requirements for retaining data on securities transactions, and 21 CFR Part 11 requirements for protecting records required by the FDA.
- **Financial Information:** Used for SEC reporting and compliance with Sarbanes-Oxley and other investor protection regulations.
- **Documents with Legal and Contractual Implications:** Whose admissibility as evidence needs to be protected.

- **Intellectual Property:** Such as engineering and patent documents, trade secrets and business plans, whose date and provenance might need to be proved in court.
- **Records Management Applications:** Where documents and files might need to be retrieved and validated after years or even decades.

CONCLUSION

Security assessment and risk management plan must be integrated with the overall enterprise continuity management approach and must be tested through drills and exercises that test the plans, the people involve, and the available tools. To avoid the occurrence of attack or failure as a result of disaster, cloud computing companies must concentrate on identifying the set of resources that will bring the most value to its customers, users, or employees. IT managers must decide what information is required and how this can best be distributed. However, regardless of our approaches, we must recognize that addressing the technical challenges of modern security and privacy in information technology will be a long march. There is no quick fixes, no silver bullets. Therefore the process and research in this field is a continuous and dynamic in nature. However, the sooner we perform a proper plan the better. It is worth recognizing that no system will be made totally effective. The level of security must be based on the recognition that it is a business decision to incorporate a cost effective level of security, which has been derived from considering the potential exposure and the cost of countermeasures.

REFERENCES

Allen, H. (2002). Computer Attack Trends Challenge Internet Security. In *Security & Privacy* (pp. 5–7). IEEE Computer Society.

Ars Technica. (2012), Why passwords have never been weaker and crackers have never been stronger. *Ars Technica*. Retrieved from http://arstechnica.com/security/2012/08/passwords-under-assault/

Brooks, C. (2009). Amazon EC2 Attack Prompts Customer Support Changes. *Tech Target*. Retrieved October 12, 2009 from: http://searchcloudcomputing.techtarget.com/news/article/0,289142,sid201_gci1371090,00.html

Drobox. (2012). Dropbox Admits Hack, Adds More Security Features. *Information-Week*. Retrieved August 1, 2012 from: http://www.informationweek.com/security/client/dropbox-admits-hack-adds-more-security-f/240004697

FEMA. (1996). *Emergency Management Guide for Business and Industry*. FEMA.

Garfinkel, T., & Rosenblum, M. (2005). When Virtual is Harder than Real. HotOS'05, Santa Fe, NM.

Global Technology Adoption Index. (2015). Retrieved from: https://powermore.dell.com/2015-global-technology-adoption-index/

Hardy, K. (1992, Spring). Contingency Planning. *Business Quarterly*, *56*(4), 26–28.

Horwath, C., Chan, W., Leung, E., & Pili, H. (2012). *Enterprise Risks Management For Cloud Computing*. The Committee of Sponsoring Organizations of the Treadway Commission (COSO).

IDC. (2015). Retrieved from: https://www.idc.com/prodserv/4Pillars/cloud

Jansen, W., & Grance, T. (2011). *Guidelines on security and privacy in public cloud computing*. NIST special publication, 800, 144

Jensen, M., Schwenk, J., Gruschka, N., & Iacono, L. L. (2009). On Technical Security Issues in Cloud Computing. *IEEE International Conference on Cloud Computing*, Bangalore, India. doi:10.1109/CLOUD.2009.60

Kalpana, P. (2012). Cloud Computing–Wave of the Future. *International Journal of Electronics Communication and Computer Engineering*, *3*(3).

Leavitt, N. (2009). Is Cloud Computing Really Ready for Prime Time? *IEEE Computer*.

LinkedIn. (2012a). An Update On Taking Steps To Protect Our Members. *LinkedIn Blog*. June 7, 2012, Retrieved from: http://blog.linkedin.com/2012/06/09/an-update-on-taking-steps-to-protect-our-members/

LinkedIn. (2012b). LinkedIn sued over hacking incident that exposed six million passwords. *Gigaom*. Retrieved from: http://gigaom.com/2012/06/19/linkedin-will-connect-with-a-federal-judge-after-privacy-breach/

McConnell, M., & Hamilton, B. A. (2002). Information Assurance in the Twenty-First Century. *Security & Privacy, IEEE. Computers & Society*, 16–19.

Metz, C. (2009). DDoS Attack Rains Down on Amazon Cloud. *The Register*. Retrieved from: http://www.theregister.co.uk/2009/10/05/amazon_bitbucket_outage/

Parker, D. B. (1998). *Fighting Computer Crime: A new Framework for Protecting Information*. New York: John Wiley & Sons Inc.

Rohrmann. (2000). Risk Information and Communication. *The Australasian Journal of Disaster and Trauma Studies, 2*.

Schulze, H. (2015). *Cloud Security Spotlight Report – 2015, Crowd Research Partners*. Retrieved from: http://go.alertlogic.com/

Slaviero, M. (2009). BlackHat presentation demo vids: Amazon, part 4 of 5. *AMI-Bomb*. Retrieved from: http://www.sensepost.com/blog/3797.html

Vieira, K., Schulter, A., & Westphall, C. (2009). Westphall, Ca. (2009). Intrusion Detection Techniques in Grid and Cloud Computing Environment. *IT Professional, IEEE. Computers & Society*, 26.

Wired. (2012a). How Apple and Amazon Security Flaws Led to My Epic Hacking. *Wired*. Retrieved from: http://www.wired.com/gadgetlab/2012/08/apple-amazon-mat-honan-hacking/all/

Wired. (2012b). Amazon Quietly Closes Security Hole After Journalist's Devastating Hack. *Wired*. Retrieved from: http://www.wired.com/gadgetlab/2012/08/amazon-changes-policy-wont-add-new-credit-cards-to-accounts-over-the-phone/

Chapter 5
On the Role of Game Theory in Modelling Incentives and Interactions in Mobile Distributed Systems

Mohammed Onimisi Yahaya
University of Hafr Albatin, Saudi Arabia

ABSTRACT

Advances in wireless networking has led to a new paradigm of Mobile Distributed Systems (MDS), where data, devices and software are mobile. Peer-to-Peer (P2P) networks is a form of distributed system in which sharing of resources has some similarities to our traditional market in terms of goods and relationship. Game theory provides a mathematical framework for understanding the complexity of interdependent decision makers with similar or conflicting objectives. Games could be characterized by number of players who interact, possibly threaten each other and form coalitions, take actions under uncertain conditions. The players receive some reward or possibly some punishment or monetary loss. Our primary objective is to provide an insight into the role and suitability of game theory in the study of Economics of P2P systems. In order to achieve this objectives, we investigate different classes of game theory, review and analyze their use in the modelling of P2P system.

DOI: 10.4018/978-1-5225-0602-7.ch005

INTRODUCTION

Distributed Systems is a form of computing paradigm that the applications and popularity has exploded over the years. Distributed system is a collection of autonomous computer systems connected together via networks and distribution middleware. These enable connected devices to coordinate their activities and to share the resources of the system, so that the users perceive the system as a single integrated computing facility. P2P network is a form of distributed systems that have received significant attention in recent years, due to the advancement in the world of information technology. P2P networks have inspired the design of social networking sites that made large scale interaction of people and businesses possible. Mobile P2P paradigm is a form of mobile distributed systems (MDS) that focuses on sharing of storage, software, and data amongst network devices. Peer-to-Peer (P2P) systems have been adopted as a viable alternative to client-server networks. This is due to the inadequacy of client-server architecture to cope with ever increasing demand for expansion and scalability. Servers in client-server systems sometimes constitute a bottleneck to expansion and attack on the server may results into a single point of failure. P2P system is a distributed system that eliminates partially or completely the need for a central server. A P2P system is described as a system that relies on computing power and bandwidth of nodes at the ends of a connection rather than concentrating on low number of servers within the network (P.Pradeep, Kumar, Shekar, & Krishna, 2012). In (Roussopoulos, Baker, & Rosenthal, 2004), the authors defined P2P systems as any network that exhibits the following characteristics: distributed control, self-organized and symmetric communication. There are many types of P2P systems, mostly used for large scale content distribution, file sharing, platform sharing, communication, distributed computation and collaboration. Peers in P2P networks are autonomous - the desire to do anything without external influence. This autonomy guarantee peers' independent activities; this may include voluntary sharing, free will entry and exit from the network, change of identity, honesty or dishonest dispositions to others and carry out trustworthy or untrustworthy transactions. Furthermore, peers in P2P networks have equal role. A server this time might become a client after a while. The features of P2P networks made modelling peers interactions a complex task. Incentives are incorporated in the design of P2P systems so as to: (1) Ensuring fairness among all participating peers. (2) Enhancement of cooperation, and (3) Alleviating the untrustworthy resources. Incentives have been identified to encourage cooperation amongst participating peers in P2P Systems. These incentives could be monetary such as digital coin and other kinds of non-priced incentives that designers deem fit. Incentives used in the literature are TTL (Time-to-live), bandwidth, service, delay times, network membership, peer rating and trust (Krishnan & Smith, 2002). Moreover, most of the incentive approaches differ in the type of incentive used and the methods of managing the incentives.

Game theory offers a rich mathematical framework for the analysis of interactions in a strategic environment like P2P system. Though the interaction in real P2P systems are more complex, game theory provides us with an acceptable understanding of complex interactions such as between peers in P2P networks. Game theory modelling is appealing to model interactions of peers in P2P networks due to the fact that difference of cost and incentives are natural net benefit that can easily be modelled as payoff function. Also, the rationality assumption of game theory that every player tends to maximize their utility tends to fit exactly the situations in P2P system.

Game Theory has been applied in modeling human behaviour in politics, social and economics, to study interaction between or amongst players. Game models decision making in an interaction between or amongst rational participants, hence it is an analytical tool that help us to understand our observation when decision makers interacts (Osbourne, 2003). Games can be used to predict, describe and prescribe interplay between competition and cooperations (Coopetition) (Adam & Nalebuff, 1997). Specifically, Behavioural game theory (Camerer, 2003) deals with the study of individual behaviour in an interaction in which the outcome, success or failure of the decision maker depends on the choice of others.

In this paper, an overview of game theory and classifications based on some criteria related to the players, their actions, moves and outcomes. Furthermore, we presents a taxonomy of peers in P2P system based on the strategies of peers may apply during their interactions. A complete description of suitable game to describe P2P interactions is proposed and discussions of challenges. The remaining part of this paper is organized as follows: Section II provides the analogy of P2P systems to traditional market and crowd. In section III, we present game basics, game classifications with some illustrating examples. In section IV, we present taxonomy of peers in P2P systems.

P2P AS A NETWORK, MARKET, AND CROWD

The concept of P2P systems is different from that of client-server model in the design principles. Researchers in (Aberer & Hauswirth, 2002) identified the principles of P2P as principle of sharing, decentralization and self-organization. In addition, the authors in (Fan et al., 2012) identified anonymity, autonomy and open nature as principles of P2P systems. In order to provide a better understanding of P2P paradigm, we list the design principles of P2P systems as follows:

- **Equal Standing:** This is a fundamental design principle of any P2P system. It requires that every peer in the networks acts as a servent, that is either as a client or server. This principle, exemplify the P2P paradigm as an alternative to the traditional client/server model which uses servers for service provision, monitoring and access. P2P systems eliminate the need for central servers which are known to constitute a bottleneck to the expansion of the networks as well as creating a single point of failure. Peers' equal standing gives rise to some peculiar characteristics exhibited by these systems due to lack of central control. For instance, high degree of entry and exit, high degree of autonomy from central server.

- **Autonomy:** Autonomy of an entity refers to the impossibility of external control in an interaction (Veijalainen, 2007). This freewill to do anything without external influence includes mobility-the will to join and leave the networks at any time. Resource sharing is based on voluntary collaboration; therefore, peers have the freedom to share or not to share, to be selfish or generous. The leeway for peers to change identity, the decision to be trustworthy or untrustworthy, honest or liar. All these actions are under the control of an autonomous peer.

- **Anonymity:** This refers to the desire of a peer in a network to be publicly unknown. In most P2P systems pseudonyms are used for access rather than full authentication. In reality, pseudoanonymity is achieved with the use of pseudonyms as in the case of student ID, bank account number, nickname etc.

- **Self Organizing:** P2P systems require that the architecture should adjust and organize itself if a new peer joins or leaves the networks. The rapid growth in P2P networks is due to it resiliency in absorbing expansion and shrinking due to itself organizing nature. A self-organizing network should automatically adapt to entry, exit and failure of nodes (Rowstron & Druschel, 2001)

- **Some Level of Decentralization:** This design principle excludes the need for architectures that requires central management. P2P systems eliminate completely or partially the need for central server. The level of decentralization depends on the design objective, application and performance requirements. But zero-level decentralization as in client-server model negates the principle of P2P systems.

In spite of these design principles that contributed to the success of P2P systems, there are challenges (Mrmol& Prez, 2009) (Banerjee, Saha, & Sen, 2005) posed by P2P systems: These challenges are:

- **Free Riding:** This is a phenomena, where a peer contribute less than what it consume.

- **Identity Management:** Persistent identity is not a stringent requirement for participating in P2P sharing, due to design goals of the networks. Thus, the availability of cheap or free pseudonyms would make a selfish or malicious peer, to exit when it is about to be discovered and rejoin with a different name, thereby evading any mechanism put in place to check such an unwanted behaviour.

- **Trust Management:** The management of Trust and Reputations of peers is another major challenge facing sharing in P2P systems. The notion of resource availability, authenticity, access control and fair trading (Daswani, Garcia-Molina, & Yang, 2002) is threatened by various trust and reputation issues such as collusion among nodes. An untrustworthy peer may pollute other peers' contents, that is adding impostor contents just to pollute the popularity of files shared by others.

- **Security Management:** Security challenges are common to all computing system. In P2P systems, the design characteristics of high rate of mobility, autonomy and anonymity pose a lot of security challenges. These include transmission of malicious content such as virus, worms and trojan by malicious peer to deliberately harm others in the networks. Furthermore, there is high level of vulnerability of P2P software and risk attached to downloaded content.

These aforementioned features are similar to that of crowd and buyers and sellers relationship in a traditional market.

PUBLIC GOODS IN ECONOMICS VS. RESOURCES IN P2P SYSTEMS

Free riders problem is not unique to distributed environment alone. The problem of free riding emerged in Economics with regards to public goods. These are goods that are both non-excludable and non-rival. An individual user cannot effectively exclude others from using the goods and use by an individual does not reduce the availability to others. Some examples of such goods are fresh air, knowledge and street lighting. However, if there is ability to impose restrictions on these goods they become private goods. Economists have studied the free riders problem (Sweeny, 1973) (Marwell & Ames, 1979) and the tragedy of the common (G.Hardin, 1968), a situation where some selfish individuals refrain from contributing to the common good. Some familiar examples in our society are, overuse of public resources such as over fishing in the deep ocean, pollution of the environment and excessive use of pesticides.

Similarly, computer resources shared in distributed systems have been compared to public and private goods in Economics. In (Krishnan & Smith, 2008), the authors pointed out that the fundamental difference in the characteristics of public goods in Economics from that of information goods in P2P networks is that while that of former is not rival-that is the use by one consumer does not affect the use by the other, the latter is affected by the fact that the provider of the content also participate in the sharing and usage of same resource. Thus, any deficit from both producer and consumer will definitely affect the quality and quantity of the goods as well as overall performance of the system. For instance, sharing in P2P networks is an act similar to the private provision of public goods (Theodore, Lawrence, & Hal, 1986).

OVERVIEW OF GAME THEORY

Games are played in numerous aspects of our life but we might not be aware that we are playing a game (Bernard, 1967). Games are being played in politics, market, war and daily interactions. For instance, a person decision to choose restaurant A instead of B due to price and quality of food offered, is playing a game. Economic activities such as auction, bargaining and price competition between firms offering the same service or producing the same product are all games. Games are modelled using game theory. Game theory has been found to provide a rich mathematical framework for analysis of complex interactions between players. In general, game theory models decision making in an interaction between rational players. The rationality assumption shows that a player has preferences and is aware of the consequences of his actions.

Each game must have one or more players. A player is a general entity of interest which may be an individual, organization, country, or a node in a network. A game must also have a non-empty set of actions (Table 1).

The overall plan of actions taken by a player is known as strategy. The set of actions taken by a player in a game is determined by the player's strategy. For instance, one can view the strategy of a game as a complete algorithm to play the game, while the actions of the game are each step in the algorithm. The result of a

Table 1. Payoff matrix for prisoner P_1 and prisoner P_1

	P_2 **(Confess)**	P_2 **(Do Not Confess)**
P_1(Confess)	(f_1^{P1}, f_1^{P2})	(f_2^{P1}, f_2^{P2})
P_1(Do not confess)	(f_3^{P1}, f_3^{P2})	(f_4^{P1}, f_4^{P2})

particular action in a game is known as payoff. Based on the strategy, an action or set of actions are taken in order to increase the payoff. A game should be played according to the rules that specify how the game can proceed.

For example, consider a classical example of a game known as prisoners dilemma. In this game, two crime suspects are remanded in prison for interrogation. The players are prisoner (P1) and prisoner (P2). The strategy of each prisoner is to spend less time in prison. Each prisoner must take an action for the game to evolve. The set of actions available to each prisoner either confess or not confess of the crime. The rules of the game specify that prisoners are kept in separate cells and questioned separately. The rules also specify the payoff a prisoner gets for taking a particular action. Once a game is played by all players, the outcome is jointly determined. As shown in Table 1, if P1 confesses and P2 confesses, the outcome of the game is (f_1P_1, f_1P_2). As such, the game has four outcomes depending on the actions taken by the players.

GAME DESCRIPTIONS

In game theory, games are described using different representations. These representations include normal form and extensive form. These two representations differ in the type of game described, the amount and depth of information needed to be retained for convenience in analysis and to reduce computational complexity. A normal form game is a representation of game that does not capture the notion of sequence and time of the action. It is a game structure that is mathematically simple, abstract and analytically convenient (Morris, 1994). A normal form game is represented with a payoff matrix. An example of a normal form representation of game is as shown in Table 1. In the normal form representation, some information such as action sequence and time about the game may be lost but focuses our understanding on dominant strategies, Nash equilibria and their payoffs (Raghavan, 1994). For instance, consider a game involving two players, if the moves per player is finite, this can be reduced to a game with one move per player. The extensive form game is an explicit representation of a game that captures the dynamics of interactions of players and made the temporal structure explicit. This complete description of a game is represented by game tree revealing information such as (1) complete descriptions of the set of players (2) the move of each player (3) the time of the move of each player and the choices made by those players (4) complete description of the players' knowledge as at the time of taking an action in the game and (5) the players payoff functions. Every extensive-form game can be converted to an equivalent normal form game but this conversion process may result into an exponential increase in the size of the representation, hence, making it computationally intractable (Shoham & Leyton-Brown, 2009). An example of the extensive form of matching pennies game is shown in Figure 1.

GAME TAXONOMY

Games can be classified based on the player, action, outcome, repetition and termination as shown in Figure 2. For example, player-based classification can be based on different criteria. These criteria could be the number of players involved, the nature of players and the type of information available to players.

Figure 1. Extensive form representation of matching pennies game

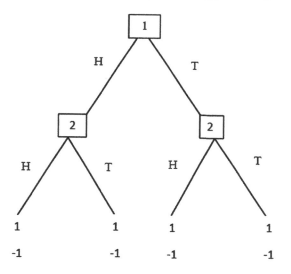

Figure 2. Classification of game

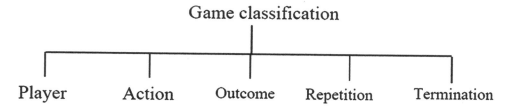

Player-Based Game Classification

This game classification is based on "who is playing the game"-the player. The criteria related to this classification are number of players, the effect of the identity of players on the outcome of the game, the nature of cooperation type of players and the information availability to players in the game as shown in Figure 3.

Game Classification Based on Identity Effects of Players

A symmetric game is a game in which the payoffs depend only on the other actions employed and not on the player playing them (Shih-Fen, Daniel, & Michael, 2004). The identities of the player do not affect the payoffs. In other word, the identities of the players can be changed without changing the payoff. Formally, a normal-form game is symmetric if the players have identical strategy spaces ($S1 = S2 = ... = SI = S$) and $u_i(si, s-i) = uj (sj, s-j)$, for $si = sj$ and $s-i = s-j$ for all $\varrho1, ..., I$. ($s-i$ denotes all the strategies in profile s except for si.) Thus, we can write $u(t, s)$ for the payoff to any player playing strategy t in profile s. We denote a symmetric game by the tuple $[I, S, u()]$ (Shih-Fen et al., 2004). On the contrary, asymmetric games are games in which the strategies are not identical for both players. Though, it may be possible sometimes for an asymmetric game to have an identical strategy for both players. In asymmetric game the identity of the players affect the payoff. For instance, if both prisoners in the prisoner's dilemma game have different payoffs for choosing the same action, then, it becomes an asymmetric game.

Game Classification Based on Number of Players

There are different types of games that may involve one, two or more players interacting in a strategic setting as shown in Figure 4.

Figure 3. Player-based classifications of game

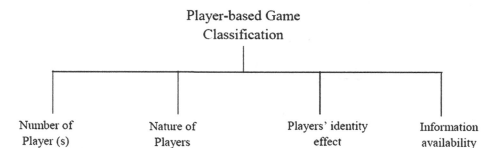

Figure 4. Player-identity effect classifications of game

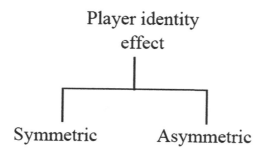

- **Two Player Game:** This is also referred to as a two person game. It involves two players interacting in a strategic environment. These are the most common category of game studied in game theory. A special case of this class of games is N-Player games. Some common examples of two player games are prisoners dilemma, stag hunt and battle of sexes.
- **N-Player Game:** This is also called multi player game. This involves three or more players interacting in a strategic setting. The analysis of this form of game is complex due to multiple and complex decision made by several players. Most N-player games can be reduced to a two player game for simplicity of analysis. Formally, N-person game is a set of n players or positions each player with a finite set of pure strategies and corresponding to each player a payoff function Pi which maps the set of all n-tuple of pure strategies into real number (Nash, 1951). An example of N-player game is an n-player coordination game.
- **One-Player Game:** In game theory, game occurs when there is conflict of interest amongst the players. In one person game there is no conflict of interest. Only a single player take decisions based on its strategy to achieve it goal. This form of game is of no much interest in game theory, but it may be interesting in probabilistic and complexity term. A one player game is model as a decision problem (Figure 5).

Game Classification Based on Nature of Cooperation

As shown in Figure 6, the nature of cooperation of players involved in a game can be used to classify game into cooperative, non-cooperative and coordination game.

- **Non-Cooperative Game:** Non-cooperative game is a class of games in which players make decisions independently. Though players may choose to cooperate, cooperation must be self-enforced. As such, there is no external en-

Figure 5. Number of player classifications of game

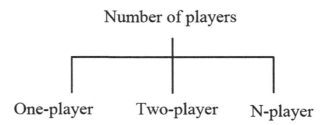

Figure 6. Nature of player classifications of game

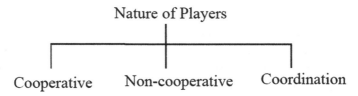

forcement for each player to plan actions with other group of players and take consensus-based decisions. Also, a game is said to be non-cooperative if it is impossible for the players to communicate in any way. In other word, if each player pursues self-interest that may partly conflict with the interest of other player, we said the game is non-cooperative (Pavel, 2012). Furthermore, in this type of games, players cannot make a credible commitment to cooperate in their strategies. The basic model of interest in this form of games is the individual player-including his interest, beliefs, preference and possible actions (Shoham & Leyton-Brown, 2009). Thus, non cooperative game theory deals with the study of interactions of competing rational individuals. Example of non-cooperative game is prisoners' dilemma game since both prisoners do not share information in taking their decisions. Both take independent decisions without necessarily considering the opponent.

- **Cooperative Game:** In cooperative games also known as coalition games (Shoham & Leyton-Brown, 2009), the term cooperative implies that players have complete freedom of communication and complete information on the structure of the game. There is a possibility of making an enforced agreement binding on one or both players to a certain policy. Co-ordination with other members in the group of players is required in cooperative games (Nash, 1951). The basic modelling unit in this class of game is the group. In this case, the outcome of any chosen strategy is a joint decision by the group. Formally, cooperative games involve a set of players, denoted by N = {1, ..., N } who seek to form cooperative groups, i.e., coalitions, in order to strengthen their positions in the game. Any coalition $S \subseteq N$ represents an agreement between the players in S to act as a single entity (Saad, Han, Debbah, & Hjrungnes, 2009). Example of cooperative game is coordination game. In this case, players need to take joint decisions, since the game is between groups of players.

- **Coordination Game:** This is a class of games somewhat in-between cooperative and non cooperative games. In these games, there exist some element of cooperation and competition. This class of games usually has multiple equilibria. Coordination games are formalization of coordination problems. There are variations in coordination games depending on the level of conflict of interest and preference with reference to the payoffs. In pure (common interest) coordination game, both players prefer the same action. Hence, their preference will yield a higher payoff than the other action in which they do not have same preference. Another forms of coordination game is the one in which both players get a better payoff if they coordinate, but less if they do not. This is the case in the stag hunt game. Lastly, the conflicting interest coordination game also refers to as Battle of Sexes. In this case, both players have to agree on a mutual gain, though some compromises exist.

Game Classification Based on Information Availability

- **Complete Information Game:** The payoff functions and the strategy sets of this type of game is a common knowledge. Hence, decisions are based on the available knowledge to all the players in the game. The players know each element in the game definition (Harsanyi, 1967). In incomplete information game, none of the players knows the type and action of the other until both of them makes their move (Harsanyi, 1967). In the other word, the game being played is not a common knowledge. A game is said to be a common knowledge if the players know the structure of the game and they are all aware that other player knows the structure of the game and so on (David & Jon, 2010). The difference between complete and incomplete information game is that players in incomplete information game or at least some of them, lack full information about the structure of the game as define by its normal form (John, 1994). Furthermore, by suitable modelling and transformation all forms of incomplete information game can be reduced to complete but imperfect information game.

- **Perfect Information Game:** A game in which the state of the game and all moves are known to all players are said to have perfect information. The player with the move knows the full history of the game so far. That is, the moves previously made by all other players. For example, a game without chance element like Chess is a perfect information game. On the other hand, in imperfect information game, the players do not know the full history of previous moves made by others.

To clearly distinguish between the often confused concept of complete and perfect, incomplete and imperfect information game. The author in (Harsanyi, 1967) differentiates them as follows, complete and incomplete information deals with the amount of information the players have about the rules of the game. On the other hand, perfect and imperfect information deals with the amount of information each player has of other players and their moves. Game classification based on information available to players is illustrated in Figure 7.

Action-Based Game Classification

Games can also be classified based on the features of the set of actions. The size of the action set which can either be finite or infinite. Also, the occurrence of these actions and the payoffs associated with the outcome as illustrated in Figure 8. A player in a game may choose a pure action and apply it or randomize it, thus, resulting in pure or mixed strategy game. Moreover, games may have a known outcome, which is deterministic or may occur with known probability distributions. Pure Strategy and Mixed Strategy: In this game, each player selects a single action and applies it. The columns or rows of the payoff matrix represent both an action and a pure strategy while in mixed strategy, players randomize over the set of available actions according to some probability distribution (David & Jon, 2010). Formally, A mixed strategy for player $n \varrho P$ is a probability distribution say $\xi n = (\xi in) i \varrho Sn$ over his pure strategies in Sn. That is, $(i \varrho Sn) \xi in$ and $i \varrho SN \xi in = 1$ (Robert, 1971). The prediction outcome of a mixed strategy is stochastic, hence less accurate than the pure strategy. As such, the outcome is computed as expected utility. Pure strategy can be seen as a special case of mixed strategies.

Figure 7. Information availability to player classifications of game

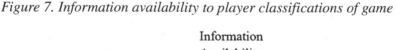
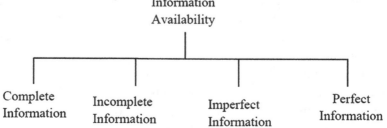

Figure 8. Action-based classifications of game

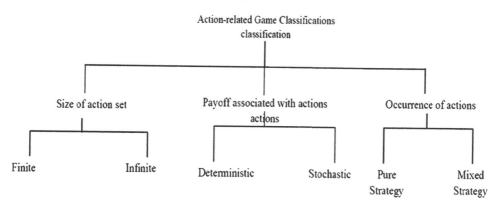

Finite game is a type of game that each player has a finite number of actions alternatives to choose; otherwise, the game is an infinite game. As such, the player has a continuous action set; this might be a vector of alternatives. Finite games are also known as matrix games. Deterministic game: If the players' actions uniquely determine the outcome of the game, as captured in the objective functions, hence the game is deterministic. On the other hand, if the objective function of at least one player depends on an additional variable (state of nature) with a known probability distribution, then the game is a stochastic game (Basar, 2010).

Outcome-Based Game Classification

As shown in Figure 9, games can be classified based on their outcome. In this class, we have constant-sum and non-zero sum game. Constant-sum game: This is a type of game in which the sum of payoff of every outcome of each player is constant. It

Figure 9. Outcome-based classifications of game

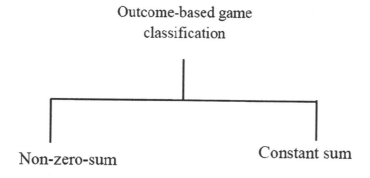

is a game of pure competition. Poker game is an example of constant-sum game, since the total wealth of both players adds up to constant. Zero-sum game is a class of constant-sum game in which the total gains for both players sum to zero. Formally, given a two person game with one move per player. If each player selects independently and simultaneously from the finite set of action plan that results into a payoff for each player. Let i, j be their independent choices, then the game is described by a real matrix Xij = (xij) and Yij = (yij). Where xij is the payoff for player 1 and yij is the payoff for player 2. The game is zero sum if and only if xij + yij ≡ 0 (Raghavan, 1994). Thus, zero sum game is a real game of conflict, a player benefits only at the expense of the opponent, hence, the gain of one player equal the loss of the other player. Examples of such games are chess, poker, matching pennies. On the other hand, in non-zero sum game, the gain of one player may not necessarily be the loss of the other player. As such, the payoff may not add up to zero. For instance, in prisoner dilemma, the sum of both players payoff may be greater or less than zero, depending on the actions of both players.

Repetition-Based Game Classification

Repeated Games: This is sometime referred to as supergame. It is a scenario in which the same stage of strategic form of a game is played at each time t for some duration of T periods. It is an infinitely repeated game if T = ∞ (Fudenberg & Tirole, 1991; Mailath & Larry, 2006). A stage game is a one-period simultaneous move game of complete information. Repeated game is used to study interactions that go on over time. Repeated game could be of perfect monitoring. This means that at the end of every time period, every player is aware of the action chosen by all other players at that period. But in imperfect monitoring, the actions of other players are not observable. Unrepeated (one) shot games are games played once without repetition (Figure 10).

Figure 10. Repetition-based classifications of game

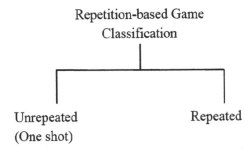

Termination-Based Game Classification

The outcome of a game is determined at the end of the game. The question here is what determine the end of the game? The end of a game could be determined by time and action. Games can also be classified in the dimension of how the game terminates as illustrated in Figure 11. If a game is duration specified game, this is time constrained game in which the expiry of this designer specified duration marks the end of the game. As in the game of soccer, two 45 minutes make a complete 90 minutes regulation time. Also, the end of a game could be determined by moves taken by either one or both players in a two-player game. The action that determines the end of the game may be taken simultaneously by both players and sequentially one after the other.

- **Sequential (Dynamic) Game:** The action is taken sequentially until a particular point in the game or the player chooses not to move further. Players in dynamic games are aware of earlier actions of other players before taking an action. The orders of play are strictly observed hence, there is possibility of learning since players are aware of others' actions. The simplest case of a sequential game is a two player game with one move each per player. In this case, the first player takes an action and the second player takes it action after

Figure 11. Termination-based classification of game

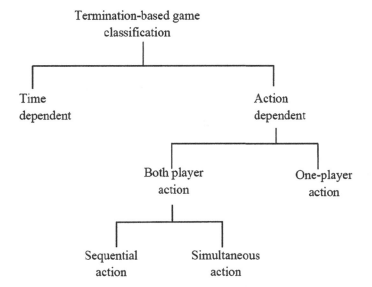

observing the action of the first player. Examples of sequential games are auction, bargaining and price competition.

- **Simultaneous (Static) Game:** The actions in this category of game are applied by all players simultaneously. The players might not take the action exactly simultaneously but the second player is not aware of the action of the first player while taking its action. Example of simultaneous game is prisoners' dilemma.

CASE STUDIES OF APPLICATION OF GAMES IN P2P NETWORKS

Prisoners Dilemma Game

The description of the prisoners' dilemma game goes as follows. Two individuals are arrested over a serious crime. Each is known to be guilty of a minor crime prior to this time, but there is no evidence to convict them of the serious crime unless one (or both of them) confesses. The suspects are separated and interrogated differently. During interrogation each of them is told that if he testifies about the other's guilt, he will get an amnesty of reduced sentence for the crime he is already found guilty. It is modeled as follows, if both suspects did not confess they both get a reduced sentence of 1 year each, if neither of them confesses, they both get a sentence of 3 years each. if one betray and testify against the other he is set free (that is 0 year) and the other get the maximum sentence of 4 years and vice versa. The payoff matrix is presented in Table 4. Note that each value in the table represent years in jail. Ordinarily higher payoff is desirable but in this case, lower is better. Rationally, every player would want to minimize his jail term. In this case, the best choice for each player is to confess. But note that irrespective of whatever suspect 1 does, it is better for suspect 2 to confess (3 <4) and (0 <1). The strategy (confess, confess) yield 3 years jail term for both and strategy (Dont confess, Dont confess) yield 1 year behind bar for both. The Nash equilibrium of this game is that both confess (or Both dont confess). No single player can gain by unilaterally changing his strategy. This is a dilemma, because each player would have been better off if both chooses not to confess.

Adaptation of PD to Model P2P Network

Each game consists of two players which can defect or cooperate. To present a social dilemma, one player is the client and the other is the server in the game. The decision of the server is meaningful in determining the outcome of the game. A player can be a server in one game and a client in another game. Where T, R, P and S stand for Temptation, Reward, Punishment and Sucker respectively. Rc, Tc, Pc and Sc are the client payoff and Rs, Ts, Ps and Ss are the server's payoff. It possesses the following characteristics to create the social dilemma (please see Tables 2 and 3).

1. Mutual cooperation leads to a higher payoff than mutual defection.
2. Mutual cooperation leads to a higher payoff than one player sucking the other
3. Defection dominates cooperation (at least weakly) as the individual level for the player that decides to cooperate or defect. (Ts $\geq$ Rs and Ps $\geq$ Ss) and (Ts >Rs and Ps >Ss)

Discussions

We drew an inference above that both players are better off when sometimes they choose the same strategy, as in both confess or both not confess in the case of Prisoners Dilemma game. This phenomenon is referred to as Social Optimality (David & Jon, 2010), a situation in which the sum of the total payoffs is maximized, considering the strategy of each player. It is noteworthy to mention that this outcome is the desired results of interactions in P2P systems, where ideally all participants contributes to the network resources at reasonable level and still gain an acceptable level of utility from the system. In this case, the common good is neither overused by some peer nor under-utilized. Furthermore, this attest to the suitability of the choice of non-cooperative game for the analysis of interactions between peers in P2P systems.

Table 2. Payoff matrix for a two PD file sharing game

	Server/Cooperate	Server/Defect
Client/Cooperate	R_c/R_s	S_c/T_s
Client/Defect	T_c/S_s	P_c/P_s

Table 3. Payoff matrix for application like P2P file sharing or overlay routing game

	Server/Request Service	Server/Ignore Service
Client/Request service	(7, -1)	(0, 0)
Client/Dont Request service	(0, 0)	(0,0)

However, interactions in real P2P system are more complex. First, peers cannot accurately predict the need from another peer in the future. In P2P game, the decision of one of the players significantly affect the outcome of the game. For example, in an interaction between two peers modeled as a game with two strategies (share, not share), if a providing peer choose the strategy not share, the game is automatically over. Hence, the outcome is significantly influenced by one of the players.

Other challenges facing game modeling in P2P are heterogeneity of interest. Each user in the system may have different interests, needs and objectives. For instance, peer x may be interested in a resource owned by peer y, while peer y may want resource from z. Peer z may be interested in a resource possessed by x. Furthermore, behaviourally, peer x may be an altruist, peer y may be a free rider while z may have behaviour inbetween these two.

In addition, the heterogeneity of environment is also a great challenge. Users of P2P systems are scattered over a vast geographically distributed over the world. These users have different computational power, storage capability and bandwidth.

GIFT-GIVING GAME

In a gift giving game model (Philip & Levine, 2001), players are randomly selected and match to play a game in a large population n. Each player is assumed to have information of the past behaviour of his opponent. In (Kandori & R., 1993), the author provided this assumption that this information is distributed by what he termed as 'information system' The game assumptions are as follows: (1) There are two types of agent named young and old; (2) each agents live for two periods; (3) there are equal number of each agent type alive in every time period.

The game is described as follows: The objective of every player is to maximize his payoff in both time periods. In the first time period the player is refers to as young and in the second period is refers to as old. Each young player is match with an old player to play a game. This young player must choose between a gift of 0 or 1. The old player has no decision to make. But if the young player selects gift of value 0, both players receive a payoff of 0; if he chooses a gift of value 1, he gets a payoff of -1 and the old player receive a payoff $\alpha > 1$. The lifetime utility is the sum of utility over the two period of life. The payoff matrix of this game is as shown in Table 5.

Adaptation to Model P2P Multimedia Sharing

Yu and Schaa (2012) models a stage game of chunk sharing in a multimedia P2P sharing as a gift giving game. With two actions = {Serve = s, Not serve =NS}, If a= S, the server incurs cost c and the server receives a benefit of r. if a = NS, both

Table 4. The payoff matrix of Prisoners Dilemma

	Confess	Don't Confess
Confess	(3,3)	(0,4)
Dont confess	(4,0)	(1,1)

Table 5. Payoff matrix for gift giving game

	Young/Give	Young/Keep
Old	$(\alpha, -1)$	$(0, 0)$

r and C equal 0. They considered constant r and c for every chunk. They claimed it can be extended to consider peer dependent and time varying cost.

With the assumption that r >c, and the ability of peers to have multiple connection, the social utility U is the sum of all utility derived from all connections. If a = NS, the short term equilibrium =0 which is undesirable for the utility of all system to be 0. The payoff matrix for this model is as shown in Table 6.

DISCUSSIONS

Game theory modelling is appealing to researchers of incentives and interactions in P2P networks due to the fact that difference of cost and incentives are natural net benefit that can easily be model as payoff function. Also, the rationality assumption of game theory that every player tends to maximize their utility tends to fit exactly the situations in P2P system. However, the system dynamics affect this model, since contribution level of each peer affect the global resource availability. For instance in storage sharing, CPU sharing networks, if contribution is optimal further contribution of the same resource would yield less utility. Hence, payoff function may vary with time, situation due to variation in cost and benefit. Furthermore, the presence of altruists in the system also affect the rationality assumptions. Altruists are peers

Table 6. Payoff matrix for multimedia sharing gift giving game

	Server/Serve	Server/Not Serve
Client/Request service	(r, c)	(0, 0)

that contribute to the common good irrespective of their gain from the system.In addition, system variation, peer variational behaviour and decisions under uncertainties poses challenges to the design of payoff functions.

THE CHALLENGES OF DESIGNING PAYOFF FUNCTIONS

To illustrate this problem, we analyze an example. Example 1: We discuss the generic game model of P2P in (Gupta & Somani, 2005). The general assumptions of the game. It assume the network lifetime is infinitely long, hence discretize time t = 0, 1, 2∞. Every user is rational and pursues maximum payoff or profit. A game is played during each time period. In a game, denoted by G, nodes request service for themselves, and decide whether to serve others or not. All players are selfish and same in the network. Precisely, the game G is defined as follows:

- **Players:** All the peers.
- **Actions:** Each player's set of actions is Serve, Don't serve.
- **Preferences:** Each player's preferences are represented by the expected value of a payoff function that assigns value U when service is received and cost C when service is provided.

Analysis and Discussions: In the pure strategy game of this model, the only Nash equilibrium in this game is (Don't serve, Don't serve). Which means that no service is provided to the network at all? This is highly unlikely, since there are altruists that will always give irrespective of what they get from the system. To further their analysis, a mixed strategy analysis is provided. The expected payoff of a player in time t if it chooses to serve with probability p

$$P \text{ ayof fserve} = p(-C * Rtserve * U) \tag{1}$$

The expected payoff of a player in time t if it chooses Don't serve with probability (1-p). P ayof fdont = (1 − p) * (RtDont * U) (2)

The payoff in 1 and 2 need to be computed to be able to evaluate the peers interactions. A reputation equation has to be incorporated as follows (see Tables 6 and 7).

$$Rtserve = Rt-1(1 − \alpha) + \alpha \tag{3}$$

$$RtDontserve = Rt-1(1 − \alpha) \tag{4}$$

Table 7. Payoff matrix for P2P model in Gupta and Somani (2005)

	Player2/Serve	**Player2/Don't Serve**
Player1/Service	(U-C, U-C)	(U-C, U)
Player1/Dont serve	(U, U-C)	(0,0)

Substituting the reputation equations into the payoff and equate them provide the means to compute the probability p. The mixed strategy at equilibrium is given as;

$$p(-C * (Rt-1(1 - \alpha) + \alpha) * U) = (1 - p) * (Rt-1(1 - \alpha) * U) \qquad (5)$$

A fixed ratio of U to C is assumed to be able to compute p. This attest to the problem of modelling the cost, benefit in a dynamic form as the game progresses. Furthermore, repetition is needed to be able to compute the reputation. Hence, we conclude that modelling interactions between peers in a P2P system with incomplete information remains a thorny research issue.

In (Hua, Huang, & Chena, 2012). The game model is given as follows: The authors classified players in the network game as altruist, in-between and free riders, but model the game between altruists and free riders. Altruists and free riders have the same strategy set {upload resource, not upload resource}. The payoff function is designed as follows: If a peer receives a resource of quantity Qd, the peer gets profit f1(Qd) and if a peer uploads resource of quantity Qu, it incur cost −g1(Qu). Both f1(.) and g1'(.) is a monotonically increasing function. Furthermore, altruists get extra profit f2(Qu), iff f2(.) − g1(.)>0. Hence the payoff of Altruist is given as = f1(Qd)+f2(Qu) − g1(Qu) and payoff of free rider = f1(Qd) -g1(Qu).

ANALYSIS AND DISCUSSION

Consider the model above. Some peers, In-between peers may uses flip flip strategy. That is, sometime give or sometime do not share. This variation may be random, oscilatory, spontaneous adaptive based on learning (Zhao, Lui, & Chiu, 2012). The function Ui equals to utility derived by peer i, that is net gain. This is the difference between the benefit and cost function(f1(.) and g1(.)). The extra benefit function f_2(Qu) derived from altruism could be based on subjective parameters such as self-esteem, self-satisfaction, reputation, additional TTL. The benefit function f1(.) could depend on parameters such as; Size of file or size of a chunk (SF), Download priority (DP), Download speed (DS) and Variety of download options (DO) (Golle, Leyton-brown, Mironov, & Lillibridge, 2001) and the cost function g1(.) a monotonically increasing functions that may depends on Bandwidth (B), Disk space Used (DS). In this work, the model is based only on size of file. The game model was analysed offline based on the assumption. The model was simulated using threshold, repetition history and complete information. The real time variation of cost and benefit was not model. The challenging peer type that exhibit flip flip phenomena was not modeled. We conclude that though game theory offer a rich mathematical framework to model interactions in P2P system. There are still many part of the complex interactions in real P2P that existing simplified model have not been able to tackle. We conclude this analysis by posing some open questions that arises from this analysis are;

- How do we associate or computing a numerical value for these parameters?
- Where do we get the probability of different peer type in the whole system?
- How do we ensure repetition of transactions to measure sharing behaviour?

STRATEGY-BASED TAXONOMY OF PEERS IN P2P SYSTEMS

The autonomy of peers and the similarity of public goods in Economics to that of information goods in P2P systems brought about the influence of human behaviour on the attitude of peers in a P2P system. Users' behaviour such as generosity, selfishness and rationality directly affect node characteristics in P2P systems.

Peers may exhibit different strategy during interactions. In order to improve our understanding of these complex interactions in P2P systems, there is a need for behavioral type classification of peers based on strategy peers may employ during interactions. Cooperative strategy: A peer is said to use a cooperative strategy, if it always share a trustworthy resources. Peers that use this strategy are refers to as Altruist (Zhang & Antonopoulos, 2013) (Hua et al., 2012), Contributors (Karakaya, Korpeoglu, & Ulusoy, 2008), Cooperators (Zhao et al., 2012), Enthusiastic nodes (Li, Chen, & Zhou, 2011). Flip flop strategy: A peer is said to use flip flop strategy, if its behaviour may vary with time during interactions. Peers that use this strategy may share or free ride based on conditions. The shared resources from these peers may be trustworthy or untrustworthy. Peers in this category are refers to in literature as In-between (Hua et al., 2012), Rational (Zhang & Antonopoulos, 2013) (Li et al., 2011), Reciprocators (Zhao et al., 2012), Droppers (Karakaya et al., 2008). Selfish strategy: A peer that uses this strategy is always free riding. This type of peers are often refers to in the literature as Defectors (Zhao et al., 2012), Free riders (Zhang

& Antonopoulos, 2013), Selfish nodes (Li et al., 2011). One can observe from these classifications, the divergent interest of various peers interacting in P2P systems as shown in Figure 12.

DISCUSSION AND CONCLUSION

Having classified different classes of peers in P2P networks, in this section, we present a game theory model of a unit of interactions between two peers. Consider a file sharing P2P networks in which two peers p1 and p2 is to share a file. Assuming that the network lifetime is infinitely long, hence discretize time t = 0, 1, 2 ...∞. Every user is rational and is aware of his preference and consequences of their actions. A game is played during each time period. In a game, nodes request service for themselves, and decide whether to serve others or not. A unit of interactions between both peers can be described with a game with the following features: two or more-players, non-cooperative and cooperative, non-zero sum, incomplete information, imperfect information, symmetric/ asymmetric, pure/mixed, sequential/ simultaneous and finite.

Figure 12. Strategy-based classification of peers in P2P systems

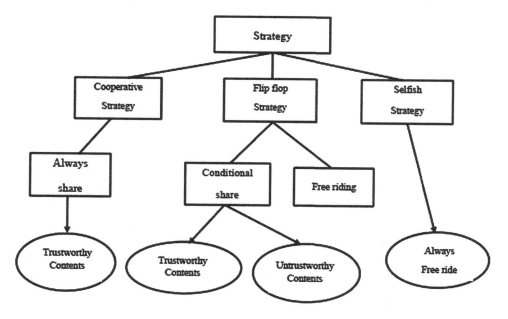

- **Two-Player:** The two peers p1 and p2 are the players in this game. Though, every unit of transaction in a P2P system is between two peers, which can be modeled as a two player game, but the outcome of the game is significantly influenced by the peer acting as a resource provider at that time. For instance, in a sharing game between two peers, if the serving pair chooses the strategy not serves. The game is cannot continue between this duo until another time period, if it is repeated. The game will automatically be concluded, if it is a one shot game.

- **Non-Cooperative:** Both peer p1 and p2 are autonomous, hence they take independent decisions, hence- it a non-cooperative interaction since there are no means to enforce cooperation. But sometimes peers may choose to cooperate, though it is self-enforced. However, it is better for players to cooperate. For instance, consider the prisoner's dilemma example, both players are better off when sometimes they choose the same strategy, as in both confess or both not confess. This phenomenon is referred to as Social Optimality (David & Jon, 2010), a situation in which the sum of the total payoffs is maximized, considering the strategy of each player. It is noteworthy to mention that this outcome is the desired results of interactions in P2P systems, where ideally all participants contributes to the network resources at reasonable level and still gain an acceptable level of utility from the system. In this case, the common good is neither overused by some peer nor under-utilized. Furthermore, this attest to the suitability of the choice of non-cooperative game for the analysis of interactions between peers in P2P systems.

- **Non-Zero Sum:** The game of interactions between two peers may not necessarily a pure game of conflict, hence it is described as non-zero sum game. For instance, if peer p1 is an altruist, it may provide file to peer p2 without expecting any file in return. This behaviour is not true for peers that need file from others in the network.

- **Incomplete Information:** Peers may not necessarily have any information about each other in a P2P system. This is due to high degree of exit and entry of peers, availability of cheap pseudonyms may allow peer to change their identity at will, and hence it is a situation of incomplete information. Furthermore, repetition is needed to be able to compute the reputation. Hence, we conclude that modelling interactions between peers in a P2P system with incomplete information remains a thorny research issue.

- **Imperfect Information:** In some model of P2P, if there is some degree of centralization to provide information about peer. This situation occurs when repetition of transaction is enforced and it is modeled as a repeated game. The information may not be perfect. That is for the peer to know the moves-the transactions of that peer so far. Thus, we can also describe the game as complete imperfect information.

- **Symmetric:** Peers in P2P has equal standing and equal capability, hence the communication, gain or loss in any transaction has equal weight between the players.

- **Pure and Mixed Strategy:** strategy is plan of actions. Peers variational behaviour will be better represented as a mixed strategy. Though, some peers may hold onto one transaction behaviour for a long time, which can be viewed as a pure strategy.

- **Sequential/Simultaneous:** Both peer p1 and p2 may carry out transaction sequentially or simultaneously depending on the model. For example, if peer p1 and p2 exchange file at the same time, it can be modelled as simultaneous game. Moreover, if the game is modeled as repeated and peer p2 observed the actions of peer p1 that is, the contribution history, then is a sequential game model.

- **Finite:** Every peer has a finite set of actions to choose from share not share. However, the sharing may be malicious or trustworthy.

REFERENCES

Aberer, K., & Hauswirth, M. (2002). An Overview on Peer-to-Peer Information Systems. In *18th international conference on data engineering* (pp. 1–14).

Adam, M. B., & Nalebuff, B. J. (1997). *Co-opetition: A revolution mindset that combines competition and cooperation: The game theory strategy that's changing the game of business*. Currency and Doubleday.

Banerjee, D., Saha, S., & Sen, S. (2005). Reciprocal resource sharing in P2P environments. In *Proceedings of the Fourth International Conference on Autonoumous and Multiagent System*. Retrieved from http:// dl.acm.org/citation.cfm?id=1082603

Basar, T. (2010). *Lecture notes on non-cooperative game theory. Electrical and Computer Engineering*. University of Illinois at Urbana Champaign.

Bernard, S. (1967). Is life a game we are playing. *Ethics*, 77(3), 209–219. doi:10.1086/291634

Camerer, F. C. (2003). *Behavioral game theory: Experiments in strategic interaction*. Princeton University Press.

Daswani, N., Garcia-Molina, H., & Yang, B. (2002). Open problems in data-sharing peer-to-peer systems. In Proceedings of the 9th international conference on database theory (pp. 1–15). London, UK: Springer-Verlag. Retrieved from http://dl.acm.org/citation.cfm?id=645505.656446

David, E., & Jon, K. (2010). *Networks, crowds, and markets: Reasoning about a highly connected world*. Cambridge University press.

Fan, X., Li, M., Ma, J., Ren, Y., Zhao, H., & Su, Z. (2012, November). Behavior-based reputation management in p2p file-sharing networks. *Journal of Computer and System Sciences*, *78*(6), 1737–1750. doi:10.1016/j.jcss.2011.10.021

Fudenberg, D., & Tirole, T. (1991). *Game theory*. MIT Press.

Hardin, G. (1968). The Tragedy of the Commons. *Science*, (162): 1243–1248. PMID:5699198

Golle, P., Leyton-brown, K., Mironov, I., & Lillibridge, M. (2001). *Incentives for Sharing in Peer-to-Peer Networks*. Electronic Commerce. doi:10.1145/501158.501193

Gupta, R., & Somani, A. K. (2005). Game theory as a tool to strategize as well as predict nodes behavior in peer-to-peer networks. In *Proceedings of the 11th international conference on parallel and distributed systems* (pp. 244–249). Washington, DC: IEEE Computer Society. Retrieved from doi:doi:10.1109/ICPADS.2005.157 doi:10.1109/ICPADS.2005.157 doi:10.1109/ICPADS.2005.157

Harsanyi, J. C. (1967). Games with incomplete information played by bayesian players, parts i, ii, and iii. *Management Science*, *14*(3), 159–182. doi:10.1287/mnsc.14.3.159

Hua, J. S., Huang, D. C., Yen, S. M., & Chena, C. W. (2012). A dynamic game theory approach to solve the free riding problem in the peer-to-peer networks. *Journal of Simulation*, *6*(1), 43–55. doi:10.1057/jos.2011.11

John, H. C. (1994). *Games with incomplete information*. Nobel Lectures.

Kandori, G., Mailath, M., & Rob, R. (1993). Learning, mutations and long run equilibria in games. *Econometrica*, *61*(1), 27–56. doi:10.2307/2951777

Karakaya, M., Korpeoglu, I., & Ulusoy, O. (2008, February). Counteracting free riding in Peer-to-Peer networks. *Computer Networks*, *52*(3), 675–694. doi:10.1016/j.comnet.2007.11.002

Krishnan, R., & Smith, M. (2002). *The economics of peer-to-peer networks*. Heinz Research Showcase, Carnegie Mellon University. Retrieved from http://repository.cmu.edu/heinzworks/52/

Krishnan, R., & Smith, M. D. (2008). The Virtual Commons: Why Free-Riding Can Be Tolerated in File Sharing Networks. In *International Conference on Information Systems*.

Li, W., Chen, J., & Zhou, B. (2011). Game theory analysis for graded punishment mechanism restraining free-riding in p2p networks. In *Proceedings of the 2011 international symposium on computer science and society* (pp. 262–266). Washington, DC: IEEE Computer Society. doi:doi:10.1109/ISCCS.2011.78 doi:10.1109/ISCCS.2011.78

Mailath, G. J., & Larry, S. (2006). *Repeated games and reputations: long-run relationships*. Oxford University Press. doi:10.1093/acprof:oso/9780195300796.001.0001

Marwell, G., & Ames, R. (1979). Experiments in the provision of public goods: Resources, interest, group size, and the free-rider problem. *American Journal of Sociology*, 84.

Morris, P. (1994). *Introduction to game theory*. Springer New York. doi:10.1007/978-1-4612-4316-8

Mrmol, F. G., & Prez, G. M. (2009). Security threats scenarios in trust and reputation models for dis-tributed systems. *Computers & Security*, 28(7), 545–556. doi:10.1016/j.cose.2009.05.005

Nash, J. (1951). Non-cooperative games. *The Annals of Mathematics*, 54, 286–295.

Osbourne, M. J. (2003). *An introduction to game theory*. Oxford University Press.

Pavel, L. (2012). *Game theory for control of optical networks, static and dynamic game theory: Foundations and applications*. Springer Science. doi:10.1007/978-0-8176-8322-1

Philip, J., & Levine, D. K. (2001). Evolution and information in a gift-giving game. *Journal of Economic Theory*, 100(1), 1–21. doi:10.1006/jeth.2001.2823

Pradeep, , Kumar, N., & Shekar, R. S., Reddy, & Krishna, C. (2012, February). Preventive measures for malware in p2p networks. *International Journal of Engineering Research and Applications*, 2(1), 391–400.

Robert, W. (1971). Computing equilibria of n-person games. *Society for Industrial and Applied Mathematics Journal*, 21(1), 80–87. doi:10.1137/0121011

Roussopoulos, M., Baker, M., & Rosenthal, D. S. H. (2004). 2 P2P or Not 2 P2P? In *Iptps'04 proceedings of the third international conference on peer-to-peer systems* (pp. 1–6).

Rowstron, A., & Druschel, P. (2001). Pastry: Scalable, decentralized object location and routing for large-scale peer-to-peer systems. In In ifip/acm international conference on distributed system platforms (pp. 329–350).

Saad, W., Han, Z., Debbah, M., & Hjrungnes, A. (2009). Coalitional game theory for communication networks: A tutorial. IEEE Signal Processing Magazine, 77–97. doi:doi:10.1109/MSP.2009.000000 doi:10.1109/MSP.2009.000000

Shih-Fen, C., Daniel, V. M., Reeves, Y., & Michael, P. W. (2004). Notes on equilibria in symmetric games. In *International joint conference on autonomous agents multi agent systems, 6th workshop on game theoretic and decision theoretic agents*.

Shoham, Y., & Leyton-Brown, K. (2009). *Multiagent system: Algorithmic, game theoretic and logic foundation*. New York: Cambridge University Press.

Sweeny, J. (1973). An experimental investigation of the free-rider problem. *Social Science Research*, ▪▪▪, 2.

Theodore, B., Lawrence, B., & Hal, R. V. (1986). On the private provision of public goods. *Journal of Public Economics*, (29): 25–49.

Veijalainen, J. (2007). Autonomy, Heterogeneity, Trust, Security, and Privacy in Mobile P2P Environments. *International Journal of Security and Its Applications*, *1*(1), 57–72.

Yu, Z. (2012). Peer-to-peer multimedia sharing based on social norms. *Signal Processing Image Communication*, *27*(5), 383–400. doi:10.1016/j.image.2012.02.003

Zhang, K., & Antonopoulos, N. (2013, January). A novel bartering exchange ring based incentive mechanism for peer-to-peer systems. *Future Gener. Comput. Syst.,* *29*(1), 361–369. doi: 10.1016/j.future.2011.06.005

Zhao, B. Q., Lui, J. C. S., & Chiu, D.-M. (2012, April). A mathematical framework for analyzing adaptive incentive protocols in p2p networks. *IEEE/ACM Trans. Netw.,* *20*(2), 367–380. doi: 10.1109/TNET.2011.2161770

Chapter 6
Security and Privacy Issues, Solutions, and Tools for MCC

Darshan M. Tank
Gujarat Technological University, India

ABSTRACT

With the development of cloud computing and mobility, mobile cloud computing has emerged and become a focus of research. Mobile Cloud Computing (MCC) integrates mobile computing and cloud computing aiming to extend mobile devices capabilities. By the means of on-demand self-service and extendibility, it can offer the infrastructure, platform, and software services in a cloud to mobile users through the mobile network. There is huge market for mobile based e-Commerce applications across the globe. Security and privacy are the key issues for mobile cloud computing applications. The limited processing power and memory of a mobile device dependent on inherently unreliable wireless channel for communication and battery for power leaves little scope for a reliable security layer. Thus there is a need for a lightweight secure framework that provides security with minimum communication and processing overhead on mobile devices. The security and privacy protection services can be achieved with the help of secure mobile-cloud application services.

DOI: 10.4018/978-1-5225-0602-7.ch006

INTRODUCTION

Mobile Cloud Computing (MCC) integrates mobile computing and cloud computing aiming to extend mobile devices capabilities. By the means of on-demand self-service and extendibility, it can offer the infrastructure, platform, and software services in a cloud to mobile users through the mobile network.

There is huge market for mobile based e-Commerce applications across the globe. Security and privacy are the key issues for mobile cloud computing applications. The limited processing power and memory of a mobile device dependent on inherently unreliable wireless channel for communication and battery for power leaves little scope for a reliable security layer. Thus there is a need for a lightweight secure framework that provides security with minimum communication and processing overhead on mobile devices. The security and privacy protection services can be achieved with the help of secure mobile-cloud application services. There are many frameworks and models suggested by different researcher in concern with privacy and security. However, there is still plenty of scope for improvement. Taking support from a proximate cloud a security service could be devised for a mobile device which works as an interface and adaptively provides optimum security solutions based on communication channel capacity, available system resources both hardware and software and user-defined parameters (Dinh 2011).

Mobile Cloud Computing (MCC) is the combination of cloud computing, mobile computing and wireless networks to bring rich computational resources to mobile users, network operators, as well as cloud computing providers. The ultimate goal of MCC is to enable execution of rich mobile applications on a plethora of mobile devices, with a rich user experience. MCC provides business opportunities for mobile network operators as well as cloud providers.

MCC can be defined as a rich mobile computing technology that leverages unified elastic resources of varied clouds and network technologies toward unrestricted functionality, storage, and mobility to serve a multitude of mobile devices anywhere, anytime through the channel of Ethernet or Internet regardless of heterogeneous environments and platforms based on the pay as you use principle. Mobile Cloud Computing refers to an infrastructure where both the data storage and the data processing occur outside of the mobile device. Mobile cloud applications move the computing power and data storage away from mobile phones and into the cloud, bringing applications and mobile computing not only to smart phone users but also to a much broader range of mobile subscribers (Zissis and Lekkas 2012).

Mobile devices are increasingly becoming an essential part of human life as the most effective and convenient communication tools not bounded by time and place. Mobile users accumulate rich experience of various services from mobile applications, which run on the devices and/or on remote servers via wireless networks. The rapid progress of mobile computing becomes a powerful trend in the development of IT technology as well as commerce and industry fields. However, the mobile devices are facing many challenges in their resources and communications. The limited resources significantly impede the improvement of service qualities (Fernando 2013).

There are so many cloud storage service providers around e.g. One Drive (Microsoft Corporation), Dropbox (Dropbox Inc), Google Drive (Google Inc), Box, Amazon Cloud Drive and Apple icloud. Cloud computing applications are the cloud-based services e.g. Mobile Email, Google Maps, Google Cloud Print (Google Inc), Other Apps (Real Estate, Insurance, Surveying, Navigation app) (Ranbijay Kumar and Rajalakshmi 2013). Recently, the mobile cloud computing is becoming a new hot technology. And the security solution for it has become a research focus. With the development of the mobile cloud computing, new security issues will happen, which needs more security approaches.

ARCHITECTURE OF MOBILE CLOUD COMPUTING

MCC uses computational augmentation approaches by which resource constraint mobile devices can utilize computational resources of varied cloud based resources. In MCC, there are four types of cloud based resources, namely distant immobile clouds, proximate immobile computing entities, proximate mobile computing entities, and hybrid. Giant clouds such as Amazon EC2 are in the distant immobile groups whereas cloudlet or surrogates are member of proximate immobile computing entities. Smart phones, tablets, handheld devices, and wearable computing devices are part of the third group of cloud based resources which is proximate mobile computing entities.

Mobile devices are connected to the mobile networks via base stations that establish and control the connections and functional interfaces between the networks and mobile devices. Mobile users' requests and information are transmitted to the central processors that are connected to servers providing mobile network services. The subscribers' requests are delivered to a cloud through the Internet. In the cloud, cloud controllers process the requests to provide mobile users with the corresponding cloud services.

Advantages of MCC (Mobile Cloud Computing)

1. Extending battery lifetime.
2. Improving data storage capacity and processing power.
3. Improving reliability.
4. Dynamic provisioning.

5. Scalability.
6. Multi-tenancy.
7. Ease of integration.

Applications of MCC (Mobile Cloud Computing)

Mobile applications gain increasing share in a global mobile market. Various mobile applications have taken the advantages of MCC.

1. Mobile commerce.
2. Mobile learning.
3. Mobile healthcare.
4. Mobile gaming.
5. Other practical applications.
   a. Keyword-based searching.
   b. Voice-based searching.
   c. Tag-based searching.

MCC Issues

1. Mobile communication issues:
   a. Low bandwidth: One of the biggest issues, because the radio resource for wireless networks is much more scarce than wired networks.
   b. Service availability: Mobile users may not be able to connect to the cloud to obtain a service due to traffic congestion, network failures, mobile signal strength problems.
   c. Heterogeneity: Handling wireless connectivity with highly heterogeneous networks to satisfy MCC requirements (always-on connectivity, on-demand scalability, energy efficiency) is a difficult problem (Dev & Baishnab 2014).
2. Computing issues:
   a. Computation offloading:
      i. One of the main features of MCC.
      ii. Offloading is not always effective in saving energy.
      iii. It is critical to determine whether to offload and which portions of the service codes to offload (Wang 2014).
      iv. Two types: Offloading in a static environment and Offloading in a dynamic environment.

MCC Security Issues

1. Protecting user privacy and data/application secrecy from adversaries is a key to establish and maintain consumers' trust in the mobile platform, especially in MCC.
2. MCC security issues have two main categories.
    a. Security for mobile users:
        i.   Mobile devices are exposed to numerous security threats like malicious codes and their vulnerability.
        ii.   GPS can cause privacy issues for subscribers.
        iii. Security for mobile applications: Installing and running security software are the simplest ways to detect security threats. Mobile devices are resource constrained, protecting them from the threats is more difficult than that for resourceful devices.
    b. Securing data on clouds.

Privacy Issues in MCC

1. Location based services (LBS) faces a privacy issue on mobile users' provide private information such as their current location. This problem becomes even worse if an adversary knows user's important information.
2. Zhangwei and Mingjun propose the Location Trusted Server (LTS) approach. After receiving mobile users' requests, LTS gathers their location information and cloaks the information called "cloaked region" to conceal user's information. The "cloaked region" is sent to LBS, so LBS know only general information about the users but cannot identify them.

SECURITY-RELATED ISSUES IN MCC

Protecting user privacy and data/application secrecy from adversary is a key to establish and maintain consumers' trust in the mobile platform, especially in MCC. The security related issues in MCC are introduced in two categories: the security for mobile users and the security for data.

1. Security for Mobile Users

Mobile devices such as cellular phone, personal digital assistant (PDA), and smart phone are exposed to numerous security threats like malicious codes (e.g., virus, worm, and Trojan horses) and their vulnerability. In addition, with mobile phones integrated global positioning system (GPS) device, they can cause privacy issues for subscribers (Suo 2013).

2. Securing Data on Clouds

Although both mobile users and application developers benefit from storing a large amount of data/applications on a cloud, they should be careful of dealing with the data/applications in terms of their integrity, authentication, and digital rights.

3. Security for Mobile Applications

Presently Mobile devices run security checks on devices itself, which costs in terms of computation and power. MCC sows the seeds of a new model where detection services are carried out on cloud, saving the device CPU and memory requirements, but demanding the increase of bandwidth. One such approach has been proposed in, but it has its own privacy issues to battle up (Suo 2013).

4. Privacy

Providing sensitive or private information such as providing user's current location creates scenarios for privacy issues. The best example is global positioning system (GPS), which provides the use of location based services (LBS) (Sanaei 2014).

SECURITY THREATS AND COUNTER MEASURES

There are numerous challenges existing in the field of MCC, including data replication, consistency, and limited scalability, and unreliability, unreliable availability of cloud resources, portability, trust, security, and privacy. The above-mentioned challenges have become a barrier in the rapid growth of MCC's subscriber. According to survey, 74% of IT Executives and Chief Information Officers are not willing to adopt cloud services due to the risks associated with security and privacy. To attract potential consumers, the cloud service provider has to target all the security issues to provide a completely secure environment. Research organizations and academia have undertaken a massive amount of work to secure a cloud computing environment. There are still some grey areas that need to be addressed, such as the security and privacy of user's data stored on cloud servers, security threats caused by multiple virtual machines, and intrusion detection. As MCC is based on cloud computing, all the security issues are inherited in MCC with the extra limitation of resource constraint mobile devices. Due to resource limitation, the security algorithms proposed for the cloud computing environment cannot be directly run on a mobile device. There is a need for a lightweight secure framework that provides security with minimum communication and processing overhead on mobile devices (Huang 2010).

The security and privacy protection services can be achieved with the help of secure cloud application services. In addition to security and privacy, the secure cloud application services provide the user management, key management, encryption on demand, intrusion detection, authentication, and authorization services to mobile users. There is a need for a secure communication channel between cloud and the mobile device. The secure routing protocols can be used to protect the communication channel between the mobile device and cloud.

Virtualization improves the utilization of cloud resources but introduces new security issues due to the lack of perfect isolation of virtual machines hosted on a single server. The security issues imposed by virtualization can be tackled to some extent with the help of virtual machine secure monitoring, mirror, and migration. To provide the transparent cloud environment, mobile users must have the facility to audit the security level of the hosted services. The audit can be done with the help of a cloud service monitor. The cloud service monitor examines the security level and flows of the running environment. The security level should meet the user security requirements and the flow of the running environment should be normal. The security verification of uploaded data on cloud can be done using a storage security verification service. The physical security of the datacenter plays a very important role to achieve security and privacy. Physical security deals with the measures taken to avoid unauthorized personnel physically accessing the resources of the cloud service provider. Physical security can be achieved with the help of security guards, video surveillance, security lighting, sensors, and alarms (Jia 2011).

The researchers have done a massive amount of work to provide an energy-aware high performance computing environment. However, there is also a need for energy-efficient security frameworks for mobile devices to provide security and privacy services in an MCC environment. For the last few years, MCC has been an active research area. As MCC is in the preliminary stages, limited surveys are available in various domains of MCC. The mobile communication issues are associated with low bandwidth, service availability, and heterogeneity. The computing issues are linked with computing offloading, security, data access, and context-aware mobile cloud services.

TRUST MANAGEMENT IN MOBILE CLOUD COMPUTING ENVIRONMENT

The concept of trust, adjusted to the case of two parties involved in a transaction, can be described as follows: "An entity A is considered to trust another entity B when entity A believes that entity B will behave exactly as expected and required". Thereinafter, an entity can be considered trustworthy, if the parties or people involved in transactions with that entity rely on its credibility. In general, the concept described above can be verbally represented by the term reliability, which refers to the quality of a person or entity that is worthy of trust. Trust in the information society is built on various different grounds, based on calculus, on knowledge or on social reasons. The notion of trust in an organization could be defined as the customer's certainty that the organization is capable of providing the required services accurately and infallibly. A certainty which also expresses the customer's faith in its moral integrity, in the soundness of its operation, in the effectiveness of its security mechanisms, in its expertise and in its abidance by all regulations and laws, while at the same time, it also contains the acknowledgement of a minimum risk factor, by the relying party. The notion of security refers to a given situation where all possible risks are either eliminated or brought to an absolute minimum.

Trust in a cloud environment depends heavily on the selected deployment model, as governance of data and applications is outsourced and delegated out of the owner's strict control. In traditional architectures, trust was enforced by an efficient security policy, which addressed constraints on functions and flow among them, constraints on access by external systems and adversaries including programs and access to data by people. In a cloud deployment, this perception is totally obscured. In the case of public or community clouds, control is delegated to the organization owning the infrastructure. When deploying on a public cloud, control is mitigated to the infrastructure owner to enforce a sufficient security policy that guarantees that appropriate security activities are being performed to ensure that risk is reduced. This introduces a number of risks and threats, as essentially security is related to trusting the processes and computing base implemented by the cloud owner. It is crucial to differentiate between deployment models, as a private cloud, where the infrastructure is operated and managed on premise by a private organization, does not introduce additional unique security challenges, as trust remains within the organization. In such a situation the infrastructures owner remains the data and process owner (Dev and Baishnab 2014).

The trust management model of mobile cloud includes identity management, key management, and security policy enforcement. An ESSI owner has the full control over the data possessed in the ESSI, and thus a user-centric identity management framework is a natural choice. The user-centric identity management allows an individual has full control of his/her identities, in which third party authenticates them. It also implies that a user has control over the data his/her sharing over the Internet, and can transfer and delete the data when required.

AUTHENTICATION AND AUTHORIZATION PROCESS

Authentication is the process of determining whether someone or something is, in fact, who or what it is declared to be. Logically, authentication precedes *authorization*. The two terms are often used synonymously but they are two different processes (Yan 2015).

Authentication is a process in which the credentials provided are compared to those on file in a database of authorized users' information on a local *operating system* or within an *authentication server*. If the credentials match, the process is completed and the user is granted authorization for access. The permissions and folders returned define both the environment the user sees and the way he can interact with it, including hours of access and other rights such as the amount of *allocated* storage space.

Authentication Factors

1. **Knowledge Factors:** A category of authentication credentials consisting of information that the user possesses, such as a personal identification number (PIN), a user name, a password or the answer to a secret question.
2. **Possession Factors:** A category of credentials based on items that the user has with them, typically a hardware device such as a security token or a mobile phone used in conjunction with software token.
3. **Inherence Factors:** A category of user authentication credentials consisting of elements that are integral to the individual in question, in the form of biometric data.

User location and current time are sometimes considered the fourth factor and fifth factor for authentication. The ubiquity of smart phones can help ease the burdens of multifactor authentication for users. Most smart phones are equipped with *GPS*, enabling reasonable surety confirmation of the login location. Lower surety measures include the *MAC* address of the login point or physical presence verifications through cards and other possession factor elements.

Authorization is the process of giving someone permission to do or have something. In multi-user computer systems, a system administrator defines for the system which users are allowed *access* to the system and what privileges of use (such as access to which file directories, hours of access, amount of allocated storage space, and so forth). Assuming that someone has logged in to a computer *operatingsystem* or *application*, the system or application may want to identify what resources the user can be given during this session. Thus, authorization is sometimes seen as both the preliminary setting up of permissions by a system administrator and the actual checking of the permission values that have been set up when a user is getting access. Logically, authorization is preceded by *authentication.*

The process of an administrator granting rights and the process of checking user account permissions for access to resources are both referred to as authorization. The privileges and preferences granted for the authorized account depend on the user's permissions, which are either stored locally or on the authentication server. The settings defined for all these environment variables are set by an administrator.

ACCESS CONTROL

Access control is a security technique that can be used to regulate who or what can view or use resources in a computing environment. There are two main types of access control: physical and logical. Physical access control limits access to campuses, buildings, rooms and physical IT assets. Logical access limits connections to computer networks, system files and data. The four main categories of access control are:

1. Mandatory access control.
2. Discretionary access control.
3. Role-based access control.
4. Rule-based access control.

Access control systems perform *authorization* identification, *authentication*, access approval, and accountability of entities through login credentials including *passwords*, personal identification numbers (PINs), *biometric* scans, and physical or electronic keys.

An access control list (ACL) is a table that tells a computer *operating system* which access rights each user has to a particular system object, such as a file *directory* or individual *file*. Each object has a security attribute that identifies its access control list. The list has an entry for each system user with access privileges. The most common privileges include the ability to read a file, to write to the file or files, and to execute the file. Microsoft Windows NT/2000, Novell's *NetWare*, Digital's *OpenVMS*, and *UNIX*-based systems are among the operating systems that use access control lists. The list is implemented differently by each operating system (Oberheide 2008).

In Windows NT/2000, an access control list (ACL) is associated with each system object. Each ACL has one or more access control entries (ACEs) consisting of the name of a user or group of users. The user can also be a role name, such as "programmer," or "tester." For each of these users, groups, or roles, the access privileges are stated in a string of bits called an access mask. Generally, the system administrator or the object owner creates the access control list for an object.

RSA ALGORITHM

RSA is a cryptosystem for public-key *encryption*, and is widely used for securing sensitive data, particularly when being sent over an insecure network such as the *Internet*. RSA was first described in 1977 by Ron Rivest, Adi Shamir and Leonard Adleman of the Massachusetts Institute of Technology. Public-key *cryptography*, also known as *asymmetric cryptography*, uses two different but mathematically linked *keys*, one public and one private. The *public key* can be shared with everyone, whereas the *private key* must be kept secret. In RSA cryptography, both the public and the private keys can encrypt a message; the opposite key from the one used to encrypt a message is used to decrypt it. This attribute is one reason why RSA has become the most widely used asymmetric *algorithm*: It provides a method of assuring the confidentiality, integrity, authenticity and non-reputability of electronic communications and data storage.

Many protocols like *SSH*, OpenPGP, *S/MIME*, and *SSL/TLS* rely on RSA for encryption and *digital signature* functions. It is also used in software programs - *browsers* are an obvious example, which need to establish a secure connection over an insecure network like the Internet or validate a digital signature. RSA signature verification is one of the most commonly performed operations in IT.

RSA derives its security from the difficulty of factoring large integers that are the product of two large *prime numbers*. Multiplying these two numbers is easy, but determining the original prime numbers from the total - factoring - is considered infeasible due to the time it would take even using today's super computers.

DATA ENCRYPTION STANDARD (DES) ALGORITHM

The Data Encryption Standard (DES) is a symmetric-key method of data *encryption*. DES works by using the same *key* to encrypt and decrypt a message, so both the sender and the receiver must know and use the same *private key*. Once the go-to, symmetric-key algorithm for the encryption of electronic data, DES has been superseded by the more secure *Advanced Encryption Standard* (AES) algorithm.

Originally designed by researchers at *IBM* in the early 1970s, DES was adopted by the U.S. government as an official Federal Information Processing Standard (*FIPS*) in 1977 for the encryption of commercial and sensitive yet unclassified government computer data. It was the first encryption *algorithm* approved by the U.S. government for public disclosure. This ensured that DES was quickly adopted by industries such as financial services, where the need for strong encryption is high. The simplicity of DES also saw it used in a wide variety of embedded systems, *smart cards*, *SIM cards* and network devices requiring encryption like *modems*, *set-top boxes* and *routers*.

ADVANCED ENCRYPTION STANDARD (AES) ALGORITHM

The Advanced Encryption Standard or AES is a symmetric *block cipher* used by the U.S. government to protect classified information and is implemented in software and hardware throughout the world to encrypt sensitive data.

The origins of AES date back to 1997 when the *National Institute of Standards and Technology (NIST)* announced that it needed a successor to the aging *Data Encryption Standard (DES)* which was becoming vulnerable to *brute-force attacks*.

This new *encryption algorithm* would be unclassified and had to be "capable of protecting sensitive government information well into the next century." It was to be easy to implement in hardware and software, as well as in restricted environments (for example, in a *smart card*) and offer good defenses against various attack techniques.

TWO-FACTOR AUTHENTICATION (2FA) SYSTEM

A password is inherently weak. It can easily be lost or forgotten; many people write their passwords down where they can be seen by others; some use the same password over and over or use weak passwords that can be easily guessed.

The use of two-factor Web authentication ensures that this won't happen. A password is one of two necessary authentication factors that must be provided before access is granted. All 2FA systems are based on two of three possible factors: a knowledge factor (something the user knows, like a password), a possession factor (something the user has, like a token; more on that below), and an inherence factor (something the user is, such as a fingerprint). In this scenario, even if a malicious party obtains a person's password, he or she would not be able to provide the relevant second element needed to complete the authentication process. This lowers risk and the potential for unscrupulous behavior, as a compromised password alone is not enough to compromise the authentication system.

In the enterprise, *two-factor Web authentication* systems rely on hardware-based security tokens that generate pass codes; these pass codes or PINs are valid for about 60 seconds and must be entered along with a password. In a consumer-oriented Web-based environment, it's cost-prohibitive for a service provider to distribute physical tokens to each and every individual user.

Instead, most websites ask users to undergo a one-time registration process during which users register one or more of their mobile devices with the website provider. This is a trusted device under the users' control that can receive a verification code via SMS or another means to verify the user's identity.

Any time a user signs into the website, a pass code is sent to the registered device. The user must enter the password and verification code to fully sign in and use the services. Two-factor Web authentication systems rely on hardware-based security tokens that generate pass codes that are valid for about 60 seconds and must be entered along with a password.

Recently Apple joined a growing number of major consumer brands like Facebook, Google, Microsoft and PayPal in offering two-factor authentication (2FA) to help customers better secure their user accounts against hacking. Apple has expanded its use of two-factor authentication to its iCloud backup service.

CLOUD COMPUTING SECURITY ATTACKS

Cloud security is an evolving sub-domain of *computer security*, *network security*, and, more broadly, *information security*. It refers to a broad set of policies, technologies, and controls deployed to protect data, applications, and the associated infrastructure of *cloud computing*.

1. Denial-of-Service Attack (DoS)

Cloud is more penetrable to DoS attacks, because so many users are involved in the usage of cloud services and resources, therefore DoS attacks can be more damaging. When workload start increasing on Cloud, Cloud Computing operating system start to provide more computational power in the form of more virtual machines, more service instances to cope with the additional workload. Thus, the server hardware boundaries for more workload start restricting. In that sense, the Cloud system is trying to work against the attacker, but actually to some extent even supports the attacker by enabling the attacker to do most possible damage on services availability, starting from a single flooding attack entry point. Thus, the attacker does not have to flood all n servers that provide a certain service in target, but merely can flood a single, Cloud-based address in order to perform a full loss of availability on the intended service. Some security concerning professionals proposed solution aims to detect and analyze Distributed Denial of Service (DDoS) attacks in cloud computing environments, using Dempster- Shafer Theory (DST) operations in 3-valued logic and Fault-Tree Analysis (FTA) for each VMbased Intrusion Detection System (IDS) (Yan 2015).

2. Cloud Malware-Injection Attack

It is the first considerable attack attempt that inject implementation of a malicious service or virtual machine into the Cloud. The purpose of malware cloud is anything that the adversary is interested in, it may include data modifications, full functionality changes/reverse or blockings. In this attack adversary creates its own malicious service implementation module (SaaS or PaaS) or virtual machine instance (IaaS), and add it to the Cloud system. Then, the adversary has to pretend to the Cloud system that it is some the new service implementation instance and among the valid instances for some particular service attacked by the adversary. If this action succeeds, the Cloud automatically redirects the requests of valid user to the malicious service implementation, and the adversary code is executed. The main scenario behind the Cloud Malware Injection attack is that an attacker transfers a manipulated/wrong copy of a victim's service instance so that malicious instance can achieve access to the service requests of the victim's service. To achieve this, the attacker has to derive control over the victim's data in the cloud. According to classification, this attack is the major representative of exploiting the service-to-cloud attack surface (Zonouz et al. 2013).

3. Side Channel Attack

An attacker attempts to compromise the cloud system by placing a malicious virtual machine in close propinquity to a target cloud server system and then debut a side channel attack. Side-channel attacks have egressed as a kind of effective security threat targeting system implementation of cryptographic algorithms. Evaluating cryptographic systems resilience to side-channel attacks is therefore important for secure system design. Side channel attacks use two steps to attack- VM CO-Residence and Placement i.e., an attacker can often place his or her instance on the same physical machine as a target instance and VM Extraction i.e., the ability of a malicious instance to utilize side channels to learn information about co-resident instances.

4. Authentication Attack

Authentication is a weak issue in the hosted and virtual services and is very frequently targeted. There are so many ways to authenticate users which can be based upon what a user knows, has, or is. The mechanisms and the methods that are used to secure the authentication process are mostly targeted by the attackers. Recently, regarding the architecture of cloud computing, SaaS, IaaS and Paas, there is only IaaS which is able to offer this kind of information protection and data encryption. If the transmitted data confidentiality is under the category high for any enterprise, the cloud computing service based on IaaS architecture will be the most suitable and possible solution for secured data communication.

5. Man-in-the-Middle Cryptographic Attacks

This attack is carried out when an attacker places himself between two users. Anytime attackers can place themselves in the communications path, there is the possibility that they can intercept and modify communications.

DENIAL OF SERVICE (DOS) ATTACK

A denial of service (DoS) attack is an incident in which a user or organization is deprived of the services of a resource they would normally expect to have. In a distributed denial-of-service, large numbers of compromised systems attack a single target.

Although a DoS attack does not usually result in the theft of information or other security loss, it can cost the target person or company a great deal of time and money. Typically, the loss of service is the inability of a particular network service, such as e-mail, to be available or the temporary loss of all network connectivity and services. A denial of service attack can also destroy programming and files in affected computer systems. In some cases, DoS attacks have forced Web sites accessed by millions of people to temporarily cease operation. Common forms of denial of service attacks are:

1.   Buffer Overflow Attacks.
2.   SYN Attack.

3.   Teardrop Attack.
4.   Smurf Attack.
5.   Viruses.
6.   Physical Infrastructure Attacks.

DISTRIBUTED DENIAL OF SERVICE (DDOS) ATTACK

A distributed denial-of-service (DDoS) attack is one in which a multitude of compromised systems attack a single target, thereby causing *denial of service* for users of the targeted system. The flood of incoming messages to the target system essentially forces it to shut down, thereby denying service to the system to legitimate users. In a typical DDoS attack, the assailant begins by exploiting vulnerability in one computer system and making it the DDoS *master*. The attack master, also known as the botmaster, identifies and identifies and infects other vulnerable systems with *malware*. Eventually, the assailant instructs the controlled machines to launch an attack against a specified target (Yan 2015).

There are two types of DDoS attacks: a network-centric attack which overloads a service by using up bandwidth and an application-layer attack which overloads a service or database with application calls. The inundation of *packets* to the target causes a denial of service. While the media tends to focus on the target of a DDoS attack as the victim, in reality there are many victims in a DDoS attack - the final target and as well the systems controlled by the intruder. Although the owners of co-opted computers are typically unaware that their computers have been compromised, they are nevertheless likely to suffer a degradation of service and not work well. A computer under the control of an intruder is known as a *zombie* or *bot*. A group of co-opted computers is known as a *botnet* or a zombie army. Both Kaspersky Labs and Symantec have identified botnets - not spam, viruses, or worms - as the biggest threat to Internet security.

HOW TO PREVENT A DENIAL-OF-SERVICE (DOS) ATTACK?

A *distributed denial-of-service attack* is an Internet assault in which a number of systems attack a single target, causing a denial of service for legitimate users of the targeted system. While many technologies today are designed to prevent various types of attacks, *preventing a distributed denial-of-service (DDoS) attack* is impossible, and stopping one once it has started can be quite a challenge.

As a top priority, make sure enough bandwidth is available to handle not only the surge in legitimate traffic, but also possible small-scale denial-of-service (DoS) attacks. I would also recommend initiating a Web infrastructure vulnerability assessment and a penetration test, including DoS testing, before the new campaign goes live. It should be noted that these attacks can last hours, days or even weeks. Any time you believe you are under a DoS attack, you should contact your ISP representative immediately.

There's no way to completely protect your network from denial-of-service attacks, especially with the prevalence of distributed denial-of-service (DDoS) attacks on the Internet today. It's extremely difficult to differentiate an attack request from a legitimate request because they often use the same protocols/ports and may resemble each other in content. However, there are some things we can do to reduce your risk:

1. Purchase a lot of bandwidth. This is not only the easiest solution, but also the most expensive. If you simply have tons of bandwidth, it makes perpetrating a DoS attack much more difficult because it's more bandwidth that an attacker has to clog.

2. Use DoS attack detection technology. Intrusion prevention system and firewall manufacturers now offer DoS protection technologies that include signature detection and connection verification techniques to limit the success of DoS attacks.

3. Prepare for DoS response. The use of throttling and rate-limiting technologies can reduce the effects of a DoS attack. One such response mode stops all new inbound connections in the event of a DoS attack, allowing established connections and new outbound connections to continue.

PHISHING ATTACK AND SPOOFING

Phishing is the attempt to acquire *sensitive information* such as usernames, passwords, and *credit card* details, often for malicious reasons, by masquerading as a trustworthy entity in an *electronic communication*. The word is a *neologism* created as a *homophone* of *fishing* due to the similarity of using fake *bait* in an attempt to catch a victim. Communications purporting to be from popular social web sites, auction sites, banks, online payment processors or IT administrators are commonly used to lure unsuspecting victims. Phishing emails may contain links to websites that are infected with *malware*. Phishing is typically carried out by *email spoofing* or *instant messaging*, and it often directs users to enter details at a fake website whose *look and feel* are almost identical to the legitimate one. Phishing is an example of *social engineering* techniques used to deceive users, and exploits the poor usability of current web security technologies. Attempts to deal with the growing number of reported phishing incidents include *legislation*, user training, public awareness, and technical security measures. Many websites have now created secondary tools for applications, like maps for games, but they should be clearly marked as to who wrote them, and users should not use the same passwords anywhere on the internet.

Phishing is a continual threat, and the risk is even larger in social media such as *Facebook*, *Twitter*, and *Google+*. Hackers could create a clone of a website and tell you to enter personal information, which is then emailed to them. Hackers commonly take advantage of these sites to attack people using them at their workplace, homes, or in public in order to take personal and security information that can affect the user or company. Phishing takes advantage of the trust that the user may have since the user may not be able to tell that the site being visited, or program being used, is not real; therefore, when this occurs, the hacker has the chance to gain the personal information of the targeted user, such as passwords, usernames, security codes, and credit card numbers, among other things.

Spoofing is the creation of TCP/IP packets using somebody else's IP address. Routers use the "destination IP" address in order to forward packets through the Internet, but ignore the "source IP" address. That address is only used by the destination machine when it responds back to the source. A common misconception is that "IP spoofing" can be used to hide your IP address while surfing the Internet, chatting on-line, sending e-mail, and so forth. This is generally not true. Forging the source IP address causes the responses to be misdirected, meaning you cannot create a normal network connection. However, IP spoofing is an integral part of many network attacks that do not need to see responses. In *computer networking*, IP address spoofing or IP spoofing is the creation of *Internet Protocol* (IP) *packets* with a forged source *IP address*, with the purpose of concealing the identity of the sender or impersonating another computing system.

SSL AND TLS

SSL is short for Secure Sockets Layer. Secure Sockets Layer (SSL) is a *protocol* developed by *Netscape* for transmitting private documents via the *Internet*. SSL uses a *cryptographic* system that uses two *keys* to *encrypt* data – a public key known to everyone and a private or secret key known only to the recipient of the message. Most *Web browsers* support SSL, and many *websites* use the protocol to obtain confidential user information, including credit card numbers. By convention, *URLs* that require an SSL connection start with https: instead of http:

When a *Web browser* tries to connect to a website using SSL, the browser will first request the web server identify itself. This prompts the web server to send the browser a copy of the *SSL Certificate*. The browser checks to see if the SSL Certificate is trusted - if the SSL Certificate is trusted, then the browser sends a message to the Web server. The server then responds to the browser with a digitally signed acknowledgement to start an SSL *encrypted* session. This allows encrypted data to be shared between the browser and the server. You may notice that your browsing session now starts with https (and not http).

Transport Layer Security (TLS) and its predecessor, Secure Sockets Layer (SSL), both of which are frequently referred to as 'SSL', are *cryptographic protocols* designed to provide *communications security* over a *computer network*. Several versions of the protocols are in widespread use in applications such as *web browsing, email, Internet faxing, instant messaging*, and *voice-over-IP* (VoIP). Major web sites use TLS to secure all communications between their servers and *web browsers*. The primary goal of the TLS protocol is to provide privacy and data integrity between two communicating computer applications.

TYPES OF CYBER ATTACK OR THREATS

A cyber attack, in simple terms, is an attack on your digital systems originating from malicious acts of an anonymous source. Cyber attack allows for an illegal access to your digital device, while gaining access or control of your digital device. A different types of cyber attacks can be defined as an offensive tactic to gain an illegal control or access to your digital device, called the target system, initiated by a person or a computer against a website, computer system or a single digital device as well as a whole, which poses a serious threat to computer systems, information stored, financial structures and the entire network itself. Cyber attacks work towards compromising the integrity of the digital device and the information stored in it.

Types of Cyber Attack or Threats

1. **Backdoors:** Backdoor is a type of cyber threat in which the attacker uses a back door to install a key logging software, thereby allowing an illegal access to your system. This threat can turn out to be potentially serious as it allows for modification of the files, stealing information, installing unwanted software or even taking control of the entire computer.

2. **Denial-of-Service Attack:** A denial-of-service or a DOS attack generally means attacking the network to bring it down completely with useless traffic by affecting the host device which is connected to the internet. A DOS attack targets websites or services which are hosted on the servers of banks and credit card payment gateways.

3. **Direct-Access Attack:** A direct-access attack simply means gaining physical access to the computer or its part and performing various functions or install-

ing various types of devices to compromise security. The attacker can install software loaded with worms or download important data, using portable devices.

4. **Eavesdropping:** As the name suggests, eavesdropping means secretly listening to a conversation between the hosts on a network. There are various programs such as Carnivore and NarusInsight that can be used to eavesdrop.

5. **Spoofing:** Spoofing is a cyber attack where a person or a program impersonates another by creating false data in order to gain illegal access to a system. Such threats are commonly found in emails where the sender's address is spoofed.

6. **Tampering:** Tampering is a web based attack where certain parameters in the URL are changed without the customer's knowledge; and when the customer keys in that URL, it looks and appears exactly the same. Tampering is basically done by hackers and criminals to steal the identity and obtain illegal access to information.

7. **Repudiation Attack:** A repudiation attack occurs when the user denies the fact that he or she has performed a certain action or has initiated a transaction. A user can simply deny having knowledge of the transaction or communication and later claim that such transaction or communication never took place.

8. **Information Disclosure:** Information disclosure breach means that the information which is thought to be secured is released to unscrupulous elements that are not trustworthy.

9. **Privilege Escalation Attack:** A privilege escalation attack is a type of network intrusion which allows the user to have an elevated access to the network which was primarily not allowed. The attacker takes the advantage of the programming errors and permits an elevated access to the network.

10. **Exploits:** An exploit attack is basically software designed to take advantage of a flaw in the system. The attacker plans to gain easy access to a computer system and gain control, allows privilege escalation or creates a DOS attack.

11. **Social Engineering:** An attack by a known or a malicious person is known as social engineering. They have knowledge about the programs used and the firewall security and thus it becomes easier to take advantage of trusted people and deceive them to gain passwords or other necessary information for a large social engineering attack.

12. **Indirect Attack:** Indirect attack means an attack launched from a third party computer as it becomes more difficult to track the origin of the attack.

13. **Computer Crime:** A crime undertaken with the use of a computer and a network is called as a computer crime.

14. **Malware:** Malware refers to malicious software that are being designed to damage or perform unwanted actions into the system. Malware is of many types

like viruses, worms, Trojan horses, etc., which can cause havoc on a computer's hard drive. They can either delete some files or a directory or simply gather data without the actual knowledge of the user.

15. **Adware:** Adware is software that supports advertisements which renders ads to its author. It has advertisements embedded in the application. So when the program is running, it shows the advertisement. Basically, adware is similar to malware as it uses ads to inflict computers with deadly viruses.

16. **Bots:** Bots is a software application that runs automated tasks which are simple and repetitive in nature. Bots may or may not be malicious, but they are usually found to initiate a DoS attack or a click fraud while using the internet.

17. **Ransomware:** Ransomware is a type of cyber security threat which will restrict access to your computer system at first and will ask for a ransom in order for the restriction to be removed. This ransom is to be paid through online payment methods only which the user can be granted an access to their system.

18. **Rootkits:** A rootkit is malicious software designed in such a way that hides certain process or programs from normal antivirus scan detection and continues to enjoy a privilege access to your system. It is that software which runs and gets activated each time you boot your system and are difficult to detect and can install various files and processes in the system.

19. **Spyware:** Spyware, as the name suggests, is software which typically spies and gathers information from the system through a user's internet connection without the user's knowledge. Spyware software is majorly a hidden component of a freeware program which can be downloaded from the internet.

20. **Scareware:** Scareware is a type of threat which acts as a genuine system message and guides you to download and purchase useless and potentially dangerous software. Such scareware pop-ups seem to be similar to any system messages, but actually aren't. The main purpose of the scareware is to create anxiety among the users and use that anxiety to coax them to download irrelevant softwares.

21. **Trojan Horses:** Trojan Horses are a form of threat that are malicious or harmful codes hidden behind genuine programs or data which can allow complete access to the system and can cause damage to the system or data corruption or loss/theft of data. It acts as a backdoor and hence it is not easily detectable.

22. **Virus:** A computer virus is a self replicating program which, when executed, replicates or even modifies by inserting copies of it into another computer file and infects the affected areas once the virus succeeds in replicating. This virus can be harmful as it spreads like wildfire and can infect majority of the system in no time.

23. **Worm:** Just like a virus, worm is a self replicating program which relies on computer network and performs malicious actions and spreads itself onto other computer networks. Worms primarily rely on security failures to access the infected system.

24. **Phishing:** Phishing is a cyber threat which makes an attempt to gain sensitive information like passwords, usernames and other details for malicious reasons. It is basically an email fraud where the perpetrator sends a legitimate looking email and attempts to gain personal information.

25. **Identity Theft:** Identity theft is a crime wherein your personal details are stolen and these details are used to commit a fraud. An identity theft is committed when a criminal impersonates individuals and use the information for some financial gain.

26. **Intellectual Property Theft:** Intellectual Property theft is a theft of copyrighted material where it violates the copyrights and the patents. It is a cybercrime to get hands onto some trade secrets and patented documents and research. It is basically a theft of an idea, plan and the methodology being used.

27. **Password Attacks:** Password attack is a form of a threat to your system security where attackers usually try ways to gain access to your system password. They either simply guess the password or use an automated program to find the correct password and gain an entry into the system.

28. **Bluesnarfing:** Bluesnarfing is a threat of information through unauthorized means. The hackers can gain access to the information and data on a Bluetooth enabled phone using the wireless technology of the Bluetooth without alerting the user of the phone.

29. **Bluejacking:** Bluejacking is simply sending of texts, images or sounds, to another Bluetooth enabled device and is a harmless way of marketing. However, there is a thin line between bluejacking and bluesnarfing and if crossed it results into an act of threat.

30. **DDoS:** DDoS basically means a Distributed Denial of Service. It is an attempt to make any online service temporarily unavailable by generating overwhelming traffic from multiple sources or suspend services of a host connected to the internet.

31. **Key Logger:** A key logger is a spyware that has the capability to spy on the happenings on the computer system. It has the capability to record every stroke on the keyboard, web sites visited and every information available on the system. This recorded log is then sent to a specified receiver.

FEATURES OF CLOUDSIM (A FRAMEWORK FOR MODELING AND SIMULATION OF CLOUD COMPUTING INFRASTRUCTURES AND SERVICES)

Cloud computing is the leading technology for delivery of reliable, secure, fault-tolerant, sustainable, and scalable computational services. For assurance of such characteristics in cloud systems under development, it is required timely, repeatable, and controllable methodologies for evaluation of new cloud applications and policies before actual development of cloud products. Because utilization of real testbeds limits the experiments to the scale of the testbed and makes the reproduction of results an extremely difficult undertaking, simulation may be used.

CloudSim goal is to provide a generalized and extensible simulation framework that enables modeling, simulation, and experimentation of emerging Cloud computing infrastructures and application services, allowing its users to focus on specific system design issues that they want to investigate, without getting concerned about the low level details related to Cloud-based infrastructures and services.

CloudSim is developed in the Cloud Computing and Distributed Systems (CLOUDS) Laboratory, at the Computer Science and Software Engineering Department of the University of Melbourne. CloudSim is powered by jProfiler.

Main Features

1. Support for modeling and simulation of large scale Cloud computing data centers.
2. Support for modeling and simulation of virtualized server hosts, with customizable policies for provisioning host resources to virtual machines.
3. Support for modeling and simulation of energy-aware computational resources.
4. Support for modeling and simulation of data center network topologies and message-passing applications.
5. Support for modeling and simulation of federated clouds.
6. Support for dynamic insertion of simulation elements, stop and resume of simulation.
7. Support for user-defined policies for allocation of hosts to virtual machines and policies for allocation of host resources to virtual machines.

FUTURE RESEARCH DIRECTIONS

Mobile cloud computing is becoming a new hot technology. And the security solution for it has become a research focus. With the development of the mobile cloud computing, new security issues will happen, which needs more security approaches.

There is huge market for mobile based e-Commerce applications across the globe. Security and privacy are the key issues for mobile cloud computing applications. The limited processing power and memory of a mobile device dependent on inherently unreliable wireless channel for communication and battery for power leaves little scope for a reliable security layer. Thus there is a need for a lightweight secure framework that provides security with minimum communication and processing overhead on mobile devices. The security and privacy protection services can be achieved with the help of secure mobile-cloud application services. There are many frameworks and models suggested by different researcher in concern with privacy and security. However, there is still plenty of scope for improvement.

CONCLUSION

Mobile cloud computing is one of mobile technology trends in the future since it combines the advantages of both mobile computing and cloud computing, thereby providing optimal services for mobile users.

This article has provided an overview of mobile cloud computing in which its definitions, architecture, advantages and challenges have been presented. The applications supported by mobile cloud computing including mobile commerce, mobile learning, and mobile healthcare have been discussed which clearly show the applicability of the mobile cloud computing to a wide range of mobile services. Then, the issues and related approaches for mobile cloud computing have been discussed. Finally, the future research directions have been outlined.

REFERENCES

Abdul Nasir Khana, M. L. (2012, August). Towards secure mobile cloud computing: A survey. *Future Generation Computer Systems*.

Al-Ahmad, A. S., & Aljunid, S. A. (2013). Mobile Cloud Computing Testing Review. *IEEE International Conference on Advanced Computer Science Applications and Technologies*.

Buyya, R. (2014). Introduction to the IEEE Transactions on Cloud Computing. *IEEE Transactions on Cloud Computing, 1*(1), 3–9. doi:10.1109/TCC.2013.13

Chow, R., Jakobsson, M., Masuoka, R., Molina, J., Niu, Y., Shi, E., & Song, Z. (2010). Authentication in the clouds: a framework and its application to mobile users. In *Proceeding ACM Cloud Computing Security Workshop, CCSW '10.* doi:10.1145/1866835.1866837

Dev, D., & Baishnab, K. L. (2014). A Review and Research towards Mobile Cloud Computing. *2nd IEEE International Conference on Mobile Cloud Computing, Services, and Engineering.* doi:10.1109/MobileCloud.2014.41

Dinh, H. T., Lee, C., Niyato, D., & Wang, P. (2013). *A survey of mobile cloud computing: Architecture, applications, and approaches.* Wireless Communications and Mobile Computing.

Fernando, Loke, & Rahayu. (2013). Mobile cloud computing: A survey. *Future Generation Computer Systems, 29*(1), 84–106.

Hoang, T. (2011). *A survey of Mobile Cloud Computing: Architecture, Applications, and Approaches.* Wireless Communications and Mobile Computing.

Hsueh, S. C., Lin, & Lin. (2011). Secure cloud storage for conventional data archive of smart phones. In *Proc. 15th IEEE Int. Symposium on Consumer Electronics.*

Hu, H., Wen, Y., Chua, T. S., & Li, X. (2014). Toward Scalable Systems for Big Data Analytics: A Technology Tutorial. *IEEE Access, 2,* 652–687. doi:10.1109/ACCESS.2014.2332453

Huang, X., Zhang, M., Kang, & Luo. (2010). MobiCloud: building secure cloud framework for mobile computing and communication. In *Proceeding 5th IEEE International Symposium on Service Oriented System Engineering, SOSE '10.* doi:10.1109/SOSE.2010.20

Jia, W., Zhu, H., Cao, Z., Wei, L., & Lin, X. (2011). SDSM: a secure data service mechanism in mobile cloud computing. In *Proceeding IEEE Conference on Computer Communications Workshops, INFOCOM WKSHPS.*

Jla, W., Zhu, H., Cao, Z., Wei, L., & Lin, X. (2011). SDSM: A secure data service mechanism in mobile cloud computing. In *Proc. IEEE Conference on Computer Communications Workshops, INFOCOM WKSHPS.*

Khalid, O., Khan, M., Khan, S., & Zomaya, A. (2014). *Omni Suggest: A Ubiquitous Cloud based Context Aware Recommendation System for Mobile Social Networks. IEEE Transactions on Services Computing.*

Khanai, & Kulkarni. (2014). Crypto-Coding as DES-Convolution for Land Mobile Satellite Channel. *International Journal of Computer Applications, 86*(18).

Khanai, R., Kulkarni, G.H., & Torse, D.A. (2014). Neural Crypto-Coding as DES: Turbo over Land Mobile Satellite (LMS) channel. In *Communications and Signal Processing (ICCSP),2014International Conference.*

Kulkarni & Khannai. (n.d.). Addressing Mobile Cloud Computing Security Issues: A Survey. *IEEE ICCSP 2015 Conference.*

Kumar, R., & Rajalakshmi. (2013). Mobile Cloud Computing Standard approach to protecting and securing of mobile cloud ecosystems. *IEEE International Conference on Computer Sciences and Applications.*

Oberheide, J., Veeraraghavan, K., Cooke, E., & Jahanian, F. (2008). Virtualized in-cloud security services for mobile devices. In *Proceedings of the 1st Workshop on Virtualization in Mobile Computing (MobiVirt).* doi:10.1145/1622103.1629656

Portokalidis, G., Homburg, P., Anagnostakis, K., & Bos, H. (2010). Paranoid Android: versatile protection for smartphones. In *Proceedings of the 26th Annual Computer Security Application Conference (ACSAC).*

Qiao Yan, Yu, Gong, & Li. (n.d.). Software-Defined Networking (SDN) and Distributed Denial of Service (DDoS) Attacks in Cloud Computing Environments: A Survey, Some Research Issues, and Challenges. *IEEE Communications Surveys & Tutorials.*

Rassan, & AlShaher. (2014). Securing Mobile Cloud Computing using Biometric Authentication (SMCBA). *IEEE International Conference on Computational Science and Computational Intelligence.*

Sanaei, Z., Abolfazli, S., Gani, A., & Buyya, R. (2014). Heterogeneity in Mobile Cloud Computing: Taxonomy and Open Challenges. *IEEE Communications Surveys and Tutorials, 16*(1), 369–392. doi:10.1109/SURV.2013.050113.00090

Shanna, & Garg. (2014). *An Efficient and Secure Data Storage in Mobile Cloud Computing through RSA and Hash Function.* IEEE.

Suo, H. (2013). *Security and Privacy in Mobile Cloud Computing.* IEEE.

Varadharajan, V. (2014). *Security as a Service Model for Cloud Environment. IEEE Transactions on Network and Service Management, 11(1).*

Wang, H., Wu, S., Chen, M., & Huazhong, W. W. (2014, March). Secunty ProtectIOn between Users and the Mobile Media Cloud. *IEEE Communications Magazine, 52*(3), 73–79. doi:10.1109/MCOM.2014.6766088

Wang, S. & Wang, X. (2010). In-device spatial cloaking for mobile user privacy assisted by the cloud. In *Proceeding 11th International Conference on Mobile Data Management, MDM '10.*

Xiao, S., & Gong, W. (2010). Mobility can help: protect user identity with dynamic credential. In *Proceeding 11th International Conference on Mobile Data Management, MDM '10.* doi:10.1109/MDM.2010.73

Yang, Wang, Wang, Tan & Yu. (2011). Provable data possession of resource constrained mobile devices in cloud computing. *Journal of Networks,* 1033–1040.

Zhang, X., Schiffman, J., Gibbs, S., Kunjithapatham, A., & Jeong, S. (2009). Securing elastic applications on mobile devices for cloud computing. In *Proceeding ACM workshop on Cloud computing security, CCSW '09.* doi:10.1145/1655008.1655026

Zissis, D., & Lekkas, D. (2012, March). Addressing cloud computing security issues. *Future Generation Computer Systems, 28*(3), 583–592. doi:10.1016/j.future.2010.12.006

Zonouz, Houmansadr, Barthier, Borisov, & Sanders. (2013). Secloud: A cloud based comprehensive and lightweight security solution for smartphones. *Science Direct Journal of Computers and Security, 37,* 215-227.

Chapter 7

Security Management in Mobile Cloud Computing:
Security and Privacy Issues and Solutions in Mobile Cloud Computing

Basudeo Singh
R. V. College of Engineering, India

Jasmine K.S.
R. V. College of Engineering, India

ABSTRACT

Mobile cloud computing is a technique or model in which mobile applications are built, powered and hosted using cloud computing technology. In Mobile Cloud computing we can store information regarding sender, data and receiver on cloud through mobile application. As we store more and more information on cloud by client, security issue will arise. This chapter presents a review on the mobile cloud computing concepts as well as security issues and vulnerabilities affecting Cloud Systems and the possible solutions available to such issues within the context of cloud computing. It also describes the pros and cons of the existing security strategy and also introduces the existing issues in cloud computing such as data integrity, data segregation, and security.

DOI: 10.4018/978-1-5225-0602-7.ch007

INTRODUCTION

The mobile cloud computing is a combination of three main parts; they are mobile device, cloud computing and mobile internet. With the help Mobile Cloud Computing, a mobile user gets a rich application delivered over the Internet and powered by cloud-backed infrastructure. The importance of Cloud Computing is increasing and it is receiving a growing attention in the scientific and industrial communities. A study by Gartner as per *Top 10 strategic technologies for 2011* considered Cloud Computing as the first among the top 10 most important technologies and with a better prospect in successive years by companies and organizations. Now a day's the top most popular concern for mobile user or any business is Security and protection. Major Security and protection concern are mainly for mobile computing, social networks and cloud computing. Mobile cloud computing refers to the availability of cloud computing services in a mobile environment. It incorporates the elements of mobile networks and cloud computing, thereby providing optimal services figure for mobile users.

MOBILE CLOUD COMPUTING

Mobile cloud computing at its simplest refers to an infrastructure where both the data storage and the data processing happen outside of the mobile device. Mobile cloud applications move the computing power and data storage away from mobile phones and into the cloud, bringing applications and mobile computing to not just smart-phone users but a much broader range of mobile subscribers.

Another definition given as per *Mobile Cloud Computing Solution Brief, AE-PONA* (2010) "Mobile cloud computing is a model for transparent elastic augmentation of mobile device capabilities via ubiquitous wireless access to cloud storage and computing resources, with context-aware dynamic adjusting of offloading in respect to change in operating conditions, while preserving available sensing and interactivity capabilities of mobile devices." by mobile computing, we mean that a set of users who conduct some joint computational and communication tasks based on their mobile devices.

Mobile cloud computing = mobile computing + cloud computing;

END TO END SECURITY ARCHITECTURE
OF MOBILE CLOUD COMPUTING

Protecting user privacy and data/application secrecy from adversary is a key to establish and maintain consumers' trust in the mobile platform, especially in MCC. A general architecture in a broader sense was as depicted in Figure1.

In the following, the security related issues in MCC are introduced in two categories: the security for mobile users and the security for data.

1. **Security for Mobile Users:** Mobile devices such as cellular phone, PDA, and smartphone are exposed to numerous security threats like malicious codes (e.g., virus, worm, and Trojan horses) and their vulnerability. In addition, with mobile phones integrated global positioning system (GPS) device, they can cause privacy issues for subscribers.

Figure 1. End to end mobile cloud computing security architecture

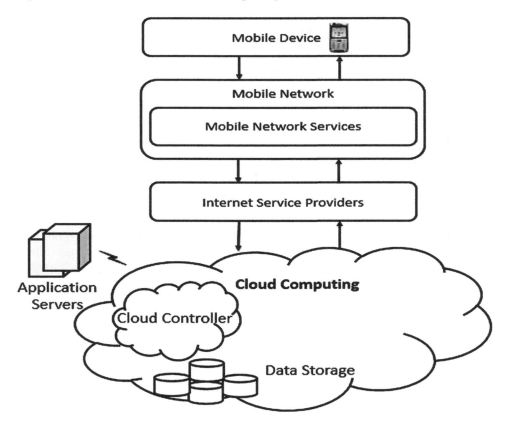

2. **Securing Data on Clouds:** Although both mobile users and application developers benefit from storing a large amount of data/applications on a cloud, they should be careful of dealing with the data/applications in terms of their integrity, authentication, and digital rights.

TYPES OF SECURITY BREACHES AND ISSUES

Data Ownership

Cloud computing provides the facility to store the personal data and purchased digital media such as e-books, video and audio files remotely. For a user, there is a chance of risk to lose the access to the purchased media data. To avoid these types of risks, the user should be aware of the different rights regarding the purchased media. MCC utilizes the context information such as locations and capabilities of devices and user profiles, which can be used by the mobile cloud server to locally optimize the access management.

Privacy

Privacy is one of the biggest challenges in the mobile cloud computing environment. Some applications which hire cloud computing store user's data remotely. Third party companies may sell this important information to some government agencies without the permission of the user. For example: Mobile devices use location based services which help their friends and other persons to get the updates about the location of the user.

Security Issues

Mobile devices are famous for malicious code. There are many chances to lose or steal the data because mobile devices are mostly unprotected. An unauthorized person can easily access the information stored on the mobile devices. The top mobile threats that affects security are:

1. Data loss from lost/ stolen devices.
2. Information stealing by mobile malware.
3. Data leakage through poorly written third party applications.
4. Vulnerabilities within devices, OS, design and third party applications.
5. Insecure network access and unreliable access points.

6.   Insecure or rogue marketplaces.
7.   Insufficient management tools, capabilities and access to APIs.
8.   Near Field Communication (NFC) and proximity based hacking.

Data can be sniffed by the intruders during wireless communications. Data access can be interrupted due to multiple points. This leads to the data locked in particular services. To protect the mobile devices from data loss, thin client like anti-malware, antivirus should be installed to monitor the malicious code. Malicious code includes not only viruses but also phishing from malicious social networks and domains, botnets, spam and identity theft. Wireless protocol encryption provides secured communication where intruders cannot hack the network.

The concept of data breach is that any malicious person or unauthorized person enters into a corporate network and stolen the sensitive or confidential data. Another serious threat is the potential incapacity to prevent data loss because many of the companies treat their data as a valuable asset. In our networked world, most people know that loss of data is unavoidable at one point or another. There is increasing amount of sensitive data which is relayed to cloud computing providers and this data could get lost in any number of ways, including through accidental deletion or corruption of stored data.

As Mobile Cloud Computing is combination of mobile computing and cloud computing, security risk in mobile computing is inherited from cloud computing. Mobile Cloud Computing suffers from following risk.

*   In mobile cloud computing, user does not know where his data is stored, so user has little or no control over the location of data.
*   Because of physical damage of cloud server, loss of encoding key or due to malicious insider, risk of data loss may arise.
*   A customer with ill intent may plant virus of phishing attack in to cloud server which may compromise data of other customers and cloud provider may not be able to track it because of privacy policy of the company.
*   A gap in security of application interface of cloud services can lead to attacks like bypass attack of API attack.
*   When cloud provider services a number of users, flaw in encryption algorithm can lead to unauthorized access to one's data.
*   As per regulatory compliance cloud provider has to maintain required security level
*   In IAAS security risk may arise due to lack of isolation in virtualization when number of virtual machines are hosted on a single server.

- Mobile user stores and transfers critical personal and corporate information while using mobile applications like online payment, social networking etc., that can be an attacker's new target.

MOBILE CLOUD COMPUTING ISSUES CLASSIFICATION AND CHALLENGES

Cloud computing is an emerging technology with shared resources, lower cost and rely on pay per use according to the user demand. The fundamental factor defining the success of any new computing technology is the level of security it provides as per *IEEE Computer Society Washington, common platform enabling security executives to share best security practices and strategic insights, Information Security Journal: A Global Perspective* (Julisch & Hall 2010). Information requiring privacy and the various privacy challenges need the specific steps to be taken in order to ensure privacy in the cloud as discussed in *39th International Conference on Parallel Processing Workshops, IEEE International Enterprise Distributed Object Computing Conference* (Chi-Chun, Huang, & Ku 2010). In case of a public-cloud computing scenario, there are multiple security issues that need to be addressed in comparison to a private cloud computing scenario. A public cloud acts as a host of a number of virtual machines, virtual machine monitors, and supporting middleware as per *IEEE International Conference on Web Services* etc. (Zhang & Zhou 2009). The security of the cloud depends on the behavior of these objects as well as on the interactions between them. Moreover, in a public cloud enabling a shared multi-tenant environment, as the number of users increase, security risks get more intensified and diverse. It is necessary to identify the attack surfaces which are prone to security attacks and mechanisms ensuring successful client-side and server-side protection as per *NIST Guidelines on Security and Privacy in Public Cloud Computing* (Jansen & Grance 2011). Because of the multifarious security issues in a public cloud, adopting a private cloud solution is more secure with an option to move to a public cloud in future, if needed can be used as per *Securing the Cloud: Addressing Cloud Computing Security Concerns with Private Cloud* (Marler 2011).

The Cloud acts as a big black box where nothing inside is visible to the clients. Therefore clients have no idea or control over what happens with their assets. Cloud Computing is about clients transferring the control of their resources (e.g. data, applications) and responsibilities to one or more third parties (cloud services providers). This brings an increased risk to which client assets are greatly exposed. Before Cloud's emergence, generally, the companies where keeping their data inside their perimeter and protecting them from any risks caused by malicious intruders. A malicious intruder was considered to be an outside attacker or a malicious employee. Now, if a company chooses to move its assets into the cloud, it is forced to trust the Cloud provider and the security solutions it offers when provided. However, even if the cloud provider is honest, it can have malicious employees (e.g. system administrators) who can tamper with the virtual machines and violate confidentiality and integrity of client's assets. In Cloud Computing the obligations in terms of security are divided between the cloud provider and the cloud user. In the case of SaaS, this means that the provider must ensure data and application security; so service levels, security, governance, compliance, and liability expectations of the service are contractually stipulated and enforced. In the case of PAAS or IAAS the security responsibility is shared between the consumer and the provider. The responsibility of the consumer's system administrators is to effectively manage the data security. The responsibility of the provider is to secure the underlying platform and infrastructure components and to ensure the basic services of availability and security.

Figure 2 represents the schematic diagram showing the hierarchy of the mobile cloud computing, with security challenges on both Deployment and Service models and also the issues related to Networks. The classification provided above reveals various common challenges under cloud computing. The security challenges with respect to network is also shown as for any internet based service, network is considered as the backbone for cloud computing.

Security Issues of Service Models

Malicious Attacks

The threat of malicious attackers is augmented for customers of cloud services by the use of various IT services which lacks the lucidity between the procedure and process relating to service providers. Malicious users may gain access to certain confidential data and thus leading to data breaches. Farzad Sabahi (2011)*Cloud Computing Security Threats and Responses* has shown malicious attacks by the unauthorized users on the victim's IP address and physical server. An access control mechanism tool can be thought of to control unauthorized user in accessing secured data. Peter Mell (2012)*what's Special about Cloud Security*, has suggested Infrastructure as a Service as one of the models that exposes challenges with using virtualization as a frontier security protection to defend against malicious cloud users.

Isolation Failure

One of the major benefits of Virtualization is Isolation as per *Virtualization security for Cloud computing service*. This benefit, if not deployed properly will generate a

Figure 2. Classification of mobile cloud issues

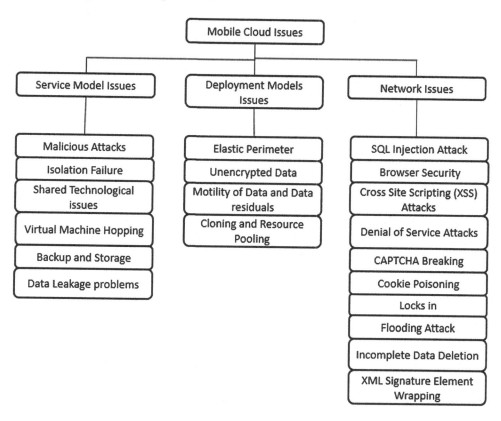

threat to the environment as per *A Survey on Concepts, Taxonomy and Associated Security Issues", IEEE* (Perez, van Doorn, & Sailer 2008). Poor isolation or inappropriate access control policy which will cause the inter-attack between two VMs or between VMs and its associated VMM. For instance, VM Escape is one of the worst cases happening if the Isolation between the host and the VMs is compromised. In case of VM Escape, the program running in a VM is able to bypass the VMM layer and get access to the host machine. Since the host machine is the root of security of a virtual system, the program which gains access to the host machine can also gains the root privilege

Shared Technological Issues

IAAS vendors transport their services in a scalable way by contributing infrastructure. But this structure does not offer strong isolation properties for a multi-tenant architecture. Hence in order to address this gap, a virtualization hypervisor intercede the access between guest operating systems and the physical compute resources. As discussed by Perez, van Doorn, and Sailer (2008)*IEEE Security and Privacy*, in spite of several advantages, these hypervisors have exhibited flaws that have permitted guest operating systems to expand inappropriate levels of control or authority on the underlying platform. This certainly led to security issues on the cloud. Lori M. Kaufman and Bruce Potter (2011)*Monitoring Cloud Computing by Layer, Part 1* has shown the implementation of IAAS by the customer to facilitate the infrastructure or hardware usage.

Virtual Machine Hopping

In VM hopping, an attacker on one VM gains rights to use another victim VM. The attacker can check the victim VM's resource procedure, change its configurations and can also delete stored data, thus, putting it in danger the VM's confidentiality, integrity, and availability. A requirement for this attack is that the two VMs must be operating on the same host, and the attacker must recognize the victim VM's IP address.

Backup and Storage

The cloud vendor must ensure that regular backup of data is implemented that even ensure security with all measures. But this backup data is generally found in unencrypted form leading to misuse of the data by unauthorized parties. Thus data backups lead to various security threats. As per the study carried by Intel IT center as per *Preparing your Virtualized Data Center for the Cloud* (Intel, n.d.), more the server virtualization increases, a very difficult problem with backup and storage is created. Data de-duplication is listed as one of the solution to reduce backup and offline storage volumes. But discussing about de-duplication, Danny Harnik, Benny Pinkas, and Alexandra Shulman-Peleg (2010)*Side Channels in Cloud Services*, have shown that de-duplication in cloud storage is carried out with the misuse of data backup.

Data Leakage Problems

Data deletion or alteration without backup leads to certain drastic data related problems like security, integrity, locality, segregation and breaches. This would lead to sensitive data being accessed by the unauthorized users. As its measure provided by Rafael Moreno et al. (2013)*Key Challenges in Cloud Computing to Enable the Future Internet of Services*, cloud platforms should provide new services in order to collect context information and to perform analysis and manage data privacy so as to support applications requesting the information. One solution to this data leakage problem, as provided by Danny Harnik et al. (2010)*Side Channels in Cloud Services:* Deduplication in Cloud Storage, is deduplication with allowing a limitation on number of user uploads per time window. The term deduplication means storing only a single copy of redundant data and providing just a link to this copy rather than storing actual copies of this data.

Security Issues of Deployment Models

Elastic Perimeter

A cloud infrastructure, particularly comprising of private cloud, creates an elastic perimeter. Various departments and users throughout the organization allow sharing of different resources to increase facility of access but unfortunately lead to data breach problem. In private clouds, according to Krishna Subramanian *Private, Public and Hybrid Clouds", whitepaper* (2011), the resources are centralized and distributed as per demand. The resource treatment transfers resources based on the requirements of the users thus leading to problems of data loss, where any user may try to access secure data with ease. Moreover, Marios D. Dikaiakos et al. (n.d.) *Cloud Computing – Distributed Internet Computing for IT and Scientific Research* states that elasticity of various cloud based resources would lead to store replicated data on untrusted hosts and this would then lead to enormous risks to data privacy.

Unencrypted Data

Data encryption is a process that helps to address various external and malicious threats. Unencrypted data is vulnerable for susceptible data, as it does not provide any security mechanism. These unencrypted data can easily be accessed by unauthorized users. According to Cong Wang et al. *IEEE (2011)transactions on parallel and distributed systems*, unencrypted data risks the user data leading cloud server to escape various data information to unauthorized users. For example, the famous file sharing service Dropbox was accused for using a single encryption key for all user data the company stored. These unencrypted, insecure data, as per Marjory S. Blumenthal (2011)*Hide and Seek in the Cloud", IEEE*, incite the malicious users to misuse the data one or the other way

Motility of Data and Data Residuals

For the best use of resources, data often is moved to cloud infrastructure. As a result the enterprise would be devoid of the location where data is put on the cloud. This is true with public cloud. With this data movement, the residuals of data is left behind which may be accessed by unauthorized users. According to Rohit Bhadauria et al. (2012)*A Survey on Security Issues in Cloud Computing and Associated Mitigation*, data-remnant causes very less security threats in private cloud but severe security issues may evolve in public cloud donations. This again may lead to data security threats like data leakage, data remnants and inconsistent data, as stated by Hassan Takabi et al. (2010)", *IEEE security and privacy*. The authors have also mentioned that in order to solve the problems with data storage the optimal solution of cryptography can be thought of effectively.

Cloning and Resource Pooling

Cloning deals with replicating or duplicating the data. According to Bernd Grobauer et al. (2011)*Understanding Cloud Computing Vulnerabilities", IEEE*, cloning leads to data leakage problems revealing the machine's authenticity. While Wayne A. Pauley (2010)*An empirical evaluation", the IEEE computer and reliability societies, IEEE* describes resource pooling as a service provided to the users by the provider to use various resources and share the same according to their application demand. Resource Pooling relates to the unauthorized access due to sharing through the same network. While the study on Virtual and Cloud Computing by various researches states that a Virtual Machine can easily be provisioned, they can also be inversed to previous cases, paused, easily restarted, readily cloned and migrated between two physical servers, leading to non-auditable security threats.

Security Issues of Mobile Cloud Network

- **SQL Injection Attacks:** In this type of attack a malicious code is inserted into a standard SQL code. Thus the attackers get unauthorized access to a database and are able to access sensitive data.
- **Browser Security:** Every client uses browser to send the information on network. The browser uses SSL technology to encrypt user's identity and credentials. But hackers from the intermediary host may acquire these credentials by the use of sniffing packages installed on the intermediary host. Steve Kirsch (2012)*the Future of Authentication* states that in order to overcome this, one should have a single identity but this.
- **Cross Site Scripting (XSS):** Hackers attack while injecting malicious scripts into Web. There are two methods for injecting the malevolent code into the web-page that is displayed to the user. Stored XSS and Reflected XSS. In case of Stored XSS, the malicious code is permanently stored into a resource managed by the web application *Proceedings of the Network and Distributed*

System (Vogt et al., n.d.). However in case of a Reflected XSS, the attack script is not permanently stored; in fact it is immediately reflected back to the user as per (Vogt et al, n.d.).

- **Denial of Service Attacks:** This attack prevents the consumer from receiving the service from the cloud.
- **CAPTCHA Breaking:** Recently, it has been found that the spammers are able to break the CAPTCHA as per *Spammers break Hotmail's CAPTCHA yet again* (Dunn 2009), provided by the Hotmail and Gmail service providers. They use audio system to read the CAPTCHA characters for the visually impaired users. Various methods such as: variable fonts of the letters used to design a CAPTCHA, implementing letter overlap, increasing the string length and using a perturbative background can be used to avoid CAPTCHA breaking as per *A Study of CAPTCHA and its Application to User Authentication* (Jeng, et al 2010). Single frame zero knowledge CAPTCHA design principles have been proposed, which will be able to oppose any attack method of static optical character recognition (OCR).
- **Cookie Poisoning:** Cookie poisoning involves changing or alerting the contents of cookie to have an illegal access to a webpage or an application. Basically cookies contain the user's identity related credentials and once these cookies are accessible, the content of these cookies can be copied to masquerade as an authorized user.
- **Locks In:** Locks in is a small tender in the manner of tools, standard data format or procedures, services edge that could embark on data, application and service portability, not leading to facilitate the customer in transferring from one cloud provider to another or transferring the services back to home IT location.
- **Flooding Attacks:** In this attack the invader sends the request for resources on the cloud rapidly so that the cloud gets flooded with the ample requests. As per the study carried out by IBM as per *IBM Research*, cloud has a property to expand on the basis of large amount of request. It will expand in order to fulfil the requests of invader making the resources inaccessible for the normal users.
- **Incomplete Data Deletion:** Incomplete data deletion is treated as hazardous one in cloud computing. According to Sara Qaisar et al. (2012)*Cloud Computing: Network/Security Threats and counter measures*, when data is deleted, it does not remove the replicated data placed on a dedicated backup server. The operating system of that server will not delete data unless it is specifically commanded by network service provider. Precise data deletion is majorly impossible because copies of data are saved in replica but are not available for usage

- **XML Signature Element Wrapping:** As clients are typically able to connect to cloud computing via a web browser or web service, the web service attacks also affect cloud computing. XML signature element wrapping is the eminent attack for web service. Although Cloud security uses XML signature in order to protect an element's name, attributes and value from unauthorized parties, it is unable to protect the particulars in the document. An attacker is able to manipulate a SOAP message by copying the target element and inserting whatever value the attacker would like and moving the original element to somewhere else on the SOAP message. This method can trick the web service to process the malicious message created by the attack.

SECURING INFORMATION ON THE MOBILE CLOUD COMPUTING

In the last few years Mobile Cloud Computing has been an active research field, as mobile cloud computing is in initial stage, limited surveys are available in various domain of MCC. In this paper our main focus is on securing information on mobile cloud computing. Table 1 illustrates the Comparisons between Researches in Privacy and Security Issues in Mobile Cloud Computing.

Jia et al. (2011)*IEEE Conference on Computer Communications Workshops* provide a secure data service mechanism through Identity based proxy re-encryption. This mechanism provides confidentiality and fine grained access control for data stored in cloud by outsourcing data security management to mobile cloud in trusted way. The goal of this protocol is that only authorized persons/sharer can access the data while unauthorized sharer will learn nothing. Identity based encryption is that user encrypt the data through his identity (Id). This encryption scheme is based on bilinear pairing.

A bilinear map is e: G1 ×G2 →Where G1 and GT be cyclic multiplicative group with prime order q and g be generator of G1, having the properties of linearity, non-degeneracy and computability. Proxy based re-encryption is used by mobile user to provide access control capability to cloud, which could grant access to an authorized users by transferring cipher text encrypted by data owner's identity to one with sharer's identity. In this mechanism 3 entities are involved: Data owner (DO), Data Sharer (DS) and Cloud Servers (CSs). Both DO and DS utilize data storage service to store and retrieve file. CSs provide services to mobile clients.

This protocol has following phases:

1. **Setup Phase:** Here system master key (SEK) and system parameters are generated, where SEK is private to data owner.

Table 1. Comparisons between researches in privacy and security issues in mobile cloud computing

Researchers	Year	Approach /Cloud Trust Level	Security Attribute Provided	Trusted Third Party	Advantages	Disadvantages
J. Oberheide et al. *Virtualized in-cloud security services for mobile devices*	2008	Cloud AV/ Fully trusted	Antivirus, Security as a Service	No	Reduced On Device software complexity and power consumption	Disconnected operation and privacy loss
Zhang et al. *ACM workshop on Cloud computing security*	2009	Cloudlet/ Semi-trusted	Task partitioning	No	Good tradeoffs between processing overhead and communication cost	Security of Web-let can be improved with other techniques.
Xiao and Gong *International Conference on Mobile Data Management*	2010	Lightweight algorithm/ Semi trusted	Authorization of user's data in cloud	No	Automatic Dynamic updating of credential information	More processing and energy burden on mobile device
Wang and Wang *11th International Conference on Mobile Data Management, MDM*	2010	Top down spatial cloaking/ Distrusted	Privacy preserving framework in location based Scheme	No	Reduced communication cost by doing spatial cloaking based on the historical data in cloud.	More energy consumption and processing burden on mobile device
Huang et al. *MobiCloud: building secure cloud framework for mobile computing and communication*	2010	MobiCloud/ distrusted	Security in Storage as a Service in MANET	Yes	Secured data while using Public Cloud	Increased cost due to two cloud providers
G. Portokalidis et al. *Annual Computer Security Application Conference (ACSAC)*	2010	Threat detection in Smartphone based on CloudAV/ Fully trusted	Security as a Service	No	Reduced transmission overhead and energy consumption	More Cloud usage cost.
R.Chow et al. *ACM Cloud Computing Security Workshop*	2010	Policy based cloud authentication n platform/ Fully trusted	Authentication of user.	No	Authentication based on behavioral data of user	Privacy threat
Jia et al. *IEEE Conference on Computer Communications Workshops, INFOCOM WKSHPS*	2011	Proxy re encryption (PRE) scheme and Identity based encryption (IDE) scheme/ Semi trusted	Secure data Service	No	Reduced cost of updating of access policy and communication cost	More processing and energy burden on mobile device for encrypting the secret information
Yang et al. *Provable data possession of resource constrained mobile devices in cloud computing*	2011	extended the public provable data possession scheme/ Distrusted	ensures privacy, confidentiality and integrity of user data stored on cloud	Yes	Reduced energy and processing requirement on mobile device	Degradation of performance with the increase in no. of users in Trusted Party Agent (TPA). Cost also increases due to two cloud service providers.
Saman Zonouz et al. *Science Direct journal of Computers and security*	2013	cloud for smartphones/ Trusted	cloud based comprehensive and lightweight security for smart phones	No	Reduced energy and processing requirement on mobile device for providing security in mobile device	Cloud assumes to be fully trusted which needs to be reconsidered .The personal data of users accessed to the cloud can affect the privacy issues

2. **Key Generation Phase:** In this phase decryption key corresponding to user's identity (dkid) is generated by following equation:

dkid=H1 (Id) s

where, Id∈ {0, 1}*, H1: {0,1}*→G1 and s∈Zq is randomly selected.

3. **Encryption Phase:** Here file F is divided into k blocks such that F= (n1,n2........ nk), for each block ni data owner performs encryption by:

$$Ni=(gr,n,e(gs,H1(ID)r)) \tag{2}$$

where, r∈Zp is randomly selected.

After implementing encryption of F, mobile user uploads encrypted file (EF)=(N1,N2............Nk) to cloud.

4. **Re-Encryption Key Generation:** On basis of SEKid generated in second phase and identity of Sharer (IDB), re-encryption key of sharer (REK) is generated.

$$REK=(H1(IDA)-s,IBEIDB(X)). \tag{3}$$

where, X is randomly selected from GT and IBE is Identity based encryption.

5. **Re-Encryption Phase:** Re-encryption key is send to cloud for re-encryption phase. Here re-encryption cipher textC=(C1,C2,C3)=(gr,m.e(gr,H2(X)),IBE IDB(X))

6. **De-Encryption Phase:** Sharer request cloud server for re-encrypted file, cloud checks the re-encrypted key to sharer.

If key existed, cloud server sends corresponding file to sharer. Now, sharer can decrypt the file without involvement of data owner. Where ni=)) By doing so sharer gets the entire file F= (n1,n2........nk).

7. **Policy Updating:** Mobile user may want to update the list of sharers, so he can update the list without retrieving and decrypting cipher text from cloud.

Yang et al. (2011)*Provable data possession of resource constrained mobile devices in cloud computing* provides provable data possession scheme of resource constrained mobile devices by using Diffie-Hellman key exchange, Bilinear mapping and Merkle Hash Tree (MHT). Provable Data Possession (PDP) scheme ensures confidentiality, privacy and integrity of mobile user's data stored on cloud. Diffie-Hellman key exchange is used to securely distribute symmetric key. A bilinear map is e: $G1 \times G2 \rightarrow GT$ where G1 and GT be cyclic multiplicative group with prime order q and g be generator of G1.MerkleHash Tree (MHT) is constructed as binary tree where leaves in MHT are the hash value of authentic data. Verifier only needs to verify the root of the tree. There are 3 participants involved in this scheme:

Mobile end user/client: Mobile user has Trusted Platform Model (TPM) chip in mobile device to produce and store secret key. Mobile end user uses the services provided by cloud. Trusted Party Auditor (TPA): TPA performs all encryption/decryption on behalf of mobile user. Cloud Storage Service Provider (CSP): CSP provides storage services to client and also provide proof of data possession by any number of times whenever needed. PDP schemes includes following phases:

1. **Set-Up Phase:** It is assumed in this scheme that end user has already completed remote identification with TPA. In this phase firstly Diffie-Hellman scheme is used to exchange key between client and TPA.

Client to TPA: g, $g\alpha$. TPA to Client: $g\beta$.

Now client and TPA shares a symmetric key $g\alpha\beta$. Client encrypt the file with this key and sends it to TPA. TPA generates a combination of symmetric key (ek, dk) for encryption and decryption respectively. Now TPA encrypt file F under ek and calculate the hash value of root of MHT (H(R)). TPA sends H(R) and dkto client encrypted with shared key $g\alpha\beta$. Client signs H(R) with private key (SK) to get Sigsk (H(R))=(H(R))$\alpha$and sends it to TPA. TPA sends { Sigsk(H(R)), F,φ} to CSP. Here, F={mi}, φ={σi}={H(mi) umiβ where $1 \leq i \leq N$, u is randomly chosen from G1and mi is ith chunk of file.

2. **Integrity Verification:** A client or TPA may send a challenge to CSP for integrity verification. According to challenge (chal) CSP performs verification and sends it back to TPA, TPA after verifying proof sends result to client. In this phase TPA sends server a challenge chal={i,vi}, where $1 \leq i \leq c$, c is random number in the set {1,N} to constitute sequence subset I for each i$\in$I, vi$\in$Zp is randomly selected. After receiving chal CSP perform verification by generating proof={μ, ω,[H(mi), Ωi],Sigsk(H(R))}, where Ωi is additional information used for rebuilding the root H(R) of MHT.

$\mu=\Sigma v$ i mi$\in$Zp and $\omega=\Pi\sigma$ ivi$\in$Giare computed by CSP as part of proof.

After receiving proof TPA performs verification by testing these two equations:

$$E(Sigsk(H(R)),g)?=e(H(R),g\alpha) \text{ and} \qquad (4)$$

$$e(\omega, g\alpha)?= e(\Pi(H(mi)vi) u\mu, g\alpha\beta) \qquad (5)$$

If these two equations are equal then it will return true; otherwise false and result is sends back to client.

3. **File Retrieval:** For retrieving a file client and TPA needs to negotiate a symmetric session key ks through Diffie-Hellman. Client sends request for file F to TPA along with decryption key dk encrypted by ks. Now TPA request for file FtoCSP; CSP send the file to TPA. Then TPA decrypt the encrypted file Funder decryption key dk and sends the file F to end user through secure communication channel.

CONCLUSION AND LIMITATIONS

Today, cloud computing is being defined and talked about across the ICT industry under different contexts and with different definitions attached to it. The core point is that cloud computing means having a server firm that can host the services for users connected to it by the network. Technology has moved in this direction because of the advancement in computing, communication and networking technologies. Fast and reliable connectivity is a must for the existence of cloud computing. Cloud computing is clearly one of the most enticing technology areas of the current times due, at least in part to its cost-efficiency and flexibility. However, despite the surge in activity and interest, there are Significant, persistent concerns about cloud computing that are impeding the momentum and will eventually compromise the vision of cloud computing as a new IT procurement model. Despite the trumpeted business and technical advantages of cloud computing, many potential cloud users have yet to join the cloud, and those major corporations that are cloud users are for the most part putting only their less sensitive data in the cloud. Lack of control is transparency in the cloud implementation – somewhat contrary to the original promise of cloud computing in which cloud implementation is not relevant. Transparency is needed for regulatory reasons and to ease concern over the potential for data breaches. Because of today's perceived lack of control, larger companies are testing the waters with smaller projects and less sensitive data. In short, the potential of the cloud is not yet being realized. When thinking about solutions to cloud computing's adoption problem, it is important to realize that many of the issues are essentially old problems in a new setting, although they may be more acute. For example, corporate partnerships and offshore outsourcing involve similar trust and regulatory issues. Similarly, open source software enables IT department to quickly build and deploy applications, but at the cost of control and governance. Similarly, virtual machine attacks and web service vulnerabilities existed long before cloud computing became fashionable. Indeed, this very overlap is reason for optimism; many of these cloud computing roadblocks have long been studied and the foundations for solutions exist. For the enhancement of technology, and hence healthy growth of global economy, it is extremely important to iron out any issues that can cause road-blocks in this new paradigm of computing. Former studies, however, lack the higher level perspective of the security factors that affect cloud environments because they were also more focused. The taxonomy proposed in this article revolves around eight main categories: software, storage and computing, virtualization, Internet and services, network, access, trust, and compliance and legality.

REFERENCES

Bhadauria, R., Chaki, R., Chaki, N., & Sanyal, S. (2012). A Survey on Security Issues in Cloud Computing and Associated Mitigation. *International Journal of Computers and Applications*, *47*(June), 47–66. doi:10.5120/7292-0578

Blumenthal. (2010). *Hide and Seek in the Cloud*. IEEE.

Chow, R., Jakobsson, M., Masuoka, R., Molina, J., Niu, Y., Shi, E., & Song, Z. (2010). Authentication in the clouds: a framework and its application to mobile users. In *ProceedingACM Cloud Computing Security Workshop*. doi:10.1145/1866835.1866837

Dikaiakos, Pallis, Katsaros, Mehra, & Vakali. (2009). Cloud Computing – Distributed Internet Computing for IT and Scientific Research. *IEEE Internet Computing*, 10–13.

Dunn. (2009, February 16). Spammers break Hotmail's CAPTCHA yet again. *Tech-world*.

Gartner Inc. (2011). *Gartner identifies the Top 10 strategic technologies for2011*. Author.

Grobauer, Walloschek, & Stöcker. (2011). *Understanding Cloud Computing Vulnerabilities*. IEEE.

Harnik, D. (2010). *Side Channels in Cloud Services: Deduplication in Cloud Storage*. IEEE.

Hoang, T. (2011). *A survey of Mobile Cloud Computing: Architecture, Applications, and Approaches.* Wireless Communications and Mobile Computing.

Huang, D., Zhang, X., Kang, M., & Luo, J. (2010). MobiCloud: building secure cloud framework for mobile computing and communication. In *Proceeding 5th IEEE International Symposium on Service Oriented System Engineering, SOSE '10.* doi:10.1109/SOSE.2010.20

Hulme. (2011). *NIST formalizes cloud computing definition, issues security and privacy guidance.* Retrieved from http://www.csoonline.com/article/661620/nistformalizes-cloud-computing-definition-issuessecurity-and-privacy-guidance

Intel IT Center. (n.d.). *Preparing your Virtualized Data Center for the Cloud.* Intel.

Jansen, W., & Grance, T. (2011). *NIST Guidelines on Security and Privacy in Public Cloud Computing.* Retrieved from http://csrc.nist.gov/publications/drafts/800-144/DraftSP-800-144_cloud-computing.pdf

Jeng, Tseng, Tseng, & Wang. (2010). A Study of CAPTCHA and its Application to User Authentication. *In Proc. of 2nd Intl. Conference on Computational Collective Intelligence: Technologies and Applications.*

Jia, W., Zhu, H., Cao, Z., Wei, L., & Lin, X. (2011). SDSM: a secure data service mechanism in mobile cloud computing. In *ProceedingIEEE Conference on Computer Communications Workshops, INFOCOM WKSHPS.* doi:10.1109/INFCOMW.2011.5928784

Julisch, K., & Hall, M. (2010). Security and control in the cloud. Information Security Journal: A Global Perspective, 19(6), 299-309.

Kaufman, & Potter. (n.d.). *Monitoring Cloud Computing by Layer, Part 1.* IEEE.

Kirsch. (2012). *The Future of Authentication.* IEEE.

Lo, Huang, & Ku. (2010). A Cooperative Intrusion Detection System Framework for Cloud Computing Networks. *ICPPW '10 Proceedings of the 201039th International Conference on Parallel Processing Workshops.* IEEE Computer Society.

Luo, S. (2011). *Virtualization security for Cloud computing service.* IEEE.

Marler, J. (2011). *Securing the Cloud: Addressing Cloud Computing Security Concerns with Private Cloud.* Rackspace Knowledge Centre. Retrieved from http://www.rackspace.com/knowledge_center/privatecloud/securing-the-cloud-addressing-cloud-computingsecurity-concerns-with-private-cloud

Mell. (2012). What's Special about Cloud Security?. *IEEE, IT Pro*, 6 – 8.

Moreno-Vozmediano, Montero, & Llorente. (n.d.). *Key Challenges in Cloud Computing to Enable the Future Internet of Services.* IEEE. .10.1109/MIC.2012.69

Motahari-Nezhad, Bartolini, Graupner, Singhal, & Spence. (2010). IT Support Conversation Manager: A Conversation-Centered Approach and Tool for Managing Best Practice IT Processes. *Proceedings of the 2010 14thIEEE International Enterprise Distributed Object Computing Conference.*

Oberheide, J., Veeraraghavan, K., Cooke, E., & Jahanian, F. (2008). Virtualized in-cloud security services for mobile devices. In *Proceedings of the 1st Workshop on Virtualization in Mobile Computing (MobiVirt).* doi:10.1145/1622103.1629656

Paper, W. (2010). *Mobile Cloud Computing Solution Brief.* AEPONA.

Pauley. (2010). Cloud Provider Transparency – An empirical evaluation. *IEEE Computer and Reliability Societies.*

Pearson, S. (2009). Taking account of privacy when designing cloud computing services. *CLOUD '09 Proc. of ICSE Workshop on Software Engineering Challenges of Cloud Computing*, (pp. 44-52). IEEE. doi:10.1109/CLOUD.2009.5071532

Perez, R., van Doorn, L., & Sailer, R. (2008). Virtualization and hardware-based security. *IEEE Security and Privacy*, 6(5), 24–31. doi:10.1109/MSP.2008.135

Portokalidis, G., Homburg, P., Anagnostakis, K., & Bos, H. (2010). Paranoid Android: versatile protection for smartphones. In *Proceedings of the 26thAnnual Computer Security Application Conference (ACSAC).*

Qaisar, S., & Khawaja, K. F. (2012). Cloud Computing: Network/Security Threats and counter measures. *Interdisciplinary Journal of Contemporary Research in Business, 3*(9), 1323 – 1329.

Sabahi, F. (2011). *Cloud Computing Security Threats and Responses.* IEEE.

Sahoo, J. (2010). *Virtualization: A Survey on Concepts, Taxonomy and Associated Security Issues.* IEEE.

Subramanian, K. (2011). *Private, Public and Hybrid Clouds. Whitepaper.* Trend Micro.

Takabi, H., Joshi, J. B. D., & Ahn, G.-J. (2010). University of Pittsburgh, Gail – Joon and Ahn Arizona State University, "Security and Privacy Challenges in Cloud Computing Environments. *IEEE Security and Privacy*, 8(6), 24–31. doi:10.1109/ MSP.2010.186

Vogt, P., Nentwich, F., Jovanovic, N., Kirda, E., Kruegel, C., & Vigna, G. (n.d.). Cross-Site Scripting Prevention with Dynamic Data Tainting and Static Analysis. *Proceedings of the Network and Distributed System.*

Wang, Cao, Ren, & Lou. (2011). Enabling Secure and Efficient Ranked Keyword Search over Outsourced Cloud Data. *IEEE Transactions on Parallel and Distributed Systems.*10.1109/TPDS.2011.282

Wang, S., & Wang, X. (2010). In-device spatial cloaking for mobile user privacy assisted by the cloud. In *Proceeding11th Interantional Conference on Mobile Data Management.*

Xiao, S., & Gong, W. (2010). Mobility can help: protect user identity with dynamic credential. In *Proceeding 11thInternational Conference on Mobile Data Management.* doi:10.1109/MDM.2010.73

Yang, Wang, Wang, Tan, & Yu. (2011). Provable data possession of resource constrained mobile devices in cloud computing. *Journal of Networks*, 1033–1040.

Zhang, L. J., & Zhou. (2009). CCOA: Cloud Computing Open Architecture. *IEEE International Conference on Web Services.* DOI: doi:10.1109/ICWS.2009.144

Zhang, X., Schiffman, J., Gibbs, S., Kunjithapatham, A., & Jeong, S. (2009). Securing elastic applications on mobile devices for cloud computing. In Proceeding ACM workshop on Cloud computing security. doi:10.1145/1655008.1655026

Zonouz, Houmansadr, Barthier, Borisov, & Sanders. (2013). Secloud: A cloud based comprehensive and lightweight security solution for smartphones. *Science Direct journal of Computers and Security*, *37*, 215-227.

Chapter 8
Security Model for Mobile Cloud Database as a Service (DBaaS)

Kashif Munir
University of Hafr Al-Batin, Saudi Arabia

ABSTRACT

There's a big change happening in the world of databases. The industry is buzzing about Database-as-a-Service (DBaaS), a cloud offering that allows companies to rent access to these managed digital data warehouses. Database-as-a-service (DBaaS) is a cloud computing service model that provides users with some form of access to a database without the need for setting up physical hardware, installing software or configuring for performance. Since consumers host data on the Mobile Cloud, DBaaS providers should be able to guarantee data owners that their data would be protected from all potential security threats. Protecting application data for large-scale web and mobile apps can be complex; especially with distributed and NoSQL databases. Data centers are no longer confined to the enterprise perimeter. More and more enterprises take their data to the Mobile Cloud, but forget to adjust their security management practices when doing so. Unauthorized access to data resources, misuse of data stored on third party platform, data confidentiality, integrity and availability are some of the major security challenges that ail this nascent Cloud service model, which hinders the wide-scale adoption of DBaaS. In this chapter, I propose a security model for Mobile Cloud Database as a Service (DBaaS). A user can change his/her password, whenever demanded. Furthermore, security analysis realizes the feasibility of the proposed model for DBaaS and achieves efficiency. This will help Cloud community to get an insight into state-of-the-art progress in terms of secure strategies, their deficiencies and possible future directions.

DOI: 10.4018/978-1-5225-0602-7.ch008

INTRODUCTION

DBaaS provides professional databases that can get running and ready in a matter of minutes without a lot of training or personnel. A service provider chooses most of the options, offering the "best" configuration for most needs.

While individual systems can become unique "snowflake" servers, DBaaS tends to avoid that by simplifying and normalizing the customization, management, and upkeep for administrators. Overall, the service makes it easier to solve problems, correct mistakes, and transfer data from one system to the next. They can scale as large as necessary, fit the needs of the customers, and offer better availability and security than most in-house operations.

DBaaS is also accessible to a larger audience because, like other "as a service" cloud innovations, it is largely defined, configured, and driven by code—not commands typed into a terminal. So, instead of requiring database specialists, developers themselves can easily create and manage database-backed apps on cloud-based development platforms.

DBaaS is already responsible for much of the growth in some key technologies, particularly open-source databases like MySQL. In other words, traditional database deployment is somewhat stagnant, and most new deployments are DBaaS. The demand is so high that some tech giants started offering a managed "as a service" version of their own (Baron S, 2015).

DBaaS provides automated services where consumers can request database-oriented functionalities from a dedicated service hosted on Cloud. The model is end user driven and provides self-service provisioning. It is based on architectural and operational approach (Oracle, 2011), which provides new and distinctive ways of using and managing database services. There are many other database services which are available today but DBaaS differs from those traditional databases because its architecture has two major attributes (Oracle, 2011), Service-orientated as database facilities are available in the form of service. Customer self-service interaction model as organizations are allowed to use, configure and deploy the Cloud database services themselves without any IT support and without purchasing any hardware for specified purpose. These are the three main phases in the overall DBaaS architecture as depicted in Figure 1.

Figure 1. Cloud DBaaS (Krishna & Roger, 2012)

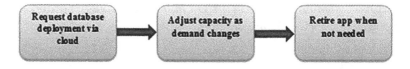

1. Consumers request the database deployment via Cloud.
2. Consumers adjust the capacity as demand changes.
3. Consumers can retire from the app when not needed.

Luca et al. (2012) advised against using any intermediary component for accessing the database on behalf of the clients, since it becomes a single point of failure. Security and availability of DBaaS services are bounded by this trusted intermediary proxy server.

Cong et al. (2013) proposed a similar approach which puts forth an idea of using third party auditors. This approach is suitable for preserving data integrity when data is outsourced to the DBaaS providers and users get access on-demand high quality services without facing maintenance burden of local data storage.

Nithiavathy (2013) proposed integrity auditing mechanism that utilizes distributed erasure-coded data for employing redundancy and homomorphic token. This techinque allows third party auditors and users to audit their logs and events at Cloud storage using light weight communication protocol at less computation cost.

Qingji et al. (2012) investigated the issues of query integrity and a solution was proposed. The solution allows users to verify executed queries in Cloud database server along with the additional support of flexible join and aggregate queries. Similarly, the solution proposed by Maciej et al. (2013) covers data key management, data encryption and data integrity which ensure high data security and access efficiency.

Cryptonite is a secure data repository solution proposed by Alok et al. (2012) which addresses availability requirements as well. It runs within Microsoft Azure and provides service APIs compatible with existing Cloud storage services.

DATABASE-AS-A-SERVICE(DBAAS) IN MOBILE CLOUD

Database-as-a-Service (DBaaS) is a service that is managed by a cloud operator (public or private) that supports applications, without the application team assuming responsibility for traditional database administration functions. With a DBaaS, the application developers should not need to be database experts, nor should they have to hire a database administrator (DBA) to maintain the database (Qingji et al., 2012). True DBaaS will be achieved when application developers can simply call a database service and it works without even having to consider the database. This would mean that the database would seamlessly scale and it would be maintained, upgraded, backed-up and handle server failure, all without impacting the developer. Database as a service (DBaaS) is a prime example of a service that's both exciting and full of difficult security issues.

Cloud providers want to offer the DBaaS service described above. In order to provide a complete DBaaS solution across large numbers of customers, the cloud providers need a high-degree of automation. Unction's that have a regular time-based interval, like backups, can be scheduled and batched. Many other functions, such as elastic scale-out can be automated based on certain business rules. For example, providing a certain quality of service (QoS) according to the service level agreement (SLA) might require limiting databases to a certain number of connections or a peak level of CPU utilization, or some other criteria. When this criterion is exceeded, the DBaaS might automatically add a new database instance to share the load. The cloud provider also needs the ability to automate the creation and configuration of database instances (Maciej et al., 2013). Much of the database administration process can be automated in this fashion, but in order to achieve this level of automation, the database management system underlying the DBaaS must expose these functions via an application programming interface.

Cloud operators must have to work on hundreds, thousands or even tens of thousands of databases at the same time. This requires automation. In order to automate these functions in a flexible manner, the DBaaS solution must provide an API to the cloud operator (Hacigumus et al., 2012) The ultimate goal of a DBaaS is that the customer doesn't have to think about the database. Today, cloud users don't have to think about server instances, storage and networking, they just work. Virtualization enables clouds to provide these services to customers while automating much of the traditional pain of buying, installing, configuring and managing these capabilities. Now database virtualization is doing the same thing for the cloud database and it is being provided as Database as a Service (DBaaS). The DBaaS can substantially reduce operational costs and perform well. It's important as well as simple thing that the goal of DBaaS is to make things easier. Cloud Control Database as a Service (DBaaS) provides:

- A shared, consolidated platform on which to provision database services.
- A self-service model for provisioning those resources.
- Elasticity to scale out and scale back database resources.
- Chargeback based on database usage.

The aggressive consolidation of information technology (IT) infrastructure and deployment of Database as a Service (DBaaS) on public or private clouds is a strategy that many enterprises are pursuing to accomplish these objectives. Both initiatives have substantial implications when designing and implementing architectures for high availability and data protection. Database consolidation and DBaaS also drive standardization of I.T. infrastructure and processes. Standardization is essential for reducing cost and operational complexity. Databases deployed in the Bronze tier include development and test databases and databases supporting smaller work group and departmental applications that are often the first candidates for database consolidation and for deployment as Database as a Service (DBaaS).

SECURITY CHALLENGES TO DATABASE-AS-A-SERVICE (DBAAS)

There has been a growing concern that DBMSs and RDBMSs are not *cloud-friendly*. This is because, unlike other technology components for cloud service such as the webservers and application servers, which can easily scale from a few machines to hundreds or even thousands of machines, DBMSs cannot be scaled very easily. There are three challenges that drive the design of Relational Cloud: efficient multi-tenancy to minimize the hardware footprint required for a given (or predicted) workload, elastic scale-out to handle growing workloads, and database privacy. In fact, past DBMS technology fails to provide adequate tools and guidance if an existing database deployment needs to scale-out from a few machines to a large number of machines (Mohammed & Eric, 2011). Cloud computing and the notion of large-scale data-centers will become a pervasive technology in the coming years. There are some technology hurdles that we confront in deploying applications on cloud computing infrastructures: DBMS scalability and DBMS security. In this paper, we will focus on the problem of making DBMS technology cloud friendly. In fact, we will argue that the success of cloud computing is critically contingent on making DBMSs scalable, elastic, available, secure and autonomic, which is in addition to the other well-known properties of database management technologies like high-level functionality, consistency, performance, and reliability.

In Table 1 security challenges of DBaaS infrastructure along with their consequences and causes has been highlighted (Kashif, 2015).

PROPOSED SECURITY MODEL

Major concerns and issues in DBaaS have been discussed in the previous sections with emphasis on security challenges. It has been observed that, despite quality research on secure data outsourcing and data services for almost a decade, existing approaches on database encryption, authentication, digital signatures (Merkle, 1989), contractual agreements etc. have not gained much success in operations. To

Table 1. Cloud DBaaS security challenges

No.	Security Challenge	Description
1	Availability	• Temporary and permanent unavailability cause service breakdown • DOS Attacks, natural disasters, equipment failure
2	Access Control Issues	• Physical, personnel and logical control missing on organization's internal and DBaaS Provider's employees • Increase development and analysis cost is incurred when user management and granular access control is implemented
3	Integrity Check	• Need to avoid modification of configuration, access and data files • Require accuracy and integrity of data
4	Auditing and Monitoring	• Configuration requirements change continuously • Important for avoiding failures, backup maintenance, configuration of auto fail-over mechanisms • Require stark network and physical device, expertise and relevant resources
5	Data Sanitization	• Recovery of data by malicious sources if not properly discarded
6	Data Confidentiality	• Unencrypted data in memory, disk or in network may cause data breaches • Co-located application data is vulnerable to software bugs and errors in the Cloud • External organizations might also generate attacks
7	Data Replication and Consistency Management	Replications between multiple servers cause management as well as consistency issues
8	Network Security	• Data flowing over the network (internet) is prone to hazardous circumstances and network performance issues. • Possible network failure reasons are: misconfiguration, lack of resource isolations, poor or untested business continuity, disaster recovery plan, network traffic modification
9	Data Locality	• Compliance and data-security privacy laws prohibit movement of sensitive data among countries • Issues faced when no one takes responsibility of data in location independent data storage
10	Data Provenance	• Complexity and time sensitiveness in provenance metadata • Intensive computations involved in getting required history • Fast algorithms, auto logs are needed
11	Insider Threats	• Employees can tap into sensitive and confidential data • Strict supply chain management and assessment is required
12	Outside Malicious Attackers	• Malicious attacks by hackers • Difficulty in synchronizing data between users and reporting corruption • Absence of authentication, authorization and accounting controls • Poor key management for encryption and decryption

date, there is minimal work done in the field of security and privacy of DBaaS as compared to traditional data storage. Different approaches for securing DBaaS are discussed under this section with assorted categories of confidentiality, privacy, integrity and availability.

State-of-the-art approaches mainly address generally adopted methods for their proposed models. Those methods are: Encryption based data security, which means hiding data content from service providers. Private information retrieval, which allows user to retrieve an item from the data server without revealing the content of that item. Information distribution, which is based on dispersing information instead of encrypting the data.

The model shown in Figure 2 used Four-layer system structure, in which each floor performs its own duty to ensure that the data security of cloud layers.

The first layer: responsible for user authentication, it is one time password authentication. User Interface Layer used to access the service via internet. This allows users to easily utilize scalable and elastic database services available on Cloud infrastructure. The second layer: is used to access software services and storage space on the Cloud. As stated previously, consumers do not need to have hardware resources to avail these services.

for user's data upload, access control. Third layer provides efficient and reliable service of managing database residing in the Cloud. It allows reuse of the query statements residing in the storage, thus saving time for querying and loading data. Fourth layer is data storage layer where Data is encrypted and decrypted at storage and retrieval stages, respectively. Data integrity and data recovery is also provided at this layer.

Storage virtualization (Moeller, 2013) is a part of data storage layer, which forms a pool of resources using multiple network storage devices. A central console is responsible for the management of the resources. Taking backups, archiving and

Figure 2. Secure model for cloud DBaaS (Kashif, 2015)

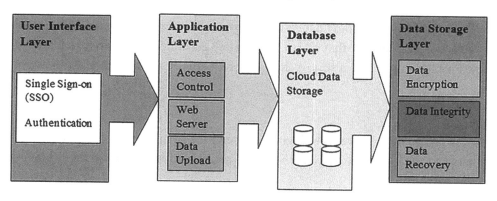

recovering data are now more feasible and less time-consuming because of these available features. Condition monitoring Error detects significant changes that cause errors in storing and managing data. Storage layer also provides data management services, such as traffic analysis, compression, virtualization, security, and replication etc., through the use of tools, policies and processes. This layer also provides database upgrades when some major changes are made in the database structure or between different releases. Our solution has three phases; Registration, Login, and Authentication.

Registration Phase

In the registration phase, user needs to register at the server by providing appropriate identification details. The server process user's data and issue a smartcard to the user. The procedure is as follows: Let f be a one-way has function, and p be a very large prime such that $p = 2q + 1$ where q is also a large prime, also let δ be a primitive element of $GF(p)$, which are all known public parameters. A random number $\eta \in [1, \ p - 1]$, with $gcd\ (\eta, \ p - 1) = 1$, is selected by the system as its private key which is used to compute the public key $\lambda = \delta^\eta mod\ p$.

Now, due to the property of $gcd\ (\eta, \ p - 1) = 1$, the public key λ is also a primitive element of $GF(p)$. Assuming that a new user U_i submits his identity IDi to the system for registration, the system computes an image of the ID_i^* as (ID_i^*) and the signature (χ_i, γ_i) of ID_i^* as

$$\gamma_i = (ID_i^* - \alpha_i \chi_i)\eta^{-1} - 1 \bmod p - 1$$

Where $\chi_i = \delta^{\alpha i} mod\ p$, and α_i is randomly selected from $[1, \ p - 1]$. We note here that due to ElGamal attack, our scheme is designed to signed the image of user identity ID_i^*, rather than directly signing the original user ID_i. Further, α_i should be used repeatedly to avoid uncovering the system's secret key η as a result of users collusion. It is clear here that γ_i is U_i secret key generated from the system's secret key. Further, this can be a sort of shared secret between the system and the user.

Login Phase

At this phase, if user i wants to login, he inserts the smart card to the input device. Then send (ID_i, χ_i) to the device. Then the smart card will perform the following computations:

1. Selects an odd random number $\nu \in \left[1,\ p\ -\ 1\right] \ni gcd\ \left(v,\ p\ -\ 1\right) = 1$, and then computes $\beta = \lambda^{\nu} mod\ p$, where λ is the public key of the system/ server.

2. Computes another value: $Z = \beta^{\nu i}\ mod\ \rho$ and sends Z to the server or system.

Authentication Phase

After receiving the authentication message Z, the remote server authenticates the login as follows:

1. Use Z and the image of U_i identity (i.e. ID_i^*) to verify that

$$\delta^{ID_i^*} = \chi_i^{ID_i^*} Z^{\nu-1} \bmod \rho$$

2. If the above condition holds, then the remote system generates a random number ρ and then sends the following to the smart card. Otherwise the request is rejected:

$$\{F(ID_i^* \oplus \rho)\}\chi_i\ or\ \{F(ID_i^* \oplus \rho)\}\kappa$$

Where κ is a predetermined secret key shared between the server and the card. Similarly, the function F is an agreed secret function.

3. User i uses its secret key γ_i or the shared key κ to decrypt the message and recover ρ, i.e:

$$[\{F(ID_i^* \oplus \rho)\}]^{-1} = (ID_i \oplus \rho)$$

and compute:

$$K = \{F(\rho)\}\lambda\ or\ K = \{F(\rho)\}\kappa$$

4. The smart card finally forwards K to the remote server. The system verifies whether $F^{-1}(K) = \rho$. If yes, the authentication process is completed. Otherwise, the request is rejected.

SECURITY ANALYSIS

To show the strength of our scheme, let's assume an intruder I knows Z, β, ρ, and $Z = \beta^{vi} \bmod \rho$. Now trying to solve yi from the information is always equivalent to computing the discrete logarithm problem over $GF(\rho)$, thus U_i's secret key γ_i will never be revealed to the public. Again, suppose an intruder impersonates U_i by developing v and V. Since $Z = \lambda^{v\gamma i} \bmod \rho$ and by knowing Z, υ, and V, the intruder can derive as $Z = Z^{v-1v} \bmod \rho$ without knowing γ_i. However, trying to compute v from β is equivalent to computing the discrete logarithm, again this attack is infeasible. Moreover, suppose ID_i is compromised, this information is not enough to derive either γ_i, or χ_i since the values where derived using ID_i^* not just ID_i.

During authentication phase, the agreed secret function F and shared secret key k are used to protect the system against any guessing attack. Moreover, for additional security, multiple shared secret keys can be used, so that whenever an encrypted message is to be sent to the system or the user, a different secret key will be used. This will ensure that even exhausted search key by an intruder will not reveal the keys, since for any guessed value for one key, there is very likely to be a corresponding value of another key such that the message will appear correlated. Additionally, the system has an option to use public key system by using γ_i to encrypt any message for U_i.

CONCLUSION

We have described the design of, a software security model for Mobile Cloud DBaaS environment. Data is possibly the most important asset a business has. Businesses today are trying hard to deal with the explosion of data and leverage it to their advantage. Database as a Service (DBaaS) is an increasingly popular Cloud service model, with attractive features like scalability, pay-as-you-go model and cost reduction that make it a perfect fit for most organizations. However, no extensive research work has been done which meticulously covers each and every aspect of DBaaS. Data storage security in Cloud is a domain which is full of challenges and is of paramount importance as customers do not want to lose their data at any cost. It is also a major hurdle in the way of adopting Cloud platform for storage services. Unfortunately, this area is still in its infancy and many research problems are yet to be identified. There is a need for effective strategies, proper measurements and methodologies to control this problem by having mature practices in the form of secure architectures to make DBaaS platform more secure, and ultimately, widely-adopted. In this chapter, I have presented a security model for cloud DBaaS environments. I have described its components, discussed existing solutions and identified possible approaches to deal with different security issues related to the DBaaS. Although many challenges remain in moving this idea from vision to implementation, the benefits of such an environment should serve to motivate the Mobile Cloud Computing research that can meet those challenges. These challenges are in addition to making the systems fault-tolerant and highly available.

FUTURE DIRECTIONS

Various techniques have been proposed for securing relational data model. However, these techniques need improvement in order to make them efficient and effective for DBaaS environment. Majority of such available solutions are based on traditional cryptographic techniques where the general idea is based on the outsourcing of encrypted data by owner only. Publishers do not manage and encrypt data; rather encryption is performed by the owner before outsourcing. Since publishers do not receive keys for decrypting the data; therefore, it is recommended to devise such techniques which allow publishers to perform queries on the encrypted data.

Thus, after conducting a thorough study on DBaaS, it can be inferred that all the practical and widely adopted approaches for providing security in relational databases can also be adopted for Cloud DBaaS model (database outsourcing) after transforming them accordingly. Moreover, all extant solutions for mitigating security challenges have room to be improved and evaluated according to a benchmark for making them more mature, practical and reliable in order to provide secure Cloud database services.

REFERENCES

Alok, K., Yogesh, S., & Viktor, P. (2012). Cryptonite: A Secure and Performant Data. *5th IEEE International Conference on*. IEEE.

Baron, S. (2015). *Why DBaaS Will Be The Next Big Thing In Database Management*. Retrieved from http://readwrite.com/2015/09/18/dbaas-trend-cloud-database-service

Cong, W., Sherman, S. M. C., Qian, W., Kui, R., & Wenjing, L. (2013). Privacy Preserving Public Auditing for Secure Cloud Storage. *IEEE Transactions on Computers, 62*(2), 362–375. doi:10.1109/TC.2011.245

Moeller. (2013). *Executive's guide to IT Governance: Improving Systems Processes with Service Management*. John Wiley & Sons.

Hacigumus, H., Iyer, B., Li, C., & Mehrotra, S. (2004). Efficient Execution of Aggregation Queries over Encrypted Relational Databases. In *Proc. of the 9th International Conference on Database Systems for Advanced Applications (DASFAA'04)*.

Krishna, K., & Roger, L. (2012). *Database as a Service (DBaaS) using Enterprise Manager 12c*. Oracle Open World.

Luca, F., Michele, C., & Mirco, M. (2012). Lecture Notes in Computer Science: Vol. 7672. *Supporting security and consistency for Cloud database*. Cyberspace Safety and Security.

Maciej, B., Gracjan, J., Michał, J., Stanisław, J., Tomasz, J., & Norbert, M. ... Sławomir, Z. (2013). National Data Storage 2: Secure Storage Cloud with Efficient and Easy Data Access. Academic Press.

Merkle, R. C. (1989). A Certified Digital Signature, Advances in Cryptology - CRYPTO '89. *9th Annual International Cryptology Conference Proceedings*, *435*, 218–238.

Mohammed, A., & Eric, P. (2011). Using Multi Shares for Ensuring Privacy in Database-as-a-Service. *Proceedings of 44th Hawaii International Conference on System Sciences*.

Munir. (2015). Security Model for Cloud Database as a Service (DBaaS). *IEEE Proceedings of the International Conference on Cloud Computing Technologies and Applications*.

Nithiavathy, R. (2013). Data Integrity and Data Dynamics with Secure Storage Service in Cloud. *Proceedings of the 2013 International Conference on Pattern Recognition, Informatics and Mobile Engineering*. IEEE. doi:10.1109/ICPRIME.2013.6496459

Oracle Corporation. (2011). *Database as a Service: Reference Architecture – An Overview*. Author.

Qingji, Z., Shouhuai, X., & Giuseppe, A. (2012). Efficient Query Integrity for Outsourced Dynamic Databases. CCSW'12, Raleigh, NC.

Related References

To continue our tradition of advancing information science and technology research, we have compiled a list of recommended IGI Global readings. These references will provide additional information and guidance to further enrich your knowledge and assist you with your own research and future publications.

Acharjya, D. P., & Mary, A. G. (2014). Privacy preservation in information system. In B. Tripathy & D. Acharjya (Eds.), *Advances in secure computing, internet services, and applications* (pp. 49–72). Hershey, PA: Information Science Reference; doi:10.4018/978-1-4666-4940-8.ch003

Agamba, J., & Keengwe, J. (2012). Pre-service teachers' perceptions of information assurance and cyber security.[IJICTE]. *International Journal of Information and Communication Technology Education, 8*(2), 94–101. doi:10.4018/jicte.2012040108

Aggarwal, R. (2013). Dispute settlement for cyber crimes in India: An analysis. In R. Khurana & R. Aggarwal (Eds.), *Interdisciplinary perspectives on business convergence, computing, and legality* (pp. 160–171). Hershey, PA: Business Science Reference; doi:10.4018/978-1-4666-4209-6.ch015

Agwu, E. (2013). Cyber criminals on the internet super highways: A technical investigation of different shades and colours within the Nigerian cyber space. [IJOM]. *International Journal of Online Marketing, 3*(2), 56–74. doi:10.4018/ijom.2013040104

Ahmad, A. (2012). Security assessment of networks. In *Wireless technologies: Concepts, methodologies, tools and applications* (pp. 208–224). Hershey, PA: Information Science Reference; doi:10.4018/978-1-61350-101-6.ch111

Ahmed, N., & Jensen, C. D. (2012). Security of dependable systems. In L. Petre, K. Sere, & E. Troubitsyna (Eds.), *Dependability and computer engineering: Concepts for software-intensive systems* (pp. 230–264). Hershey, PA: Engineering Science Reference; doi:10.4018/978-1-60960-747-0.ch011

Al, M., & Yoshigoe, K. (2012). Security and attacks in wireless sensor networks. In *Wireless technologies: Concepts, methodologies, tools and applications* (pp. 1811–1846). Hershey, PA: Information Science Reference; doi:10.4018/978-1-61350-101-6.ch706

Al-Ahmad, W. (2011). Building secure software using XP.[IJSSE]. *International Journal of Secure Software Engineering*, 2(3), 63–76. doi:10.4018/jsse.2011070104

Al-Bayatti, A. H., & Al-Bayatti, H. M. (2012). Security management and simulation of mobile ad hoc networks (MANET). In H. Al-Bahadili (Ed.), *Simulation in computer network design and modeling: Use and analysis* (pp. 297–314). Hershey, PA: Information Science Reference; doi:10.4018/978-1-4666-0191-8.ch014

Al-Bayatti, A. H., Zedan, H., Cau, A., & Siewe, F. (2012). Security management for mobile ad hoc network of networks (MANoN). In I. Khalil & E. Weippl (Eds.), *Advancing the next-generation of mobile computing: Emerging technologies* (pp. 1–18). Hershey, PA: Information Science Reference; doi:10.4018/978-1-4666-0119-2.ch001

Al-Hamdani, W. A. (2011). Three models to measure information security compliance. In H. Nemati (Ed.), *Security and privacy assurance in advancing technologies: New developments* (pp. 351–373). Hershey, PA: Information Science Reference; doi:10.4018/978-1-60960-200-0.ch022

Al-Hamdani, W. A. (2014). Secure e-learning and cryptography. In K. Sullivan, P. Czigler, & J. Sullivan Hellgren (Eds.), *Cases on professional distance education degree programs and practices: Successes, challenges, and issues* (pp. 331–369). Hershey, PA: Information Science Reference; doi:10.4018/978-1-4666-4486-1.ch012

Al-Jaljouli, R., & Abawajy, J. H. (2012). Security framework for mobile agents-based applications. In A. Kumar & H. Rahman (Eds.), *Mobile computing techniques in emerging markets: Systems, applications and services* (pp. 242–269). Hershey, PA: Information Science Reference; doi:10.4018/978-1-4666-0080-5.ch009

Al-Jaljouli, R., & Abawajy, J. H. (2014). Mobile agents security protocols. In *Crisis management: Concepts, methodologies, tools and applications* (pp. 166–202). Hershey, PA: Information Science Reference; doi:10.4018/978-1-4666-4707-7.ch007

Related References

Al-Suqri, M. N., & Akomolafe-Fatuyi, E. (2012). Security and privacy in digital libraries: Challenges, opportunities and prospects.[IJDLS]. *International Journal of Digital Library Systems*, *3*(4), 54–61. doi:10.4018/ijdls.2012100103

Alavi, R., Islam, S., Jahankhani, H., & Al-Nemrat, A. (2013). Analyzing human factors for an effective information security management system.[IJSSE]. *International Journal of Secure Software Engineering*, *4*(1), 50–74. doi:10.4018/jsse.2013010104

Alazab, A., Abawajy, J. H., & Hobbs, M. (2013). Web malware that targets web applications. In L. Caviglione, M. Coccoli, & A. Merlo (Eds.), *Social network engineering for secure web data and services* (pp. 248–264). Hershey, PA: Information Science Reference; doi:10.4018/978-1-4666-3926-3.ch012

Alazab, A., Hobbs, M., Abawajy, J., & Khraisat, A. (2013). Malware detection and prevention system based on multi-stage rules.[IJISP]. *International Journal of Information Security and Privacy*, *7*(2), 29–43. doi:10.4018/jisp.2013040102

Alazab, M., Venkatraman, S., Watters, P., & Alazab, M. (2013). Information security governance: The art of detecting hidden malware. In D. Mellado, L. Enrique Sánchez, E. Fernández-Medina, & M. Piattini (Eds.), *IT security governance innovations: Theory and research* (pp. 293–315). Hershey, PA: Information Science Reference; doi:10.4018/978-1-4666-2083-4.ch011

Alhaj, A., Aljawarneh, S., Masadeh, S., & Abu-Taieh, E. (2013). A secure data transmission mechanism for cloud outsourced data.[IJCAC]. *International Journal of Cloud Applications and Computing*, *3*(1), 34–43. doi:10.4018/ijcac.2013010104

Ali, M., & Jawandhiya, P. (2012). Security aware routing protocols for mobile ad hoc networks. In K. Lakhtaria (Ed.), *Technological advancements and applications in mobile ad-hoc networks: Research trends* (pp. 264–289). Hershey, PA: Information Science Reference; doi:10.4018/978-1-4666-0321-9.ch016

Ali, S. (2012). Practical web application security audit following industry standards and compliance. In J. Zubairi & A. Mahboob (Eds.), *Cyber security standards, practices and industrial applications: Systems and methodologies* (pp. 259–279). Hershey, PA: Information Science Reference; doi:10.4018/978-1-60960-851-4.ch013

Aljawarneh, S. (2013). Cloud security engineering: Avoiding security threats the right way. In S. Aljawarneh (Ed.), *Cloud computing advancements in design, implementation, and technologies* (pp. 147–153). Hershey, PA: Information Science Reference; doi:10.4018/978-1-4666-1879-4.ch010

Alshaer, H., Muhaidat, S., Shubair, R., & Shayegannia, M. (2014). Security and connectivity analysis in vehicular communication networks. In D. Rawat, B. Bista, & G. Yan (Eds.), *Security, privacy, trust, and resource management in mobile and wireless communications* (pp. 83–107). Hershey, PA: Information Science Reference; doi:10.4018/978-1-4666-4691-9.ch005

Alzamil, Z. A. (2012). Information security awareness at Saudi Arabians' organizations: An information technology employee's perspective.[IJISP]. *International Journal of Information Security and Privacy, 6*(3), 38–55. doi:10.4018/jisp.2012070102

Anyiwo, D., & Sharma, S. (2011). Web services and e-business technologies: Security issues. In O. Bak & N. Stair (Eds.), *Impact of e-business technologies on public and private organizations: Industry comparisons and perspectives* (pp. 249–261). Hershey, PA: Business Science Reference; doi:10.4018/978-1-60960-501-8.ch015

Apostolakis, I., Chryssanthou, A., & Varlamis, I. (2011). A holistic perspective of security in health related virtual communities. In *Virtual communities: Concepts, methodologies, tools and applications* (pp. 1190–1204). Hershey, PA: Information Science Reference; doi:10.4018/978-1-60960-100-3.ch406

Arnett, K. P., Templeton, G. F., & Vance, D. A. (2011). Information security by words alone: The case for strong security policies. In H. Nemati (Ed.), *Security and privacy assurance in advancing technologies: New developments* (pp. 154–159). Hershey, PA: Information Science Reference; doi:10.4018/978-1-60960-200-0.ch011

Arogundade, O. T., Akinwale, A. T., Jin, Z., & Yang, X. G. (2011). A unified use-misuse case model for capturing and analysing safety and security requirements. [IJISP]. *International Journal of Information Security and Privacy, 5*(4), 8–30. doi:10.4018/jisp.2011100102

Arshad, J., Townend, P., Xu, J., & Jie, W. (2012). Cloud computing security: Opportunities and pitfalls.[IJGHPC]. *International Journal of Grid and High Performance Computing, 4*(1), 52–66. doi:10.4018/jghpc.2012010104

Asim, M., & Petkovic, M. (2012). Fundamental building blocks for security interoperability in e-business. In E. Kajan, F. Dorloff, & I. Bedini (Eds.), *Handbook of research on e-business standards and protocols: Documents, data and advanced web technologies* (pp. 269–292). Hershey, PA: Business Science Reference; doi:10.4018/978-1-4666-0146-8.ch013

Related References

Askary, S., Goodwin, D., & Lanis, R. (2012). Improvements in audit risks related to information technology frauds.[IJEIS]. *International Journal of Enterprise Information Systems*, 8(2), 52–63. doi:10.4018/jeis.2012040104

Aurigemma, S. (2013). A composite framework for behavioral compliance with information security policies.[JOEUC]. *Journal of Organizational and End User Computing*, 25(3), 32–51. doi:10.4018/joeuc.2013070103

Avalle, M., Pironti, A., Pozza, D., & Sisto, R. (2011). JavaSPI: A framework for security protocol implementation.[IJSSE]. *International Journal of Secure Software Engineering*, 2(4), 34–48. doi:10.4018/jsse.2011100103

Axelrod, C. W. (2012). A dynamic cyber security economic model: incorporating value functions for all involved parties. In M. Gupta, J. Walp, & R. Sharman (Eds.), *Threats, countermeasures, and advances in applied information security* (pp. 462–477). Hershey, PA: Information Science Reference; doi:10.4018/978-1-4666-0978-5.ch024

Ayanso, A., & Herath, T. (2012). Law and technology at crossroads in cyberspace: Where do we go from here? In A. Dudley, J. Braman, & G. Vincenti (Eds.), *Investigating cyber law and cyber ethics: Issues, impacts and practices* (pp. 57–77). Hershey, PA: Information Science Reference; doi:10.4018/978-1-61350-132-0.ch004

Baars, T., & Spruit, M. (2012). Designing a secure cloud architecture: The SeCA model.[IJISP]. *International Journal of Information Security and Privacy*, 6(1), 14–32. doi:10.4018/jisp.2012010102

Bachmann, M. (2011). Deciphering the hacker underground: First quantitative insights. In T. Holt & B. Schell (Eds.), *Corporate hacking and technology-driven crime: Social dynamics and implications* (pp. 105–126). Hershey, PA: Information Science Reference; doi:10.4018/978-1-61692-805-6.ch006

Bachmann, M., & Smith, B. (2012). Internet fraud. In Z. Yan (Ed.), *Encyclopedia of cyber behavior* (pp. 931–943). Hershey, PA: Information Science Reference; doi:10.4018/978-1-4666-0315-8.ch077

Bai, Y., & Khan, K. M. (2011). Ell secure information system using modal logic technique.[IJSSE]. *International Journal of Secure Software Engineering*, 2(2), 65–76. doi:10.4018/jsse.2011040104

Bandeira, G. S. (2014). Criminal liability of organizations, corporations, legal persons, and similar entities on law of portuguese cybercrime: A brief discussion on the issue of crimes of "false information," the "damage on other programs or computer data," the "computer-software sabotage," the "illegitimate access," the "unlawful interception," and "illegitimate reproduction of the protected program". In I. Portela & F. Almeida (Eds.), *Organizational, legal, and technological dimensions of information system administration* (pp. 96–107). Hershey, PA: Information Science Reference; doi:10.4018/978-1-4666-4526-4.ch006

Barjis, J. (2012). Software engineering security based on business process modeling. In K. Khan (Ed.), *Security-aware systems applications and software development methods* (pp. 52–68). Hershey, PA: Information Science Reference; doi:10.4018/978-1-4666-1580-9.ch004

Bedi, P., Gandotra, V., & Singhal, A. (2013). Innovative strategies for secure software development. In H. Singh & K. Kaur (Eds.), *Designing, engineering, and analyzing reliable and efficient software* (pp. 217–237). Hershey, PA: Information Science Reference; doi:10.4018/978-1-4666-2958-5.ch013

Belsis, P., Skourlas, C., & Gritzalis, S. (2011). Secure electronic healthcare records management in wireless environments.[JITR]. *Journal of Information Technology Research*, *4*(4), 1–17. doi:10.4018/jitr.2011100101

Bernik, I. (2012). Internet study: Cyber threats and cybercrime awareness and fear.[IJCWT]. *International Journal of Cyber Warfare & Terrorism*, *2*(3), 1–11. doi:10.4018/ijcwt.2012070101

Bhatia, M. S. (2011). World war III: The cyber war.[IJCWT]. *International Journal of Cyber Warfare & Terrorism*, *1*(3), 59–69. doi:10.4018/ijcwt.2011070104

Blanco, C., Rosado, D., Gutiérrez, C., Rodríguez, A., Mellado, D., Fernández-Medina, E., & Piattini, M. et al. (2011). Security over the information systems development cycle. In H. Mouratidis (Ed.), *Software engineering for secure systems: Industrial and research perspectives* (pp. 113–154). Hershey, PA: Information Science Reference; doi:10.4018/978-1-61520-837-1.ch005

Bobbert, Y., & Mulder, H. (2012). A research journey into maturing the business information security of mid market organizations. In W. Van Grembergen & S. De Haes (Eds.), *Business strategy and applications in enterprise IT governance* (pp. 236–259). Hershey, PA: Business Science Reference; doi:10.4018/978-1-4666-1779-7.ch014

Boddington, R. (2011). Digital evidence. In D. Kerr, J. Gammack, & K. Bryant (Eds.), *Digital business security development: Management technologies* (pp. 37–72). Hershey, PA: Business Science Reference; doi:10.4018/978-1-60566-806-2.ch002

Bossler, A. M., & Burruss, G. W. (2011). The general theory of crime and computer hacking: Low self-control hackers? In T. Holt & B. Schell (Eds.), *Corporate hacking and technology-driven crime: Social dynamics and implications* (pp. 38–67). Hershey, PA: Information Science Reference; doi:10.4018/978-1-61692-805-6.ch003

Bouras, C., & Stamos, K. (2011). Security issues for multi-domain resource reservation. In D. Kar & M. Syed (Eds.), *Network security, administration and management: Advancing technology and practice* (pp. 38–50). Hershey, PA: Information Science Reference; doi:10.4018/978-1-60960-777-7.ch003

Bracci, F., Corradi, A., & Foschini, L. (2014). Cloud standards: Security and interoperability issues. In H. Mouftah & B. Kantarci (Eds.), *Communication infrastructures for cloud computing* (pp. 465–495). Hershey, PA: Information Science Reference; doi:10.4018/978-1-4666-4522-6.ch020

Brodsky, J., & Radvanovsky, R. (2011). Control systems security. In T. Holt & B. Schell (Eds.), *Corporate hacking and technology-driven crime: Social dynamics and implications* (pp. 187–204). Hershey, PA: Information Science Reference; doi:10.4018/978-1-61692-805-6.ch010

Brooks, D. (2013). Security threats and risks of intelligent building systems: Protecting facilities from current and emerging vulnerabilities. In C. Laing, A. Badii, & P. Vickers (Eds.), *Securing critical infrastructures and critical control systems: Approaches for threat protection* (pp. 1–16). Hershey, PA: Information Science Reference; doi:10.4018/978-1-4666-2659-1.ch001

Bülow, W., & Wester, M. (2012). The right to privacy and the protection of personal data in a digital era and the age of information. In C. Akrivopoulou & N. Garipidis (Eds.), *Human rights and risks in the digital era: Globalization and the effects of information technologies* (pp. 34–45). Hershey, PA: Information Science Reference; doi:10.4018/978-1-4666-0891-7.ch004

Canongia, C., & Mandarino, R. (2014). Cybersecurity: The new challenge of the information society. In Crisis management: Concepts, methodologies, tools and applications (pp. 60-80). Hershey, PA: Information Science Reference. doi:10.4018/978-1-4666-4707-7.ch003

Cao, X., & Lu, Y. (2011). The social network structure of a computer hacker community. In H. Nemati (Ed.), *Security and privacy assurance in advancing technologies: New developments* (pp. 160–173). Hershey, PA: Information Science Reference; doi:10.4018/978-1-60960-200-0.ch012

Cardholm, L. (2014). Identifying the business value of information security. In T. Tsiakis, T. Kargidis, & P. Katsaros (Eds.), *Approaches and processes for managing the economics of information systems* (pp. 157–180). Hershey, PA: Business Science Reference; doi:10.4018/978-1-4666-4983-5.ch010

Cardoso, R. C., & Gomes, A. (2012). Security issues in massively multiplayer online games. In M. Cruz-Cunha (Ed.), *Handbook of research on serious games as educational, business and research tools* (pp. 290–314). Hershey, PA: Information Science Reference; doi:10.4018/978-1-4666-0149-9.ch016

Carpen-Amarie, A., Costan, A., Leordeanu, C., Basescu, C., & Antoniu, G. (2012). Towards a generic security framework for cloud data management environments. [IJDST]. *International Journal of Distributed Systems and Technologies*, *3*(1), 17–34. doi:10.4018/jdst.2012010102

Caushaj, E., Fu, H., Sethi, I., Badih, H., Watson, D., Zhu, Y., & Leng, S. (2013). Theoretical analysis and experimental study: Monitoring data privacy in smartphone communications.[IJITN]. *International Journal of Interdisciplinary Telecommunications and Networking*, *5*(2), 66–82. doi:10.4018/jitn.2013040106

Cepheli, Ö., & Kurt, G. K. (2014). Physical layer security in wireless communication networks. In D. Rawat, B. Bista, & G. Yan (Eds.), *Security, privacy, trust, and resource management in mobile and wireless communications* (pp. 61–81). Hershey, PA: Information Science Reference; doi:10.4018/978-1-4666-4691-9.ch004

Chakraborty, P., & Raghuraman, K. (2013). Trends in information security. In K. Buragga & N. Zaman (Eds.), *Software development techniques for constructive information systems design* (pp. 354–376). Hershey, PA: Information Science Reference; doi:10.4018/978-1-4666-3679-8.ch020

Chandrakumar, T., & Parthasarathy, S. (2012). Enhancing data security in ERP projects using XML.[IJEIS]. *International Journal of Enterprise Information Systems*, *8*(1), 51–65. doi:10.4018/jeis.2012010104

Related References

Chapple, M. J., Striegel, A., & Crowell, C. R. (2011). Firewall rulebase management: Tools and techniques. In M. Quigley (Ed.), *ICT ethics and security in the 21st century: New developments and applications* (pp. 254–276). Hershey, PA: Information Science Reference; doi:10.4018/978-1-60960-573-5.ch013

Chen, L., Hu, W., Yang, M., & Zhang, L. (2011). Security and privacy issues in secure e-mail standards and services. In H. Nemati (Ed.), *Security and privacy assurance in advancing technologies: new developments* (pp. 174–185). Hershey, PA: Information Science Reference; doi:10.4018/978-1-60960-200-0.ch013

Chen, L., Varol, C., Liu, Q., & Zhou, B. (2014). Security in wireless metropolitan area networks: WiMAX and LTE. In D. Rawat, B. Bista, & G. Yan (Eds.), *Security, privacy, trust, and resource management in mobile and wireless communications* (pp. 11–27). Hershey, PA: Information Science Reference; doi:10.4018/978-1-4666-4691-9.ch002

Cherdantseva, Y., & Hilton, J. (2014). Information security and information assurance: Discussion about the meaning, scope, and goals. In I. Portela & F. Almeida (Eds.), *Organizational, legal, and technological dimensions of information system administration* (pp. 167–198). Hershey, PA: Information Science Reference; doi:10.4018/978-1-4666-4526-4.ch010

Cherdantseva, Y., & Hilton, J. (2014). The 2011 survey of information security and information assurance professionals: Findings. In I. Portela & F. Almeida (Eds.), *Organizational, legal, and technological dimensions of information system administration* (pp. 243–256). Hershey, PA: Information Science Reference; doi:10.4018/978-1-4666-4526-4.ch013

Chowdhury, M. U., & Ray, B. R. (2013). Security risks/vulnerability in a RFID system and possible defenses. In N. Karmakar (Ed.), *Advanced RFID systems, security, and applications* (pp. 1–15). Hershey, PA: Information Science Reference; doi:10.4018/978-1-4666-2080-3.ch001

Cofta, P., Lacohée, H., & Hodgson, P. (2011). Incorporating social trust into design practices for secure systems. In H. Mouratidis (Ed.), *Software engineering for secure systems: Industrial and research perspectives* (pp. 260–284). Hershey, PA: Information Science Reference; doi:10.4018/978-1-61520-837-1.ch010

Conway, M. (2012). What is cyberterrorism and how real is the threat? A review of the academic literature, 1996 – 2009. In P. Reich & E. Gelbstein (Eds.), *Law, policy, and technology: Cyberterrorism, information warfare, and internet immobilization* (pp. 279–307). Hershey, PA: Information Science Reference; doi:10.4018/978-1-61520-831-9.ch011

Corser, G. P., Arslanturk, S., Oluoch, J., Fu, H., & Corser, G. E. (2013). Knowing the enemy at the gates: Measuring attacker motivation.[IJITN]. *International Journal of Interdisciplinary Telecommunications and Networking*, 5(2), 83–95. doi:10.4018/jitn.2013040107

Crosbie, M. (2013). Hack the cloud: Ethical hacking and cloud forensics. In K. Ruan (Ed.), *Cybercrime and cloud forensics: Applications for investigation processes* (pp. 42–58). Hershey, PA: Information Science Reference; doi:10.4018/978-1-4666-2662-1.ch002

Curran, K., Carlin, S., & Adams, M. (2012). Security issues in cloud computing. In L. Chao (Ed.), *Cloud computing for teaching and learning: Strategies for design and implementation* (pp. 200–208). Hershey, PA: Information Science Reference; doi:10.4018/978-1-4666-0957-0.ch014

Czosseck, C., Ottis, R., & Talihärm, A. (2011). Estonia after the 2007 cyber attacks: Legal, strategic and organisational changes in cyber security.[IJCWT]. *International Journal of Cyber Warfare & Terrorism*, 1(1), 24–34. doi:10.4018/ijcwt.2011010103

Czosseck, C., & Podins, K. (2012). A vulnerability-based model of cyber weapons and its implications for cyber conflict.[IJCWT]. *International Journal of Cyber Warfare & Terrorism*, 2(1), 14–26. doi:10.4018/ijcwt.2012010102

da Silva, F. A., Moura, D. F., & Galdino, J. F. (2012). Classes of attacks for tactical software defined radios.[IJERTCS]. *International Journal of Embedded and Real-Time Communication Systems*, 3(4), 57–82. doi:10.4018/jertcs.2012100104

Dabcevic, K., Marcenaro, L., & Regazzoni, C. S. (2013). Security in cognitive radio networks. In T. Lagkas, P. Sarigiannidis, M. Louta, & P. Chatzimisios (Eds.), *Evolution of cognitive networks and self-adaptive communication systems* (pp. 301–335). Hershey, PA: Information Science Reference; doi:10.4018/978-1-4666-4189-1.ch013

Related References

Dahbur, K., Mohammad, B., & Tarakji, A. B. (2013). Security issues in cloud computing: A survey of risks, threats and vulnerabilities. In S. Aljawarneh (Ed.), *Cloud computing advancements in design, implementation, and technologies* (pp. 154–165). Hershey, PA: Information Science Reference; doi:10.4018/978-1-4666-1879-4.ch011

Dark, M. (2011). Data breach disclosure: A policy analysis. In M. Dark (Ed.), *Information assurance and security ethics in complex systems: Interdisciplinary perspectives* (pp. 226–252). Hershey, PA: Information Science Reference; doi:10.4018/978-1-61692-245-0.ch011

Das, S., Mukhopadhyay, A., & Bhasker, B. (2013). Today's action is better than tomorrow's cure - Evaluating information security at a premier indian business school. [JCIT]. *Journal of Cases on Information Technology*, *15*(3), 1–23. doi:10.4018/jcit.2013070101

Dasgupta, D., & Naseem, D. (2014). A framework for compliance and security coverage estimation for cloud services: A cloud insurance model. In S. Srinivasan (Ed.), *Security, trust, and regulatory aspects of cloud computing in business environments* (pp. 91–114). Hershey, PA: Information Science Reference; doi:10.4018/978-1-4666-5788-5.ch005

De Fuentes, J. M., González-Tablas, A. I., & Ribagorda, A. (2011). Overview of security issues in vehicular ad-hoc networks. In M. Cruz-Cunha & F. Moreira (Eds.), *Handbook of research on mobility and computing: Evolving technologies and ubiquitous impacts* (pp. 894–911). Hershey, PA: Information Science Reference; doi:10.4018/978-1-60960-042-6.ch056

De Groef, W., Devriese, D., Reynaert, T., & Piessens, F. (2013). Security and privacy of online social network applications. In L. Caviglione, M. Coccoli, & A. Merlo (Eds.), *Social network engineering for secure web data and services* (pp. 206–221). Hershey, PA: Information Science Reference; doi:10.4018/978-1-4666-3926-3.ch010

Denning, D. E. (2011). Cyber conflict as an emergent social phenomenon. In T. Holt & B. Schell (Eds.), *Corporate hacking and technology-driven crime: Social dynamics and implications* (pp. 170–186). Hershey, PA: Information Science Reference; doi:10.4018/978-1-61692-805-6.ch009

Desai, A. M., & Mock, K. (2013). Security in cloud computing. In A. Bento & A. Aggarwal (Eds.), *Cloud computing service and deployment models: Layers and management* (pp. 208–221). Hershey, PA: Business Science Reference; doi:10.4018/978-1-4666-2187-9.ch011

Dionysiou, I., & Ktoridou, D. (2012). Enhancing dynamic-content courses with student-oriented learning strategies: The case of computer security course.[IJCEE]. *International Journal of Cyber Ethics in Education*, 2(2), 24–33. doi:10.4018/ijcee.2012040103

Disterer, G. (2012). Attacks on IT systems: Categories of motives. In T. Chou (Ed.), *Information assurance and security technologies for risk assessment and threat management: Advances* (pp. 1–16). Hershey, PA: Information Science Reference; doi:10.4018/978-1-61350-507-6.ch001

Dougan, T., & Curran, K. (2012). Man in the browser attacks.[IJACI]. *International Journal of Ambient Computing and Intelligence*, 4(1), 29–39. doi:10.4018/jaci.2012010103

Dubey, R., Sharma, S., & Chouhan, L. (2013). Security for cognitive radio networks. In M. Ku & J. Lin (Eds.), *Cognitive radio and interference management: Technology and strategy* (pp. 238–256). Hershey, PA: Information Science Reference; doi:10.4018/978-1-4666-2005-6.ch013

Dunkels, E., Frånberg, G., & Hällgren, C. (2011). Young people and online risk. In E. Dunkels, G. Franberg, & C. Hallgren (Eds.), *Youth culture and net culture: Online social practices* (pp. 1–16). Hershey, PA: Information Science Reference; doi:10.4018/978-1-60960-209-3.ch001

Dunkerley, K., & Tejay, G. (2012). The development of a model for information systems security success. In Z. Belkhamza & S. Azizi Wafa (Eds.), *Measuring organizational information systems success: New technologies and practices* (pp. 341–366). Hershey, PA: Business Science Reference; doi:10.4018/978-1-4666-0170-3.ch017

Dunkerley, K., & Tejay, G. (2012). Theorizing information security success: Towards secure e-government. In V. Weerakkody (Ed.), *Technology enabled transformation of the public sector: Advances in e-government* (pp. 224–235). Hershey, PA: Information Science Reference; doi:10.4018/978-1-4666-1776-6.ch014

Related References

Eisenga, A., Jones, T. L., & Rodriguez, W. (2012). Investing in IT security: How to determine the maximum threshold.[IJISP]. *International Journal of Information Security and Privacy, 6*(3), 75–87. doi:10.4018/jisp.2012070104

Eyitemi, M. (2012). Regulation of cybercafés in Nigeria. In *Cyber crime: Concepts, methodologies, tools and applications* (pp. 1305–1313). Hershey, PA: Information Science Reference; doi:10.4018/978-1-61350-323-2.ch606

Ezumah, B., & Adekunle, S. O. (2012). A review of privacy, internet security threat, and legislation in Africa: A case study of Nigeria, South Africa, Egypt, and Kenya. In J. Abawajy, M. Pathan, M. Rahman, A. Pathan, & M. Deris (Eds.), *Internet and distributed computing advancements: Theoretical frameworks and practical applications* (pp. 115–136). Hershey, PA: Information Science Reference; doi:10.4018/978-1-4666-0161-1.ch005

Farooq-i-Azam, M., & Ayyaz, M. N. (2014). Embedded systems security. In *Software design and development: Concepts, methodologies, tools, and applications* (pp. 980–998). Hershey, PA: Information Science Reference; doi:10.4018/978-1-4666-4301-7.ch047

Fauzi, A. H., & Taylor, H. (2013). Secure community trust stores for peer-to-peer e-commerce applications using cloud services.[IJEEI]. *International Journal of E-Entrepreneurship and Innovation, 4*(1), 1–15. doi:10.4018/jeei.2013010101

Fenz, S. (2011). E-business and information security risk management: Challenges and potential solutions. In E. Kajan (Ed.), *Electronic business interoperability: Concepts, opportunities and challenges* (pp. 596–614). Hershey, PA: Business Science Reference; doi:10.4018/978-1-60960-485-1.ch024

Fernandez, E. B., Yoshioka, N., Washizaki, H., Jurjens, J., VanHilst, M., & Pernu, G. (2011). Using security patterns to develop secure systems. In H. Mouratidis (Ed.), *Software engineering for secure systems: Industrial and research perspectives* (pp. 16–31). Hershey, PA: Information Science Reference; doi:10.4018/978-1-61520-837-1.ch002

Flores, A. E., Win, K. T., & Susilo, W. (2011). Secure exchange of electronic health records. In A. Chryssanthou, I. Apostolakis, & I. Varlamis (Eds.), *Certification and security in health-related web applications: Concepts and solutions* (pp. 1–22). Hershey, PA: Medical Information Science Reference; doi:10.4018/978-1-61692-895-7.ch001

Fonseca, J., & Vieira, M. (2014). A survey on secure software development lifecycles. In *Software design and development: Concepts, methodologies, tools, and applications* (pp. 17–33). Hershey, PA: Information Science Reference; doi:10.4018/978-1-4666-4301-7.ch002

Fournaris, A. P., Kitsos, P., & Sklavos, N. (2013). Security and cryptographic engineering in embedded systems. In M. Khalgui, O. Mosbahi, & A. Valentini (Eds.), *Embedded computing systems: Applications, optimization, and advanced design* (pp. 420–438). Hershey, PA: Information Science Reference; doi:10.4018/978-1-4666-3922-5.ch021

Franqueira, V. N., van Cleeff, A., van Eck, P., & Wieringa, R. J. (2013). Engineering security agreements against external insider threat.[IRMJ]. *Information Resources Management Journal*, *26*(4), 66–91. doi:10.4018/irmj.2013100104

French, T., Bessis, N., Maple, C., & Asimakopoulou, E. (2012). Trust issues on crowd-sourcing methods for urban environmental monitoring.[IJDST]. *International Journal of Distributed Systems and Technologies*, *3*(1), 35–47. doi:10.4018/jdst.2012010103

Fu, Y., Kulick, J., Yan, L. K., & Drager, S. (2013). Formal modeling and verification of security property in Handel C program.[IJSSE]. *International Journal of Secure Software Engineering*, *3*(3), 50–65. doi:10.4018/jsse.2012070103

Furnell, S., von Solms, R., & Phippen, A. (2011). Preventative actions for enhancing online protection and privacy.[IJITSA]. *International Journal of Information Technologies and Systems Approach*, *4*(2), 1–11. doi:10.4018/jitsa.2011070101

Gaivéo, J. (2011). SMEs e-business security issues. In M. Cruz-Cunha & J. Varajão (Eds.), *Innovations in SMEs and conducting e-business: Technologies, trends and solutions* (pp. 317–337). Hershey, PA: Business Science Reference; doi:10.4018/978-1-60960-765-4.ch018

Gaivéo, J. M. (2013). Security of ICTs supporting healthcare activities. In M. Cruz-Cunha, I. Miranda, & P. Gonçalves (Eds.), *Handbook of research on ICTs for human-centered healthcare and social care services* (pp. 208–228). Hershey, PA: Medical Information Science Reference; doi:10.4018/978-1-4666-3986-7.ch011

Gelbstein, E. E. (2013). Designing a security audit plan for a critical information infrastructure (CII). In C. Laing, A. Badii, & P. Vickers (Eds.), *Securing critical infrastructures and critical control systems: Approaches for threat protection* (pp. 262–285). Hershey, PA: Information Science Reference; doi:10.4018/978-1-4666-2659-1.ch011

Related References

Gódor, G., & Imre, S. (2012). Security aspects in radio frequency identification systems. In D. Saha & V. Sridhar (Eds.), *Next generation data communication technologies: Emerging trends* (pp. 187–225). Hershey, PA: Information Science Reference; doi:10.4018/978-1-61350-477-2.ch009

Gogolin, G. (2011). Security and privacy concerns of virtual worlds. In B. Ciaramitaro (Ed.), *Virtual worlds and e-commerce: Technologies and applications for building customer relationships* (pp. 244–256). Hershey, PA: Business Science Reference; doi:10.4018/978-1-61692-808-7.ch014

Gogoulos, F. I., Antonakopoulou, A., Lioudakis, G. V., Kaklamani, D. I., & Venieris, I. S. (2014). Trust in an enterprise world: A survey. In M. Cruz-Cunha, F. Moreira, & J. Varajão (Eds.), *Handbook of research on enterprise 2.0: Technological, social, and organizational dimensions* (pp. 199–219). Hershey, PA: Business Science Reference; doi:10.4018/978-1-4666-4373-4.ch011

Goldman, J. E., & Ahuja, S. (2011). Integration of COBIT, balanced scorecard and SSE-CMM as an organizational & strategic information security management (ISM) framework. In M. Quigley (Ed.), *ICT ethics and security in the 21st century: New developments and applications* (pp. 277–309). Hershey, PA: Information Science Reference; doi:10.4018/978-1-60960-573-5.ch014

Goldschmidt, C., Dark, M., & Chaudhry, H. (2011). Responsibility for the harm and risk of software security flaws. In M. Dark (Ed.), *Information assurance and security ethics in complex systems: Interdisciplinary perspectives* (pp. 104–131). Hershey, PA: Information Science Reference; doi:10.4018/978-1-61692-245-0.ch006

Grahn, K., Karlsson, J., & Pulkkis, G. (2011). Secure routing and mobility in future IP networks. In M. Cruz-Cunha & F. Moreira (Eds.), *Handbook of research on mobility and computing: Evolving technologies and ubiquitous impacts* (pp. 952–972). Hershey, PA: Information Science Reference; doi:10.4018/978-1-60960-042-6.ch059

Greitzer, F. L., Frincke, D., & Zabriskie, M. (2011). Social/ethical issues in predictive insider threat monitoring. In M. Dark (Ed.), *Information assurance and security ethics in complex systems: Interdisciplinary perspectives* (pp. 132–161). Hershey, PA: Information Science Reference; doi:10.4018/978-1-61692-245-0.ch007

Grobler, M. (2012). The need for digital evidence standardisation.[IJDCF]. *International Journal of Digital Crime and Forensics, 4*(2), 1–12. doi:10.4018/jdcf.2012040101

Guo, J., Marshall, A., & Zhou, B. (2014). A multi-parameter trust framework for mobile ad hoc networks. In D. Rawat, B. Bista, & G. Yan (Eds.), *Security, privacy, trust, and resource management in mobile and wireless communications* (pp. 245–277). Hershey, PA: Information Science Reference; doi:10.4018/978-1-4666-4691-9.ch011

Gururajan, R., & Hafeez-Baig, A. (2011). Wireless handheld device and LAN security issues: A case study. In D. Kerr, J. Gammack, & K. Bryant (Eds.), *Digital business security development: Management technologies* (pp. 129–151). Hershey, PA: Business Science Reference; doi:10.4018/978-1-60566-806-2.ch006

Ha, H. (2012). Online security and consumer protection in ecommerce an Australian case. In K. Mohammed Rezaul (Ed.), *Strategic and pragmatic e-business: Implications for future business practices* (pp. 217–243). Hershey, PA: Business Science Reference; doi:10.4018/978-1-4666-1619-6.ch010

Hagen, J. M. (2012). The contributions of information security culture and human relations to the improvement of situational awareness. In C. Onwubiko & T. Owens (Eds.), *Situational awareness in computer network defense: Principles, methods and applications* (pp. 10–28). Hershey, PA: Information Science Reference; doi:10.4018/978-1-4666-0104-8.ch002

Hai-Jew, S. (2011). The social design of 3D interactive spaces for security in higher education: A preliminary view. In A. Rea (Ed.), *Security in virtual worlds, 3D webs, and immersive environments: Models for development, interaction, and management* (pp. 72–96). Hershey, PA: Information Science Reference; doi:10.4018/978-1-61520-891-3.ch005

Halder, D., & Jaishankar, K. (2012). Cyber crime against women and regulations in Australia. In *Cyber crime: Concepts, methodologies, tools and applications* (pp. 757–764). Hershey, PA: Information Science Reference; doi:10.4018/978-1-61350-323-2.ch404

Halder, D., & Jaishankar, K. (2012). Cyber victimization of women and cyber laws in India. In *Cyber crime: Concepts, methodologies, tools and applications* (pp. 742–756). Hershey, PA: Information Science Reference; doi:10.4018/978-1-61350-323-2.ch403

Halder, D., & Jaishankar, K. (2012). Definition, typology and patterns of victimization. In *Cyber crime: Concepts, methodologies, tools and applications* (pp. 1016–1042). Hershey, PA: Information Science Reference; doi:10.4018/978-1-61350-323-2.ch502

Hamlen, K., Kantarcioglu, M., Khan, L., & Thuraisingham, B. (2012). Security issues for cloud computing. In H. Nemati (Ed.), *Optimizing information security and advancing privacy assurance: New technologies* (pp. 150–162). Hershey, PA: Information Science Reference; doi:10.4018/978-1-4666-0026-3.ch008

Harnesk, D. (2011). Convergence of information security in B2B networks. In E. Kajan (Ed.), *Electronic business interoperability: Concepts, opportunities and challenges* (pp. 571–595). Hershey, PA: Business Science Reference; doi:10.4018/978-1-60960-485-1.ch023

Harnesk, D., & Hartikainen, H. (2011). Multi-layers of information security in emergency response.[IJISCRAM]. *International Journal of Information Systems for Crisis Response and Management, 3*(2), 1–17. doi:10.4018/jiscrm.2011040101

Hawrylak, P. J., Hale, J., & Papa, M. (2013). Security issues for ISO 18000-6 type C RFID: Identification and solutions. In *Supply chain management: Concepts, methodologies, tools, and applications* (pp. 1565–1581). Hershey, PA: Business Science Reference; doi:10.4018/978-1-4666-2625-6.ch093

He, B., Tran, T. T., & Xie, B. (2014). Authentication and identity management for secure cloud businesses and services. In S. Srinivasan (Ed.), *Security, trust, and regulatory aspects of cloud computing in business environments* (pp. 180–201). Hershey, PA: Information Science Reference; doi:10.4018/978-1-4666-5788-5.ch011

Henrie, M. (2012). Cyber security in liquid petroleum pipelines. In J. Zubairi & A. Mahboob (Eds.), *Cyber security standards, practices and industrial applications: Systems and methodologies* (pp. 200–222). Hershey, PA: Information Science Reference; doi:10.4018/978-1-60960-851-4.ch011

Herath, T., Rao, H. R., & Upadhyaya, S. (2012). Internet crime: How vulnerable are you? Do gender, social influence and education play a role in vulnerability? In *Cyber crime: Concepts, methodologies, tools and applications* (pp. 1–13). Hershey, PA: Information Science Reference; doi:10.4018/978-1-61350-323-2.ch101

Hilmi, M. F., Pawanchik, S., Mustapha, Y., & Ali, H. M. (2013). Information security perspective of a learning management system: An exploratory study.[IJKSR]. *International Journal of Knowledge Society Research, 4*(2), 9–18. doi:10.4018/jksr.2013040102

Hommel, W. (2012). Security and privacy management for learning management systems. In *Virtual learning environments: Concepts, methodologies, tools and applications* (pp. 1151–1170). Hershey, PA: Information Science Reference; doi:10.4018/978-1-4666-0011-9.ch602

Hoops, D. S. (2012). Lost in cyberspace: Navigating the legal issues of e-commerce. [JECO]. *Journal of Electronic Commerce in Organizations, 10*(1), 33–51. doi:10.4018/jeco.2012010103

Houmb, S., Georg, G., Petriu, D., Bordbar, B., Ray, I., Anastasakis, K., & France, R. (2011). Balancing security and performance properties during system architectural design. In H. Mouratidis (Ed.), *Software engineering for secure systems: Industrial and research perspectives* (pp. 155–191). Hershey, PA: Information Science Reference; doi:10.4018/978-1-61520-837-1.ch006

Huang, E., & Cheng, F. (2012). Online security cues and e-payment continuance intention.[IJEEI]. *International Journal of E-Entrepreneurship and Innovation, 3*(1), 42–58. doi:10.4018/jeei.2012010104

Ifinedo, P. (2011). Relationships between information security concerns and national cultural dimensions: Findings in the global financial services industry. In H. Nemati (Ed.), *Security and privacy assurance in advancing technologies: New developments* (pp. 134–153). Hershey, PA: Information Science Reference; doi:10.4018/978-1-60960-200-0.ch010

Inden, U., Lioudakis, G., & Rückemann, C. (2013). Awareness-based security management for complex and internet-based operations management systems. In C. Rückemann (Ed.), *Integrated information and computing systems for natural, spatial, and social sciences* (pp. 43–73). Hershey, PA: Information Science Reference; doi:10.4018/978-1-4666-2190-9.ch003

Islam, S., Mouratidis, H., Kalloniatis, C., Hudic, A., & Zechner, L. (2013). Model based process to support security and privacy requirements engineering.[IJSSE]. *International Journal of Secure Software Engineering, 3*(3), 1–22. doi:10.4018/jsse.2012070101

Itani, W., Kayssi, A., & Chehab, A. (2012). Security and privacy in body sensor networks: Challenges, solutions, and research directions. In M. Watfa (Ed.), *E-healthcare systems and wireless communications: Current and future challenges* (pp. 100–127). Hershey, PA: Medical Information Science Reference; doi:10.4018/978-1-61350-123-8.ch005

Related References

Jansen van Vuuren, J., Grobler, M., & Zaaiman, J. (2012). Cyber security awareness as critical driver to national security.[IJCWT]. *International Journal of Cyber Warfare & Terrorism, 2*(1), 27–38. doi:10.4018/ijcwt.2012010103

Jansen van Vuuren, J., Leenen, L., Phahlamohlaka, J., & Zaaiman, J. (2012). An approach to governance of CyberSecurity in South Africa.[IJCWT]. *International Journal of Cyber Warfare & Terrorism, 2*(4), 13–27. doi:10.4018/ijcwt.2012100102

Jensen, J., & Groep, D. L. (2012). Security and trust in a global research infrastructure. In J. Leng & W. Sharrock (Eds.), *Handbook of research on computational science and engineering: Theory and practice* (pp. 539–566). Hershey, PA: Engineering Science Reference; doi:10.4018/978-1-61350-116-0.ch022

Johnsen, S. O. (2014). Safety and security in SCADA systems must be improved through resilience based risk management. In *Crisis management: Concepts, methodologies, tools and applications* (pp. 1422–1436). Hershey, PA: Information Science Reference; doi:10.4018/978-1-4666-4707-7.ch071

Johnston, A. C., Wech, B., & Jack, E. (2012). Engaging remote employees: The moderating role of "remote" status in determining employee information security policy awareness.[JOEUC]. *Journal of Organizational and End User Computing, 25*(1), 1–23. doi:10.4018/joeuc.2013010101

Jung, C., Rudolph, M., & Schwarz, R. (2013). Security evaluation of service-oriented systems using the SiSOA method. In K. Khan (Ed.), *Developing and evaluating security-aware software systems* (pp. 20–35). Hershey, PA: Information Science Reference; doi:10.4018/978-1-4666-2482-5.ch002

Kaiya, H., Sakai, J., Ogata, S., & Kaijiri, K. (2013). Eliciting security requirements for an information system using asset flows and processor deployment.[IJSSE]. *International Journal of Secure Software Engineering, 4*(3), 42–63. doi:10.4018/jsse.2013070103

Kalloniatis, C., Kavakli, E., & Gritzalis, S. (2011). Designing privacy aware information systems. In H. Mouratidis (Ed.), *Software engineering for secure systems: Industrial and research perspectives* (pp. 212–231). Hershey, PA: Information Science Reference; doi:10.4018/978-1-61520-837-1.ch008

Kamoun, F., & Halaweh, M. (2012). User interface design and e-commerce security perception: An empirical study.[IJEBR]. *International Journal of E-Business Research, 8*(2), 15–32. doi:10.4018/jebr.2012040102

Kamruzzaman, J., Azad, A. K., Karmakar, N. C., Karmakar, G., & Srinivasan, B. (2013). Security and privacy in RFID systems. In N. Karmakar (Ed.), *Advanced RFID systems, security, and applications* (pp. 16–40). Hershey, PA: Information Science Reference; doi:10.4018/978-1-4666-2080-3.ch002

Kaosar, M. G., & Yi, X. (2011). Privacy preserving data gathering in wireless sensor network. In D. Kar & M. Syed (Eds.), *Network security, administration and management: Advancing technology and practice* (pp. 237–251). Hershey, PA: Information Science Reference; doi:10.4018/978-1-60960-777-7.ch012

Kar, D. C., Ngo, H. L., Mulkey, C. J., & Sanapala, G. (2011). Advances in security and privacy in wireless sensor networks. In H. Nemati (Ed.), *Security and privacy assurance in advancing technologies: New developments* (pp. 186–213). Hershey, PA: Information Science Reference; doi:10.4018/978-1-60960-200-0.ch014

Karadsheh, L., & Alhawari, S. (2011). Applying security policies in small business utilizing cloud computing technologies.[IJCAC]. *International Journal of Cloud Applications and Computing*, *1*(2), 29–40. doi:10.4018/ijcac.2011040103

Karokola, G., Yngström, L., & Kowalski, S. (2012). Secure e-government services: A comparative analysis of e-government maturity models for the developing regions–The need for security services.[IJEGR]. *International Journal of Electronic Government Research*, *8*(1), 1–25. doi:10.4018/jegr.2012010101

Kassim, N. M., & Ramayah, T. (2013). Security policy issues in internet banking in Malaysia. In *IT policy and ethics: Concepts, methodologies, tools, and applications* (pp. 1274–1293). Hershey, PA: Information Science Reference; doi:10.4018/978-1-4666-2919-6.ch057

Kayem, A. V. (2013). Security in service oriented architectures: Standards and challenges. In *Digital rights management: Concepts, methodologies, tools, and applications* (pp. 50–73). Hershey, PA: Information Science Reference; doi:10.4018/978-1-4666-2136-7.ch004

K.C, A., Forsgren, H., Grahn, K., Karvi, T., & Pulkkis, G. (2013). Security and trust of public key cryptography for HIP and HIP multicast.[IJDTIS]. *International Journal of Dependable and Trustworthy Information Systems*, *2*(3), 17–35. doi:10.4018/jdtis.2011070102

Related References

Kelarev, A. V., Brown, S., Watters, P., Wu, X., & Dazeley, R. (2011). Establishing reasoning communities of security experts for internet commerce security. In J. Yearwood & A. Stranieri (Eds.), *Technologies for supporting reasoning communities and collaborative decision making: Cooperative approaches* (pp. 380–396). Hershey, PA: Information Science Reference; doi:10.4018/978-1-60960-091-4.ch020

Kerr, D., Gammack, J. G., & Boddington, R. (2011). Overview of digital business security issues. In D. Kerr, J. Gammack, & K. Bryant (Eds.), *Digital business security development: Management technologies* (pp. 1–36). Hershey, PA: Business Science Reference; doi:10.4018/978-1-60566-806-2.ch001

Khan, K. M. (2011). A decision support system for selecting secure web services. In *Enterprise information systems: Concepts, methodologies, tools and applications* (pp. 1113–1120). Hershey, PA: Business Science Reference; doi:10.4018/978-1-61692-852-0.ch415

Khan, K. M. (2012). Software security engineering: Design and applications.[IJSSE]. *International Journal of Secure Software Engineering*, 3(1), 62–63. doi:10.4018/jsse.2012010104

Kilger, M. (2011). Social dynamics and the future of technology-driven crime. In T. Holt & B. Schell (Eds.), *Corporate hacking and technology-driven crime: Social dynamics and implications* (pp. 205–227). Hershey, PA: Information Science Reference; doi:10.4018/978-1-61692-805-6.ch011

Kirwan, G., & Power, A. (2012). Hacking: Legal and ethical aspects of an ambiguous activity. In A. Dudley, J. Braman, & G. Vincenti (Eds.), *Investigating cyber law and cyber ethics: Issues, impacts and practices* (pp. 21–36). Hershey, PA: Information Science Reference; doi:10.4018/978-1-61350-132-0.ch002

Kline, D. M., He, L., & Yaylacicegi, U. (2011). User perceptions of security technologies.[IJISP]. *International Journal of Information Security and Privacy*, 5(2), 1–12. doi:10.4018/jisp.2011040101

Kolkowska, E., Hedström, K., & Karlsson, F. (2012). Analyzing information security goals. In M. Gupta, J. Walp, & R. Sharman (Eds.), *Threats, countermeasures, and advances in applied information security* (pp. 91–110). Hershey, PA: Information Science Reference; doi:10.4018/978-1-4666-0978-5.ch005

Korhonen, J. J., Hiekkanen, K., & Mykkänen, J. (2012). Information security governance. In M. Gupta, J. Walp, & R. Sharman (Eds.), *Strategic and practical approaches for information security governance: Technologies and applied solutions* (pp. 53–66). Hershey, PA: Information Science Reference; doi:10.4018/978-1-4666-0197-0.ch004

Korovessis, P. (2011). Information security awareness in academia.[IJKSR]. *International Journal of Knowledge Society Research*, 2(4), 1–17. doi:10.4018/jksr.2011100101

Koskosas, I., & Sariannidis, N. (2011). Project commitment in the context of information security.[IJITPM]. *International Journal of Information Technology Project Management*, 2(3), 17–29. doi:10.4018/jitpm.2011070102

Kotsonis, E., & Eliakis, S. (2013). Information security standards for health information systems: The implementer's approach. In *User-driven healthcare: Concepts, methodologies, tools, and applications* (pp. 225–257). Hershey, PA: Medical Information Science Reference; doi:10.4018/978-1-4666-2770-3.ch013

Krishna, A. V. (2014). A randomized cloud library security environment. In S. Dhamdhere (Ed.), *Cloud computing and virtualization technologies in libraries* (pp. 278–296). Hershey, PA: Information Science Reference; doi:10.4018/978-1-4666-4631-5.ch016

Kruck, S. E., & Teer, F. P. (2011). Computer security practices and perceptions of the next generation of corporate computer users. In H. Nemati (Ed.), *Pervasive information security and privacy developments: Trends and advancements* (pp. 255–265). Hershey, PA: Information Science Reference; doi:10.4018/978-1-61692-000-5.ch017

Kumar, M., Sareen, M., & Chhabra, S. (2011). Technology related trust issues in SME B2B E-Commerce.[IJICTHD]. *International Journal of Information Communication Technologies and Human Development*, 3(4), 31–46. doi:10.4018/jicthd.2011100103

Kumar, P., & Mittal, S. (2012). The perpetration and prevention of cyber crime: An analysis of cyber terrorism in India.[IJT]. *International Journal of Technoethics*, 3(1), 43–52. doi:10.4018/jte.2012010104

Kumar, P. S., Ashok, M. S., & Subramanian, R. (2012). A publicly verifiable dynamic secret sharing protocol for secure and dependable data storage in cloud computing. [IJCAC]. *International Journal of Cloud Applications and Computing*, 2(3), 1–25. doi:10.4018/ijcac.2012070101

Kumar, S., & Dutta, K. (2014). Security issues in mobile ad hoc networks: A survey. In D. Rawat, B. Bista, & G. Yan (Eds.), *Security, privacy, trust, and resource management in mobile and wireless communications* (pp. 176–221). Hershey, PA: Information Science Reference; doi:10.4018/978-1-4666-4691-9.ch009

Lawson, S. (2013). Motivating cybersecurity: Assessing the status of critical infrastructure as an object of cyber threats. In C. Laing, A. Badii, & P. Vickers (Eds.), *Securing critical infrastructures and critical control systems: Approaches for threat protection* (pp. 168–189). Hershey, PA: Information Science Reference; doi:10.4018/978-1-4666-2659-1.ch007

Leitch, S., & Warren, M. (2011). The ethics of security of personal information upon Facebook. In M. Quigley (Ed.), *ICT ethics and security in the 21st century: New developments and applications* (pp. 46–65). Hershey, PA: Information Science Reference; doi:10.4018/978-1-60960-573-5.ch003

Li, M. (2013). Security terminology. In A. Miri (Ed.), *Advanced security and privacy for RFID technologies* (pp. 1–13). Hershey, PA: Information Science Reference; doi:10.4018/978-1-4666-3685-9.ch001

Ligaarden, O. S., Refsdal, A., & Stølen, K. (2013). Using indicators to monitor security risk in systems of systems: How to capture and measure the impact of service dependencies on the security of provided services. In D. Mellado, L. Enrique Sánchez, E. Fernández-Medina, & M. Piattini (Eds.), *IT security governance innovations: Theory and research* (pp. 256–292). Hershey, PA: Information Science Reference; doi:10.4018/978-1-4666-2083-4.ch010

Lim, J. S., Chang, S., Ahmad, A., & Maynard, S. (2012). Towards an organizational culture framework for information security practices. In M. Gupta, J. Walp, & R. Sharman (Eds.), *Strategic and practical approaches for information security governance: Technologies and applied solutions* (pp. 296–315). Hershey, PA: Information Science Reference; doi:10.4018/978-1-4666-0197-0.ch017

Lin, X., & Luppicini, R. (2011). Socio-technical influences of cyber espionage: A case study of the GhostNet system.[IJT]. *International Journal of Technoethics*, 2(2), 65–77. doi:10.4018/jte.2011040105

Lindström, J., & Hanken, C. (2012). Security challenges and selected legal aspects for wearable computing.[JITR]. *Journal of Information Technology Research*, 5(1), 68–87. doi:10.4018/jitr.2012010104

Maheshwari, H., Hyman, H., & Agrawal, M. (2012). A comparison of cyber-crime definitions in India and the United States. In *Cyber crime: Concepts, methodologies, tools and applications* (pp. 714–726). Hershey, PA: Information Science Reference; doi:10.4018/978-1-61350-323-2.ch401

Malcolmson, J. (2014). The role of security culture. In I. Portela & F. Almeida (Eds.), *Organizational, legal, and technological dimensions of information system administration* (pp. 225–242). Hershey, PA: Information Science Reference; doi:10.4018/978-1-4666-4526-4.ch012

Mantas, G., Lymberopoulos, D., & Komninos, N. (2011). Security in smart home environment. In A. Lazakidou, K. Siassiakos, & K. Ioannou (Eds.), *Wireless technologies for ambient assisted living and healthcare: Systems and applications* (pp. 170–191). Hershey, PA: Medical Information Science Reference; doi:10.4018/978-1-61520-805-0.ch010

Maple, C., Short, E., Brown, A., Bryden, C., & Salter, M. (2012). Cyberstalking in the UK: Analysis and recommendations.[IJDST]. *International Journal of Distributed Systems and Technologies*, 3(4), 34–51. doi:10.4018/jdst.2012100104

Maqousi, A., & Balikhina, T. (2011). Building security awareness culture to serve e-government initiative. In A. Al Ajeeli & Y. Al-Bastaki (Eds.), *Handbook of research on e-services in the public sector: E-government strategies and advancements* (pp. 304–311). Hershey, PA: Information Science Reference; doi:10.4018/978-1-61520-789-3.ch024

Martin, N., & Rice, J. (2013). Spearing high net wealth individuals: The case of online fraud and mature age internet users.[IJISP]. *International Journal of Information Security and Privacy*, 7(1), 1–15. doi:10.4018/jisp.2013010101

Martino, L., & Bertino, E. (2012). Security for web services: Standards and research issues. In L. Jie-Zhang (Ed.), *Innovations, standards and practices of web services: Emerging research topics* (pp. 336–362). Hershey, PA: Information Science Reference; doi:10.4018/978-1-61350-104-7.ch015

Massonet, P., Michot, A., Naqvi, S., Villari, M., & Latanicki, J. (2013). Securing the external interfaces of a federated infrastructure cloud. In *IT policy and ethics: Concepts, methodologies, tools, and applications* (pp. 1876–1903). Hershey, PA: Information Science Reference; doi:10.4018/978-1-4666-2919-6.ch082

Related References

Maumbe, B., & Owei, V. T. (2013). Understanding the information security landscape in South Africa: Implications for strategic collaboration and policy development. In B. Maumbe & C. Patrikakis (Eds.), *E-agriculture and rural development: Global innovations and future prospects* (pp. 90–102). Hershey, PA: Information Science Reference; doi:10.4018/978-1-4666-2655-3.ch009

Mazumdar, C. (2011). Enterprise information system security: A life-cycle approach. In *Enterprise information systems: Concepts, methodologies, tools and applications* (pp. 154–168). Hershey, PA: Business Science Reference; doi:10.4018/978-1-61692-852-0.ch111

McCune, J., & Haworth, D. A. (2012). Securing America against cyber war.[IJCWT]. *International Journal of Cyber Warfare & Terrorism*, 2(1), 39–49. doi:10.4018/ijcwt.2012010104

Melvin, A. O., & Ayotunde, T. (2011). Spirituality in cybercrime (Yahoo Yahoo) activities among youths in south west Nigeria. In E. Dunkels, G. Franberg, & C. Hallgren (Eds.), *Youth culture and net culture: Online social practices* (pp. 357–380). Hershey, PA: Information Science Reference; doi:10.4018/978-1-60960-209-3.ch020

Miller, J. M., Higgins, G. E., & Lopez, K. M. (2013). Considering the role of e-government in cybercrime awareness and prevention: Toward a theoretical research program for the 21st century. In *Digital rights management: Concepts, methodologies, tools, and applications* (pp. 789–800). Hershey, PA: Information Science Reference; doi:10.4018/978-1-4666-2136-7.ch036

Millman, C., Whitty, M., Winder, B., & Griffiths, M. D. (2012). Perceived criminality of cyber-harassing behaviors among undergraduate students in the United Kingdom.[IJCBPL]. *International Journal of Cyber Behavior, Psychology and Learning*, 2(4), 49–59. doi:10.4018/ijcbpl.2012100104

Minami, N. A. (2012). Employing dynamic models to enhance corporate IT security policy.[IJATS]. *International Journal of Agent Technologies and Systems*, 4(2), 42–59. doi:10.4018/jats.2012040103

Mirante, D. P., & Ammari, H. M. (2014). Wireless sensor network security attacks: A survey. In *Crisis management: Concepts, methodologies, tools and applications* (pp. 25–59). Hershey, PA: Information Science Reference; doi:10.4018/978-1-4666-4707-7.ch002

Mishra, A., & Mishra, D. (2013). Cyber stalking: A challenge for web security. In J. Bishop (Ed.), *Examining the concepts, issues, and implications of internet trolling* (pp. 32–42). Hershey, PA: Information Science Reference; doi:10.4018/978-1-4666-2803-8.ch004

Mishra, S. (2011). Wireless sensor networks: Emerging applications and security solutions. In D. Kar & M. Syed (Eds.), *Network security, administration and management: Advancing technology and practice* (pp. 217–236). Hershey, PA: Information Science Reference; doi:10.4018/978-1-60960-777-7.ch011

Mitra, S., & Padman, R. (2012). Privacy and security concerns in adopting social media for personal health management: A health plan case study.[JCIT]. *Journal of Cases on Information Technology, 14*(4), 12–26. doi:10.4018/jcit.2012100102

Modares, H., Lloret, J., Moravejosharieh, A., & Salleh, R. (2014). Security in mobile cloud computing. In J. Rodrigues, K. Lin, & J. Lloret (Eds.), *Mobile networks and cloud computing convergence for progressive services and applications* (pp. 79–91). Hershey, PA: Information Science Reference; doi:10.4018/978-1-4666-4781-7.ch005

Mohammadi, S., Golara, S., & Mousavi, N. (2012). Selecting adequate security mechanisms in e-business processes using fuzzy TOPSIS.[IJFSA]. *International Journal of Fuzzy System Applications, 2*(1), 35–53. doi:10.4018/ijfsa.2012010103

Mohammed, L. A. (2012). ICT security policy: Challenges and potential remedies. In *Cyber crime: Concepts, methodologies, tools and applications* (pp. 999–1015). Hershey, PA: Information Science Reference; doi:10.4018/978-1-61350-323-2.ch501

Molok, N. N., Ahmad, A., & Chang, S. (2012). Online social networking: A source of intelligence for advanced persistent threats.[IJCWT]. *International Journal of Cyber Warfare & Terrorism, 2*(1), 1–13. doi:10.4018/ijcwt.2012010101

Monteleone, S. (2011). Ambient intelligence: Legal challenges and possible directions for privacy protection. In C. Akrivopoulou & A. Psygkas (Eds.), *Personal data privacy and protection in a surveillance era: Technologies and practices* (pp. 201–221). Hershey, PA: Information Science Reference; doi:10.4018/978-1-60960-083-9.ch012

Moralis, A., Pouli, V., Grammatikou, M., Kalogeras, D., & Maglaris, V. (2012). Security standards and issues for grid computing. In N. Preve (Ed.), *Computational and data grids: Principles, applications and design* (pp. 248–264). Hershey, PA: Information Science Reference; doi:10.4018/978-1-61350-113-9.ch010

Mouratidis, H., & Kang, M. (2011). Secure by design: Developing secure software systems from the ground up.[IJSSE]. *International Journal of Secure Software Engineering*, 2(3), 23–41. doi:10.4018/jsse.2011070102

Murthy, A. S., Nagadevara, V., & De', R. (2012). Predictive models in cybercrime investigation: An application of data mining techniques. In J. Wang (Ed.), *Advancing the service sector with evolving technologies: Techniques and principles* (pp. 166–177). Hershey, PA: Business Science Reference; doi:10.4018/978-1-4666-0044-7.ch011

Nabi, S. I., Al-Ghmlas, G. S., & Alghathbar, K. (2012). Enterprise information security policies, standards, and procedures: A survey of available standards and guidelines. In M. Gupta, J. Walp, & R. Sharman (Eds.), *Strategic and practical approaches for information security governance: Technologies and applied solutions* (pp. 67–89). Hershey, PA: Information Science Reference; doi:10.4018/978-1-4666-0197-0.ch005

Nachtigal, S. (2011). E-business and security. In O. Bak & N. Stair (Eds.), *Impact of e-business technologies on public and private organizations: Industry comparisons and perspectives* (pp. 262–277). Hershey, PA: Business Science Reference; doi:10.4018/978-1-60960-501-8.ch016

Namal, S., & Gurtov, A. (2012). Security and mobility aspects of femtocell networks. In R. Saeed, B. Chaudhari, & R. Mokhtar (Eds.), *Femtocell communications and technologies: Business opportunities and deployment challenges* (pp. 124–156). Hershey, PA: Information Science Reference; doi:10.4018/978-1-4666-0092-8.ch008

Naqvi, D. E. (2011). Designing efficient security services infrastructure for virtualization oriented architectures. In H. Nemati (Ed.), *Pervasive information security and privacy developments: Trends and advancements* (pp. 149–171). Hershey, PA: Information Science Reference; doi:10.4018/978-1-61692-000-5.ch011

Neto, A. A., & Vieira, M. (2011). Security gaps in databases: A comparison of alternative software products for web applications support.[IJSSE]. *International Journal of Secure Software Engineering*, 2(3), 42–62. doi:10.4018/jsse.2011070103

Ngugi, B., Mana, J., & Segal, L. (2011). Evaluating the quality and usefulness of data breach information systems.[IJISP]. *International Journal of Information Security and Privacy*, 5(4), 31–46. doi:10.4018/jisp.2011100103

Nhlabatsi, A., Bandara, A., Hayashi, S., Haley, C., Jurjens, J., & Kaiya, H. … Yu, Y. (2011). Security patterns: Comparing modeling approaches. In H. Mouratidis (Ed.), Software engineering for secure systems: Industrial and research perspectives (pp. 75-111). Hershey, PA: Information Science Reference. doi:10.4018/978-1-61520-837-1.ch004

Nicho, M. (2013). An information governance model for information security management. In D. Mellado, L. Enrique Sánchez, E. Fernández-Medina, & M. Piattini (Eds.), *IT security governance innovations: Theory and research* (pp. 155–189). Hershey, PA: Information Science Reference; doi:10.4018/978-1-4666-2083-4.ch007

Nicho, M., Fakhry, H., & Haiber, C. (2011). An integrated security governance framework for effective PCI DSS implementation.[IJISP]. *International Journal of Information Security and Privacy*, 5(3), 50–67. doi:10.4018/jisp.2011070104

Nobelis, N., Boudaoud, K., Delettre, C., & Riveill, M. (2012). Designing security properties-centric communication protocols using a component-based approach. [IJDST]. *International Journal of Distributed Systems and Technologies*, 3(1), 1–16. doi:10.4018/jdst.2012010101

Ohashi, M., & Hori, M. (2011). Security management services based on authentication roaming between different certificate authorities. In M. Cruz-Cunha & J. Varajao (Eds.), *Enterprise information systems design, implementation and management: Organizational applications* (pp. 72–84). Hershey, PA: Information Science Reference; doi:10.4018/978-1-61692-020-3.ch005

Okubo, T., Kaiya, H., & Yoshioka, N. (2012). Analyzing impacts on software enhancement caused by security design alternatives with patterns.[IJSSE]. *International Journal of Secure Software Engineering*, 3(1), 37–61. doi:10.4018/jsse.2012010103

Oost, D., & Chew, E. K. (2012). Investigating the concept of information security culture. In M. Gupta, J. Walp, & R. Sharman (Eds.), *Strategic and practical approaches for information security governance: Technologies and applied solutions* (pp. 1–12). Hershey, PA: Information Science Reference; doi:10.4018/978-1-4666-0197-0.ch001

Otero, A. R., Ejnioui, A., Otero, C. E., & Tejay, G. (2013). Evaluation of information security controls in organizations by grey relational analysis.[IJDTIS]. *International Journal of Dependable and Trustworthy Information Systems*, 2(3), 36–54. doi:10.4018/jdtis.2011070103

Related References

Ouedraogo, M., Mouratidis, H., Dubois, E., & Khadraoui, D. (2011). Security assurance evaluation and IT systems' context of use security criticality.[IJHCR]. *International Journal of Handheld Computing Research, 2*(4), 59–81. doi:10.4018/jhcr.2011100104

Pal, S. (2013). Cloud computing: Security concerns and issues. In A. Bento & A. Aggarwal (Eds.), *Cloud computing service and deployment models: Layers and management* (pp. 191–207). Hershey, PA: Business Science Reference; doi:10.4018/978-1-4666-2187-9.ch010

Palanisamy, R., & Mukerji, B. (2012). Security and privacy issues in e-government. In M. Shareef, N. Archer, & S. Dutta (Eds.), *E-government service maturity and development: Cultural, organizational and technological perspectives* (pp. 236–248). Hershey, PA: Information Science Reference; doi:10.4018/978-1-60960-848-4.ch013

Pan, Y., Yuan, B., & Mishra, S. (2011). Network security auditing. In D. Kar & M. Syed (Eds.), *Network security, administration and management: Advancing technology and practice* (pp. 131–157). Hershey, PA: Information Science Reference; doi:10.4018/978-1-60960-777-7.ch008

Patel, A., Taghavi, M., Júnior, J. C., Latih, R., & Zin, A. M. (2012). Safety measures for social computing in wiki learning environment.[IJISP]. *International Journal of Information Security and Privacy, 6*(2), 1–15. doi:10.4018/jisp.2012040101

Pathan, A. K. (2012). Security management in heterogeneous distributed sensor networks. In S. Bagchi (Ed.), *Ubiquitous multimedia and mobile agents: Models and implementations* (pp. 274–294). Hershey, PA: Information Science Reference; doi:10.4018/978-1-61350-107-8.ch012

Paul, C., & Porche, I. R. (2011). Toward a U.S. army cyber security culture.[IJCWT]. *International Journal of Cyber Warfare & Terrorism, 1*(3), 70–80. doi:10.4018/ijcwt.2011070105

Pavlidis, M., Mouratidis, H., & Islam, S. (2012). Modelling security using trust based concepts.[IJSSE]. *International Journal of Secure Software Engineering, 3*(2), 36–53. doi:10.4018/jsse.2012040102

Pendegraft, N., Rounds, M., & Stone, R. W. (2012). Factors influencing college students' use of computer security. In H. Nemati (Ed.), *Optimizing information security and advancing privacy assurance: New technologies* (pp. 225–234). Hershey, PA: Information Science Reference; doi:10.4018/978-1-4666-0026-3.ch013

Petkovic, M., & Ibraimi, L. (2011). Privacy and security in e-health applications. In C. Röcker & M. Ziefle (Eds.), *E-health, assistive technologies and applications for assisted living: Challenges and solutions* (pp. 23–48). Hershey, PA: Medical Information Science Reference; doi:10.4018/978-1-60960-469-1.ch002

Picazo-Sanchez, P., Ortiz-Martin, L., Peris-Lopez, P., & Hernandez-Castro, J. C. (2013). Security of EPC class-1. In P. Lopez, J. Hernandez-Castro, & T. Li (Eds.), *Security and trends in wireless identification and sensing platform tags: Advancements in RFID* (pp. 34–63). Hershey, PA: Information Science Reference; doi:10.4018/978-1-4666-1990-6.ch002

Pieters, W., Probst, C. W., Lukszo, Z., & Montoya, L. (2014). Cost-effectiveness of security measures: A model-based framework. In T. Tsiakis, T. Kargidis, & P. Katsaros (Eds.), *Approaches and processes for managing the economics of information systems* (pp. 139–156). Hershey, PA: Business Science Reference; doi:10.4018/978-1-4666-4983-5.ch009

Pirim, T., James, T., Boswell, K., Reithel, B., & Barkhi, R. (2011). Examining an individual's perceived need for privacy and security: Construct and scale development. In H. Nemati (Ed.), *Pervasive information security and privacy developments: Trends and advancements* (pp. 1–13). Hershey, PA: Information Science Reference; doi:10.4018/978-1-61692-000-5.ch001

Podhradsky, A., Casey, C., & Ceretti, P. (2012). The bluetooth honeypot project: Measuring and managing bluetooth risks in the workplace.[IJITN]. *International Journal of Interdisciplinary Telecommunications and Networking*, 4(3), 1–22. doi:10.4018/jitn.2012070101

Pomponiu, V. (2011). Security in e-health applications. In C. Röcker & M. Ziefle (Eds.), *E-health, assistive technologies and applications for assisted living: Challenges and solutions* (pp. 94–118). Hershey, PA: Medical Information Science Reference; doi:10.4018/978-1-60960-469-1.ch005

Pomponiu, V. (2014). Securing wireless ad hoc networks: State of the art and challenges. In *Crisis management: Concepts, methodologies, tools and applications* (pp. 81–101). Hershey, PA: Information Science Reference; doi:10.4018/978-1-4666-4707-7.ch004

Pope, M. B., Warkentin, M., & Luo, X. R. (2012). Evolutionary malware: Mobile malware, botnets, and malware toolkits.[IJWNBT]. *International Journal of Wireless Networks and Broadband Technologies*, 2(3), 52–60. doi:10.4018/ijwnbt.2012070105

Related References

Prakash, S., Vaish, A., Coul, N. G. S., Srinidhi, T., & Botsa, J. (2013). Child security in cyberspace through moral cognition.[IJISP]. *International Journal of Information Security and Privacy, 7*(1), 16–29. doi:10.4018/jisp.2013010102

Pye, G. (2011). Critical infrastructure systems: Security analysis and modelling approach.[IJCWT]. *International Journal of Cyber Warfare & Terrorism, 1*(3), 37–58. doi:10.4018/ijcwt.2011070103

Rahman, M. M., & Rezaul, K. M. (2012). Information security management: Awareness of threats in e-commerce. In M. Gupta, J. Walp, & R. Sharman (Eds.), *Threats, countermeasures, and advances in applied information security* (pp. 66–90). Hershey, PA: Information Science Reference; doi:10.4018/978-1-4666-0978-5.ch004

Rak, M., Ficco, M., Luna, J., Ghani, H., Suri, N., Panica, S., & Petcu, D. (2012). Security issues in cloud federations. In M. Villari, I. Brandic, & F. Tusa (Eds.), *Achieving federated and self-manageable cloud infrastructures: Theory and practice* (pp. 176–194). Hershey, PA: Business Science Reference; doi:10.4018/978-1-4666-1631-8.ch010

Ramachandran, M., & Mahmood, Z. (2011). A framework for internet security assessment and improvement process. In M. Ramachandran (Ed.), *Knowledge engineering for software development life cycles: Support technologies and applications* (pp. 244–255). Hershey, PA: Information Science Reference; doi:10.4018/978-1-60960-509-4.ch013

Ramachandran, S., Mundada, R., Bhattacharjee, A., Murthy, C., & Sharma, R. (2011). Classifying host anomalies: Using ontology in information security monitoring. In R. Santanam, M. Sethumadhavan, & M. Virendra (Eds.), *Cyber security, cyber crime and cyber forensics: Applications and perspectives* (pp. 70–86). Hershey, PA: Information Science Reference; doi:10.4018/978-1-60960-123-2.ch006

Ramamurthy, B. (2014). Securing business IT on the cloud. In S. Srinivasan (Ed.), *Security, trust, and regulatory aspects of cloud computing in business environments* (pp. 115–125). Hershey, PA: Information Science Reference; doi:10.4018/978-1-4666-5788-5.ch006

Raspotnig, C., & Opdahl, A. L. (2012). Improving security and safety modelling with failure sequence diagrams.[IJSSE]. *International Journal of Secure Software Engineering, 3*(1), 20–36. doi:10.4018/jsse.2012010102

Reddy, A., & Prasad, G. V. (2012). Consumer perceptions on security, privacy, and trust on e-portals.[IJOM]. *International Journal of Online Marketing, 2*(2), 10–24. doi:10.4018/ijom.2012040102

Richet, J. (2013). From young hackers to crackers.[IJTHI]. *International Journal of Technology and Human Interaction, 9*(3), 53–62. doi:10.4018/jthi.2013070104

Rjaibi, N., Rabai, L. B., Ben Aissa, A., & Mili, A. (2013). Mean failure cost as a measurable value and evidence of cybersecurity: E-learning case study.[IJSSE]. *International Journal of Secure Software Engineering, 4*(3), 64–81. doi:10.4018/jsse.2013070104

Roberts, L. D. (2012). Cyber identity theft. In *Cyber crime: Concepts, methodologies, tools and applications* (pp. 21–36). Hershey, PA: Information Science Reference; doi:10.4018/978-1-61350-323-2.ch103

Rodríguez, J., Fernández-Medina, E., Piattini, M., & Mellado, D. (2011). A security requirements engineering tool for domain engineering in software product lines. In N. Milanovic (Ed.), *Non-functional properties in service oriented architecture: Requirements, models and methods* (pp. 73–92). Hershey, PA: Information Science Reference; doi:10.4018/978-1-60566-794-2.ch004

Roldan, M., & Rea, A. (2011). Individual privacy and security in virtual worlds. In A. Rea (Ed.), *Security in virtual worlds, 3D webs, and immersive environments: Models for development, interaction, and management* (pp. 1–19). Hershey, PA: Information Science Reference; doi:10.4018/978-1-61520-891-3.ch001

Rowe, N. C., Garfinkel, S. L., Beverly, R., & Yannakogeorgos, P. (2011). Challenges in monitoring cyberarms compliance.[IJCWT]. *International Journal of Cyber Warfare & Terrorism, 1*(2), 35–48. doi:10.4018/ijcwt.2011040104

Rwabutaza, A., Yang, M., & Bourbakis, N. (2012). A comparative survey on cryptology-based methodologies.[IJISP]. *International Journal of Information Security and Privacy, 6*(3), 1–37. doi:10.4018/jisp.2012070101

Sadkhan, S. B., & Abbas, N. A. (2014). Privacy and security of wireless communication networks. In J. Rodrigues, K. Lin, & J. Lloret (Eds.), *Mobile networks and cloud computing convergence for progressive services and applications* (pp. 58–78). Hershey, PA: Information Science Reference; doi:10.4018/978-1-4666-4781-7.ch004

Saedy, M., & Mojtahed, V. (2011). Machine-to-machine communications and security solution in cellular systems.[IJITN]. *International Journal of Interdisciplinary Telecommunications and Networking, 3*(2), 66–75. doi:10.4018/jitn.2011040105

San Nicolas-Rocca, T., & Olfman, L. (2013). End user security training for identification and access management.[JOEUC]. *Journal of Organizational and End User Computing, 25*(4), 75–103. doi:10.4018/joeuc.2013100104

Satoh, F., Nakamura, Y., Mukhi, N. K., Tatsubori, M., & Ono, K. (2011). Model-driven approach for end-to-end SOA security configurations. In N. Milanovic (Ed.), *Non-functional properties in service oriented architecture: Requirements, models and methods* (pp. 268–298). Hershey, PA: Information Science Reference; doi:10.4018/978-1-60566-794-2.ch012

Saucez, D., Iannone, L., & Bonaventure, O. (2014). The map-and-encap locator/identifier separation paradigm: A security analysis. In M. Boucadair & D. Binet (Eds.), *Solutions for sustaining scalability in internet growth* (pp. 148–163). Hershey, PA: Information Science Reference; doi:10.4018/978-1-4666-4305-5.ch008

Schell, B. H., & Holt, T. J. (2012). A profile of the demographics, psychological predispositions, and social/behavioral patterns of computer hacker insiders and outsiders. In *Cyber crime: Concepts, methodologies, tools and applications* (pp. 1461–1484). Hershey, PA: Information Science Reference; doi:10.4018/978-1-61350-323-2.ch705

Schmidt, H. (2011). Threat and risk-driven security requirements engineering. [IJMCMC]. *International Journal of Mobile Computing and Multimedia Communications*, *3*(1), 35–50. doi:10.4018/jmcmc.2011010103

Schmidt, H., Hatebur, D., & Heisel, M. (2011). A pattern-based method to develop secure software. In H. Mouratidis (Ed.), *Software engineering for secure systems: Industrial and research perspectives* (pp. 32–74). Hershey, PA: Information Science Reference; doi:10.4018/978-1-61520-837-1.ch003

Seale, R. O., & Hargiss, K. M. (2011). A proposed architecture for autonomous mobile agent intrusion prevention and malware defense in heterogeneous networks. [IJSITA]. *International Journal of Strategic Information Technology and Applications*, *2*(4), 44–54. doi:10.4018/jsita.2011100104

Sen, J. (2013). Security and privacy challenges in cognitive wireless sensor networks. In N. Meghanathan & Y. Reddy (Eds.), *Cognitive radio technology applications for wireless and mobile ad hoc networks* (pp. 194–232). Hershey, PA: Information Science Reference; doi:10.4018/978-1-4666-4221-8.ch011

Sen, J. (2014). Security and privacy issues in cloud computing. In A. Ruiz-Martinez, R. Marin-Lopez, & F. Pereniguez-Garcia (Eds.), *Architectures and protocols for secure information technology infrastructures* (pp. 1–45). Hershey, PA: Information Science Reference; doi:10.4018/978-1-4666-4514-1.ch001

Sengupta, A., & Mazumdar, C. (2011). A mark-up language for the specification of information security governance requirements.[IJISP]. *International Journal of Information Security and Privacy*, 5(2), 33–53. doi:10.4018/jisp.2011040103

Shaqrah, A. A. (2011). The influence of internet security on e-business competence in Jordan: An empirical analysis. In *Global business: Concepts, methodologies, tools and applications* (pp. 1071–1086). Hershey, PA: Business Science Reference; doi:10.4018/978-1-60960-587-2.ch413

Shareef, M. A., & Kumar, V. (2012). Prevent/control identity theft: Impact on trust and consumers' purchase intention in B2C EC.[IRMJ]. *Information Resources Management Journal*, 25(3), 30–60. doi:10.4018/irmj.2012070102

Sharma, K., & Singh, A. (2011). Biometric security in the e-world. In H. Nemati & L. Yang (Eds.), *Applied cryptography for cyber security and defense: Information encryption and cyphering* (pp. 289–337). Hershey, PA: Information Science Reference; doi:10.4018/978-1-61520-783-1.ch013

Sharma, R. K. (2014). Physical layer security and its applications: A survey. In D. Rawat, B. Bista, & G. Yan (Eds.), *Security, Privacy, Trust, and Resource Management in Mobile and Wireless Communications* (pp. 29–60). Hershey, PA: Information Science Reference; doi:10.4018/978-1-4666-4691-9.ch003

Shaw, R., Keh, H., & Huang, N. (2011). Information security awareness on-line materials design with knowledge maps.[IJDET]. *International Journal of Distance Education Technologies*, 9(4), 41–56. doi:10.4018/jdet.2011100104

Shebanow, A., Perez, R., & Howard, C. (2012). The effect of firewall testing types on cloud security policies.[IJSITA]. *International Journal of Strategic Information Technology and Applications*, 3(3), 60–68. doi:10.4018/jsita.2012070105

Shen, Y., Li, Y., Wu, L., Liu, S., & Wen, Q. (2014). Data protection in the cloud era. In Y. Shen, Y. Li, L. Wu, S. Liu, & Q. Wen (Eds.), *Enabling the new era of cloud computing: Data security, transfer, and management* (pp. 132–154). Hershey, PA: Information Science Reference; doi:10.4018/978-1-4666-4801-2.ch007

Shen, Y., Li, Y., Wu, L., Liu, S., & Wen, Q. (2014). Enterprise security monitoring with the fusion center model. In Y. Shen, Y. Li, L. Wu, S. Liu, & Q. Wen (Eds.), *Enabling the new era of cloud computing: Data security, transfer, and management* (pp. 116–131). Hershey, PA: Information Science Reference; doi:10.4018/978-1-4666-4801-2.ch006

Related References

Shore, M. (2011). Cyber security and anti-social networking. In *Virtual communities: Concepts, methodologies, tools and applications* (pp. 1286–1297). Hershey, PA: Information Science Reference; doi:10.4018/978-1-60960-100-3.ch412

Siddiqi, J., Alqatawna, J., & Btoush, M. H. (2011). Do insecure systems increase global digital divide? In *Global business: Concepts, methodologies, tools and applications* (pp. 2102–2111). Hershey, PA: Business Science Reference; doi:10.4018/978-1-60960-587-2.ch717

Simpson, J. J., Simpson, M. J., Endicott-Popovsky, B., & Popovsky, V. (2012). Secure software education: A contextual model-based approach. In K. Khan (Ed.), *Security-aware systems applications and software development methods* (pp. 286–312). Hershey, PA: Information Science Reference; doi:10.4018/978-1-4666-1580-9.ch016

Singh, S. (2012). Security threats and issues with MANET. In K. Lakhtaria (Ed.), *Technological advancements and applications in mobile ad-hoc networks: Research trends* (pp. 247–263). Hershey, PA: Information Science Reference; doi:10.4018/978-1-4666-0321-9.ch015

Sockel, H., & Falk, L. K. (2012). Online privacy, vulnerabilities, and threats: A manager's perspective. In *Cyber crime: Concepts, methodologies, tools and applications* (pp. 101–123). Hershey, PA: Information Science Reference; doi:10.4018/978-1-61350-323-2.ch108

Spruit, M., & de Bruijn, W. (2012). CITS: The cost of IT security framework. [IJISP]. *International Journal of Information Security and Privacy*, 6(4), 94–116. doi:10.4018/jisp.2012100105

Srinivasan, C., Lakshmy, K., & Sethumadhavan, M. (2011). Complexity measures of cryptographically secure boolean functions. In R. Santanam, M. Sethumadhavan, & M. Virendra (Eds.), *Cyber security, cyber crime and cyber forensics: Applications and perspectives* (pp. 220–230). Hershey, PA: Information Science Reference; doi:10.4018/978-1-60960-123-2.ch015

Srivatsa, M., Agrawal, D., & McDonald, A. D. (2012). Security across disparate management domains in coalition MANETs. In *Wireless technologies: Concepts, methodologies, tools and applications* (pp. 1494–1518). Hershey, PA: Information Science Reference; doi:10.4018/978-1-61350-101-6.ch521

Stojanovic, M. D., Acimovic-Raspopovic, V. S., & Rakas, S. B. (2013). Security management issues for open source ERP in the NGN environment. In *Enterprise resource planning: Concepts, methodologies, tools, and applications* (pp. 789–804). Hershey, PA: Business Science Reference; doi:10.4018/978-1-4666-4153-2.ch046

Stoll, M., & Breu, R. (2012). Information security governance and standard based management systems. In M. Gupta, J. Walp, & R. Sharman (Eds.), *Strategic and practical approaches for information security governance: Technologies and applied solutions* (pp. 261–282). Hershey, PA: Information Science Reference; doi:10.4018/978-1-4666-0197-0.ch015

Sundaresan, M., & Boopathy, D. (2014). Different perspectives of cloud security. In S. Srinivasan (Ed.), *Security, trust, and regulatory aspects of cloud computing in business environments* (pp. 73–90). Hershey, PA: Information Science Reference; doi:10.4018/978-1-4666-5788-5.ch004

Takabi, H., Joshi, J. B., & Ahn, G. (2013). Security and privacy in cloud computing: Towards a comprehensive framework. In X. Yang & L. Liu (Eds.), *Principles, methodologies, and service-oriented approaches for cloud computing* (pp. 164–184). Hershey, PA: Business Science Reference; doi:10.4018/978-1-4666-2854-0.ch007

Takabi, H., Zargar, S. T., & Joshi, J. B. (2014). Mobile cloud computing and its security and privacy challenges. In D. Rawat, B. Bista, & G. Yan (Eds.), *Security, privacy, trust, and resource management in mobile and wireless communications* (pp. 384–407). Hershey, PA: Information Science Reference; doi:10.4018/978-1-4666-4691-9.ch016

Takemura, T. (2014). Unethical information security behavior and organizational commitment. In T. Tsiakis, T. Kargidis, & P. Katsaros (Eds.), *Approaches and processes for managing the economics of information systems* (pp. 181–198). Hershey, PA: Business Science Reference; doi:10.4018/978-1-4666-4983-5.ch011

Talib, S., Clarke, N. L., & Furnell, S. M. (2011). Establishing a personalized information security culture.[IJMCMC]. *International Journal of Mobile Computing and Multimedia Communications*, *3*(1), 63–79. doi:10.4018/jmcmc.2011010105

Talukder, A. K. (2011). Securing next generation internet services. In R. Santanam, M. Sethumadhavan, & M. Virendra (Eds.), *Cyber security, cyber crime and cyber forensics: Applications and perspectives* (pp. 87–105). Hershey, PA: Information Science Reference; doi:10.4018/978-1-60960-123-2.ch007

Tchepnda, C., Moustafa, H., Labiod, H., & Bourdon, G. (2011). Vehicular networks security: Attacks, requirements, challenges and current contributions. In K. Curran (Ed.), *Ubiquitous developments in ambient computing and intelligence: Human-centered applications* (pp. 43–55). Hershey, PA: Information Science Reference; doi:10.4018/978-1-60960-549-0.ch004

Tereshchenko, N. (2012). US foreign policy challenges of non-state actors' cyber terrorism against critical infrastructure.[IJCWT]. *International Journal of Cyber Warfare & Terrorism*, 2(4), 28–48. doi:10.4018/ijcwt.2012100103

Thurimella, R., & Baird, L. C. (2011). Network security. In H. Nemati & L. Yang (Eds.), *Applied cryptography for cyber security and defense: Information encryption and cyphering* (pp. 1–31). Hershey, PA: Information Science Reference; doi:10.4018/978-1-61520-783-1.ch001

Thurimella, R., & Mitchell, W. (2011). Cloak and dagger: Man-in-the-middle and other insidious attacks. In H. Nemati (Ed.), *Security and privacy assurance in advancing technologies: New developments* (pp. 252–270). Hershey, PA: Information Science Reference; doi:10.4018/978-1-60960-200-0.ch016

Tiwari, S., Singh, A., Singh, R. S., & Singh, S. K. (2013). Internet security using biometrics. In *IT policy and ethics: Concepts, methodologies, tools, and applications* (pp. 1680–1707). Hershey, PA: Information Science Reference; doi:10.4018/978-1-4666-2919-6.ch074

Tomaiuolo, M. (2012). Trust enforcing and trust building, different technologies and visions.[IJCWT]. *International Journal of Cyber Warfare & Terrorism*, 2(4), 49–66. doi:10.4018/ijcwt.2012100104

Tomaiuolo, M. (2014). Trust management and delegation for the administration of web services. In I. Portela & F. Almeida (Eds.), *Organizational, legal, and technological dimensions of information system administration* (pp. 18–37). Hershey, PA: Information Science Reference; doi:10.4018/978-1-4666-4526-4.ch002

Touhafi, A., Braeken, A., Cornetta, G., Mentens, N., & Steenhaut, K. (2011). Secure techniques for remote reconfiguration of wireless embedded systems. In M. Cruz-Cunha & F. Moreira (Eds.), *Handbook of research on mobility and computing: Evolving technologies and ubiquitous impacts* (pp. 930–951). Hershey, PA: Information Science Reference; doi:10.4018/978-1-60960-042-6.ch058

Traore, I., & Woungang, I. (2013). Software security engineering – Part I: Security requirements and risk analysis. In K. Buragga & N. Zaman (Eds.), *Software development techniques for constructive information systems design* (pp. 221–255). Hershey, PA: Information Science Reference; doi:10.4018/978-1-4666-3679-8.ch012

Tripathi, M., Gaur, M., & Laxmi, V. (2014). Security challenges in wireless sensor network. In D. Rawat, B. Bista, & G. Yan (Eds.), *Security, privacy, trust, and resource management in mobile and wireless communications* (pp. 334–359). Hershey, PA: Information Science Reference; doi:10.4018/978-1-4666-4691-9.ch014

Trösterer, S., Beck, E., Dalpiaz, F., Paja, E., Giorgini, P., & Tscheligi, M. (2012). Formative user-centered evaluation of security modeling: Results from a case study.[IJSSE]. *International Journal of Secure Software Engineering*, *3*(1), 1–19. doi:10.4018/jsse.2012010101

Tsiakis, T. (2013). The role of information security and cryptography in digital democracy: (Human) rights and freedom. In C. Akrivopoulou & N. Garipidis (Eds.), *Digital democracy and the impact of technology on governance and politics: New globalized practices* (pp. 158–174). Hershey, PA: Information Science Reference; doi:10.4018/978-1-4666-3637-8.ch009

Tsiakis, T., Kargidis, T., & Chatzipoulidis, A. (2013). IT security governance in e-banking. In D. Mellado, L. Enrique Sánchez, E. Fernández-Medina, & M. Piattini (Eds.), *IT security governance innovations: Theory and research* (pp. 13–46). Hershey, PA: Information Science Reference; doi:10.4018/978-1-4666-2083-4.ch002

Turgeman-Goldschmidt, O. (2011). Between hackers and white-collar offenders. In T. Holt & B. Schell (Eds.), *Corporate hacking and technology-driven crime: Social dynamics and implications* (pp. 18–37). Hershey, PA: Information Science Reference; doi:10.4018/978-1-61692-805-6.ch002

Tvrdíková, M. (2012). Information system integrated security. In M. Gupta, J. Walp, & R. Sharman (Eds.), *Strategic and practical approaches for information security governance: Technologies and applied solutions* (pp. 158–169). Hershey, PA: Information Science Reference; doi:10.4018/978-1-4666-0197-0.ch009

Uffen, J., & Breitner, M. H. (2013). Management of technical security measures: An empirical examination of personality traits and behavioral intentions.[IJSODIT]. *International Journal of Social and Organizational Dynamics in IT*, *3*(1), 14–31. doi:10.4018/ijsodit.2013010102

Vance, A., & Siponen, M. T. (2012). IS security policy violations: A rational choice perspective.[JOEUC]. *Journal of Organizational and End User Computing, 24*(1), 21–41. doi:10.4018/joeuc.2012010102

Veltsos, C. (2011). Mitigating the blended threat: Protecting data and educating users. In D. Kar & M. Syed (Eds.), *Network security, administration and management: Advancing technology and practice* (pp. 20–37). Hershey, PA: Information Science Reference; doi:10.4018/978-1-60960-777-7.ch002

Venkataraman, R., Pushpalatha, M., & Rao, T. R. (2014). Trust management and modeling techniques in wireless communications. In D. Rawat, B. Bista, & G. Yan (Eds.), *Security, privacy, trust, and resource management in mobile and wireless communications* (pp. 278–294). Hershey, PA: Information Science Reference; doi:10.4018/978-1-4666-4691-9.ch012

Venkataraman, R., & Rao, T. R. (2012). Security issues and models in mobile ad hoc networks. In K. Lakhtaria (Ed.), *Technological advancements and applications in mobile ad-hoc networks: Research trends* (pp. 219–227). Hershey, PA: Information Science Reference; doi:10.4018/978-1-4666-0321-9.ch013

Viney, D. (2011). Future trends in digital security. In D. Kerr, J. Gammack, & K. Bryant (Eds.), *Digital business security development: Management technologies* (pp. 173–190). Hershey, PA: Business Science Reference; doi:10.4018/978-1-60566-806-2.ch009

Vinod, P., Laxmi, V., & Gaur, M. (2011). Metamorphic malware analysis and detection methods. In R. Santanam, M. Sethumadhavan, & M. Virendra (Eds.), *Cyber security, cyber crime and cyber forensics: Applications and perspectives* (pp. 178–202). Hershey, PA: Information Science Reference; doi:10.4018/978-1-60960-123-2.ch013

von Solms, R., & Warren, M. (2011). Towards the human information security firewall.[IJCWT]. *International Journal of Cyber Warfare & Terrorism, 1*(2), 10–17. doi:10.4018/ijcwt.2011040102

Wall, D. S. (2011). Micro-frauds: Virtual robberies, stings and scams in the information age. In T. Holt & B. Schell (Eds.), *Corporate hacking and technology-driven crime: Social dynamics and implications* (pp. 68–86). Hershey, PA: Information Science Reference; doi:10.4018/978-1-61692-805-6.ch004

Wang, H., Zhao, J. L., & Chen, G. (2012). Managing data security in e-markets through relationship driven access control.[JDM]. *Journal of Database Management, 23*(2), 1–21. doi:10.4018/jdm.2012040101

Warren, M., & Leitch, S. (2011). Protection of Australia in the cyber age.[IJCWT]. *International Journal of Cyber Warfare & Terrorism, 1*(1), 35–40. doi:10.4018/ijcwt.2011010104

Weber, S. G., & Gustiené, P. (2013). Crafting requirements for mobile and pervasive emergency response based on privacy and security by design principles.[IJISCRAM]. *International Journal of Information Systems for Crisis Response and Management, 5*(2), 1–18. doi:10.4018/jiscrm.2013040101

Wei, J., Lin, B., & Loho-Noya, M. (2013). Development of an e-healthcare information security risk assessment method.[JDM]. *Journal of Database Management, 24*(1), 36–57. doi:10.4018/jdm.2013010103

Weippl, E. R., & Riedl, B. (2012). Security, trust, and privacy on mobile devices and multimedia applications. In *Cyber crime: Concepts, methodologies, tools and applications* (pp. 228–244). Hershey, PA: Information Science Reference; doi:10.4018/978-1-61350-323-2.ch202

White, G., & Long, J. (2012). Global information security factors. In H. Nemati (Ed.), *Optimizing information security and advancing privacy assurance: New technologies* (pp. 163–174). Hershey, PA: Information Science Reference; doi:10.4018/978-1-4666-0026-3.ch009

White, S. C., Sedigh, S., & Hurson, A. R. (2013). Security concepts for cloud computing. In X. Yang & L. Liu (Eds.), *Principles, methodologies, and service-oriented approaches for cloud computing* (pp. 116–142). Hershey, PA: Business Science Reference; doi:10.4018/978-1-4666-2854-0.ch005

Whyte, B., & Harrison, J. (2011). State of practice in secure software: Experts' views on best ways ahead. In H. Mouratidis (Ed.), *Software engineering for secure systems: Industrial and research perspectives* (pp. 1–14). Hershey, PA: Information Science Reference; doi:10.4018/978-1-61520-837-1.ch001

Wu, Y., & Saunders, C. S. (2011). Governing information security: Governance domains and decision rights allocation patterns.[IRMJ]. *Information Resources Management Journal, 24*(1), 28–45. doi:10.4018/irmj.2011010103

Yadav, S. B. (2011). SEACON: An integrated approach to the analysis and design of secure enterprise architecture–based computer networks. In H. Nemati (Ed.), *Pervasive information security and privacy developments: Trends and advancements* (pp. 309–331). Hershey, PA: Information Science Reference; doi:10.4018/978-1-61692-000-5.ch020

Yadav, S. B. (2012). A six-view perspective framework for system security: Issues, risks, and requirements. In H. Nemati (Ed.), *Optimizing information security and advancing privacy assurance: New technologies* (pp. 58–90). Hershey, PA: Information Science Reference; doi:10.4018/978-1-4666-0026-3.ch004

Yamany, H. F., Allison, D. S., & Capretz, M. A. (2013). Developing proactive security dimensions for SOA. In *IT policy and ethics: Concepts, methodologies, tools, and applications* (pp. 900–922). Hershey, PA: Information Science Reference; doi:10.4018/978-1-4666-2919-6.ch041

Yan, G., Rawat, D. B., Bista, B. B., & Chen, L. (2014). Location security in vehicular wireless networks. In D. Rawat, B. Bista, & G. Yan (Eds.), *Security, privacy, trust, and resource management in mobile and wireless communications* (pp. 108–133). Hershey, PA: Information Science Reference; doi:10.4018/978-1-4666-4691-9.ch006

Yaokumah, W. (2013). Evaluating the effectiveness of information security governance practices in developing nations: A case of Ghana.[IJITBAG]. *International Journal of IT/Business Alignment and Governance, 4*(1), 27–43. doi:10.4018/jitbag.2013010103

Yates, D., & Harris, A. (2011). International ethical attitudes and behaviors: Implications for organizational information security policy. In M. Dark (Ed.), *Information assurance and security ethics in complex systems: Interdisciplinary perspectives* (pp. 55–80). Hershey, PA: Information Science Reference; doi:10.4018/978-1-61692-245-0.ch004

Yau, S. S., Yin, Y., & An, H. (2011). An adaptive approach to optimizing tradeoff between service performance and security in service-based systems.[IJWSR]. *International Journal of Web Services Research, 8*(2), 74–91. doi:10.4018/jwsr.2011040104

Zadig, S. M., & Tejay, G. (2012). Emerging cybercrime trends: Legal, ethical, and practical issues. In A. Dudley, J. Braman, & G. Vincenti (Eds.), *Investigating cyber law and cyber ethics: Issues, impacts and practices* (pp. 37–56). Hershey, PA: Information Science Reference; doi:10.4018/978-1-61350-132-0.ch003

Zafar, H., Ko, M., & Osei-Bryson, K. (2012). Financial impact of information security breaches on breached firms and their non-breached competitors.[IRMJ]. *Information Resources Management Journal*, 25(1), 21–37. doi:10.4018/irmj.2012010102

Zapata, B. C., & Alemán, J. L. (2013). Security risks in cloud computing: An analysis of the main vulnerabilities. In D. Rosado, D. Mellado, E. Fernandez-Medina, & M. Piattini (Eds.), *Security engineering for cloud computing: Approaches and tools* (pp. 55–71). Hershey, PA: Information Science Reference; doi:10.4018/978-1-4666-2125-1.ch004

Zboril, F., Horacek, J., Drahansky, M., & Hanacek, P. (2012). Security in wireless sensor networks with mobile codes. In M. Gupta, J. Walp, & R. Sharman (Eds.), *Threats, countermeasures, and advances in applied information security* (pp. 411–425). Hershey, PA: Information Science Reference; doi:10.4018/978-1-4666-0978-5.ch021

Zhang, J. (2012). Trust management for VANETs: Challenges, desired properties and future directions.[IJDST]. *International Journal of Distributed Systems and Technologies*, 3(1), 48–62. doi:10.4018/jdst.2012010104

Zhang, Y., He, L., Shu, L., Hara, T., & Nishio, S. (2012). Security issues on outlier detection and countermeasure for distributed hierarchical wireless sensor networks. In A. Pathan, M. Pathan, & H. Lee (Eds.), *Advancements in distributed computing and internet technologies: Trends and issues* (pp. 182–210). Hershey, PA: Information Science Publishing; doi:10.4018/978-1-61350-110-8.ch009

Zheng, X., & Oleshchuk, V. (2012). Security enhancement of peer-to-peer session initiation. In M. Gupta, J. Walp, & R. Sharman (Eds.), *Threats, countermeasures, and advances in applied information security* (pp. 281–308). Hershey, PA: Information Science Reference; doi:10.4018/978-1-4666-0978-5.ch015

Zineddine, M. (2012). Is your automated healthcare information secure? In M. Watfa (Ed.), *E-healthcare systems and wireless communications: Current and future challenges* (pp. 128–142). Hershey, PA: Medical Information Science Reference; doi:10.4018/978-1-61350-123-8.ch006

Compilation of References

Abdul Nasir Khana, M. L. (2012, August). Towards secure mobile cloud computing: A survey. *Future Generation Computer Systems*.

Aberer, K., & Hauswirth, M. (2002). An Overview on Peer-to-Peer Information Systems. In *18th international conference on data engineering* (pp. 1–14).

Abram, T. (2009). The hidden values of it risk management. *Information Systems Audit and Control Association Journal, 2009*(2), 40-45.

Ackermann, T. (2012). *IT Security Risk Management: Perceived IT Security Risks in the Context of Cloud Computing*. Berlin, Germany: Springer-Gabler.

Adam, M. B., & Nalebuff, B. J. (1997). *Co-opetition: A revolution mindset that combines competition and cooperation: The game theory strategy that's changing the game of business*. Currency and Doubleday.

Akyildiz, I. F., Su, W., Sankarasubramaniam, Y., & Cayirci, E. (2002). A survey on sensor networks. *Communications Magazine, IEEE, 40*(8), 102-114.

Al-Ahmad, A. S., & Aljunid, S. A. (2013). Mobile Cloud Computing Testing Review. *IEEE International Conference on Advanced Computer Science Applications and Technologies*.

Ali, M., Samee, U. K., & Athanasios, V. V. (2015). Security in cloud computing: Opportunities and challenges. *Information Sciences, 305*, 357–383. doi:10.1016/j.ins.2015.01.025

Alla, S. B., Ezzati, A., & Mohsen, A. (2012). *Hierarchical Adaptive Balanced Routing Protocol for Energy Efficiency in Heterogeneous Wireless Sensor Networks*. INTECH Open Access Publisher.

Allen, H. (2002). Computer Attack Trends Challenge Internet Security. In *Security & Privacy* (pp. 5–7). IEEE Computer Society.

Alok, K., Yogesh, S., & Viktor, P. (2012). Cryptonite: A Secure and Performant Data. *5th IEEE International Conference on*. IEEE.

Anderson James, P. (1980). *Computer Security Threat Monitoring and Surveillance*. Fort Washington.

Ars Technica. (2012), Why passwords have never been weaker and crackers have never been stronger. *Ars Technica*. Retrieved from http://arstechnica.com/security/2012/08/passwords-under-assault/

Aven, T. (2008). *Risk analysis: Assessing uncertainties beyond expected values and probabilities*. West Sussex, UK: John Wiely and Sons, Ltd. doi:10.1002/9780470694435

Banerjee, D., Saha, S., & Sen, S. (2005). Reciprocal resource sharing in P2P environments. In *Proceedings of the Fourth International Conference on Autonoumous and Multiagent System*. Retrieved from http:// dl.acm.org/citation.cfm?id=1082603

Baron, S. (2015). *Why DBaaS Will Be The Next Big Thing In Database Management*. Retrieved from http://readwrite.com/2015/09/18/dbaas-trend-cloud-database-service

Basar, T. (2010). *Lecture notes on non-cooperative game theory. Electrical and Computer Engineering*. University of Illinois at Urbana Champaign.

Baya, V., Mathaisel, B., & Parker, B. (2010). The cloud you don't know: An engine for new business growth. PWC Journal of Technology Forecast, 1(4), 4-16.

Bernard, S. (1967). Is life a game we are playing. *Ethics*, 77(3), 209–219. doi:10.1086/291634

Bhadauria, R., Chaki, R., Chaki, N., & Sanyal, S. (2012). A Survey on Security Issues in Cloud Computing and Associated Mitigation. *International Journal of Computers and Applications*, 47(June), 47–66. doi:10.5120/7292-0578

Blumenthal. (2010). *Hide and Seek in the Cloud*. IEEE.

Brooks, C. (2009). Amazon EC2 Attack Prompts Customer Support Changes. *Tech Target*. Retrieved October 12, 2009 from: http://searchcloudcomputing.techtarget.com/news/article/0,289142,sid201_gci1371090,00.html

Brotby, W. (2006). *Information security governance: Guidance for boards of directors and executive management*. Rolling Meadows, IL: IT Governance Institute.

Brown, W., Laird, R., Gee, C., & Mitra, T. (2008). *SOA Governance: Achieving and Sustaining Business and IT Agility*. Indianapolis, IN: IBM Press.

Brown, W. A., Moore, G., & Tegan, W. (2006). *SOA governance—IBM's approach.* Somers, NY: IBM Corporation.

Buyya, R. (2014). Introduction to the IEEE Transactions on Cloud Computing. *IEEE Transactions on Cloud Computing, 1*(1), 3–9. doi:10.1109/TCC.2013.13

Camerer, F. C. (2003). *Behavioral game theory: Experiments in strategic interaction.* Princeton University Press.

Campagna, R., Lyer, S., & Krishnan, A. (2013). *Mobile Device Security for Dummies.* Hoboken, NJ: John Wiley & Sons.

Chandrasekaran, I. (Ed.). (2011). Mobile Computing with Cloud. In Advances in Parallel Distributed Computing (pp. 513-522). Berlin: Springer-Verlag GmbH. doi :doi:10.1007/978-3-642-24037-9_51 doi:10.1007/978-3-642-24037-9_51

Chow, R., Jakobsson, M., Masuoka, R., Molina, J., Niu, Y., Shi, E., & Song, Z. (2010). Authentication in the clouds: a framework and its application to mobile users. In *Proceeding ACM Cloud Computing Security Workshop, CCSW '10.* doi:10.1145/1866835.1866837

Cisco. (2016). *Cisco visual networking index: Global mobile data traffic forecast update, 2015-2020.* Retrieved from: http://www.cisco.com/c/en/us/solutions/collateral/service-provider/visual-networking-index-vni/mobile-white-paper-c11-520862.html

Cong, W., Sherman, S. M. C., Qian, W., Kui, R., & Wenjing, L. (2013). Privacy Preserving Public Auditing for Secure Cloud Storage. *IEEE Transactions on Computers, 62*(2), 362–375. doi:10.1109/TC.2011.245

COSO. (2012). Enterprise Risk Management for Cloud Computing. Durham, NC: The Committee of Sponsoring Organizations of the Treadway Commission (COSO).

Crouhy, M., Galai, D., & Mark, R. (2006). *The essentials of risk management.* New York: McGraw-Hill Inc.

CSA (The Cloud Security Alliance). (2011). *Security guidance for critical areas of focus in cloud computing v3.0.* Retrieved September 09, 2015, from https://downloads.cloudsecurityalliance.org/initiatives/guidance/csaguide.v3.0.pdf

CSA. (2012). *CSA identifies 17 key components for effective mobile device management of BYOD and company-owned devices.* Retrieved from: https://cloudsecurityalliance.org/media/news/csa-publishes-mobile-device-management/

Dastjerdi, A. V., & Bakar, K. A. (2009). Distributed Intrusion Detection in Clouds Using Mobile Agents. *Third International Conference on Advanced Engineering Computing and Applications in Sciences* (pp.175 – 180). Sliema. doi:10.1109/ADVCOMP.2009.34

Daswani, N., Garcia-Molina, H., & Yang, B. (2002). Open problems in data-sharing peer-to-peer systems. In Proceedings of the 9th international conference on database theory (pp. 1–15). London, UK: Springer-Verlag. Retrieved from http://dl.acm.org/citation.cfm?id=645505.656446

David, E., & Jon, K. (2010). *Networks, crowds, and markets: Reasoning about a highly connected world*. Cambridge University press.

Davis, C., Schiller, M., & Wheeler, K. (2006). *IT auditing: Using controls to protect information assets*. Emeryville, CA: McGraw-Hill Osborne Media.

De Haes, S., & Grembergen, W. (2009). *Enterprise governance of information technology: Achieving strategic alignment and value*. New York: Springer. doi:10.1007/978-0-387-84882-2

Debar, H., Curry, D., & Feinstein, B. (2004). *The Intrusion Detection Message Exchange Format, Internet Draft Technical Report*. IETF Intrusion Detection Exchange Format Working Group.

Denning, D. E. (1987). An intrusion-detection model. *IEEE Transactions on Software Engineering, SE-13*(2), 222–232. doi:10.1109/TSE.1987.232894

Dev, D., & Baishnab, K. L. (2014). A Review and Research towards Mobile Cloud Computing. *2nd IEEE International Conference on Mobile Cloud Computing, Services, and Engineering*. doi:10.1109/MobileCloud.2014.41

Dikaiakos, Pallis, Katsaros, Mehra, & Vakali. (2009). Cloud Computing – Distributed Internet Computing for IT and Scientific Research. *IEEE Internet Computing*, 10 – 13.

Dinh, H. T., Lee, C., Niyato, D., & Wang, P. (2013). *A survey of mobile cloud computing: Architecture, applications, and approaches*. Wireless Communications and Mobile Computing.

Doelitzscher, F., Reich, C., Knahl, M., & Clarke, N. (2011). An autonomous agent based incident detection system for cloud environments. *Third IEEE International Conference on Cloud Computing Technology and Science* (pp. 197 – 204). doi:10.1109/CloudCom.2011.35

Drobox. (2012). Dropbox Admits Hack, Adds More Security Features. *Information-Week*. Retrieved August 1, 2012 from: http://www.informationweek.com/security/client/dropbox-admits-hack-adds-more-security-f/240004697

Dunn. (2009, February 16). Spammers break Hotmail's CAPTCHA yet again. *Tech-world*.

Eckmann, S., Vigna, G., & Kemmerer, R. (2002). Statl: An attack language for state-based intrusion detection. *Journal of Computer Security*, *10*(1-2), 71–103.

Ektefa M. & Memar S. & Memar F. & Suriani Affendey L. (2010). Intrusion Detection Using Data Mining Techniques. *Information Retrieval & Knowledge Management*, 200-203.

Fan, X., Li, M., Ma, J., Ren, Y., Zhao, H., & Su, Z. (2012, November). Behavior-based reputation management in p2p file-sharing networks. *Journal of Computer and System Sciences*, *78*(6), 1737–1750. doi:10.1016/j.jcss.2011.10.021

FEMA. (1996). *Emergency Management Guide for Business and Industry*. FEMA.

Fernando, Loke, & Rahayu. (2013). Mobile cloud computing: A survey. *Future Generation Computer Systems, 29*(1), 84–106.

Fit'o, J., & Guitart, J. (2014). Introducing Risk Management into Cloud. *Journal of Future Generation Computer Systems*, *32*(1), 41–53.

Fudenberg, D., & Tirole, T. (1991). *Game theory*. MIT Press.

GAO U.S. Government Accountability Office. (2012). *Information security: Better implementation of controls for mobile devices should be encouraged*. Retrieved from: http://www.gao.gov/products/GAO-12-757

Garfinkel, T., & Rosenblum, M. (2005). When Virtual is Harder than Real. HotOS'05, Santa Fe, NM.

Gartner Inc. (2011). *Gartner identifies the Top 10 strategic technologies for2011*. Author.

Global Technology Adoption Index. (2015). Retrieved from: https://powermore.dell.com/2015-global-technology-adoption-index/

Golle, P., Leyton-brown, K., Mironov, I., & Lillibridge, M. (2001). *Incentives for Sharing in Peer-to-Peer Networks*. Electronic Commerce. doi:10.1145/501158.501193

Goranson, H. (1999). *The agile virtual enterprise: Cases, metrics, tools.* New York: Quorum Books.

Grobauer, Walloschek, & Stöcker. (2011). *Understanding Cloud Computing Vulnerabilities.* IEEE.

Gruschka, N., & Jensen, M. (2010). Attack Surfaces: A Taxonomy for Attacks on Cloud Services. *IEEE 3rd International Conference on Cloud Computing*, (pp. 276 – 279).

Guan, Y., Ghorbani, A., & Belacel, N. (2003). Y-Means: A clustering method for intrusion detection. CCECE 2003 CCGEI 2003, (pp. 1083- 1086).

Gul, I., & Hussain, M. (2011). Distributed Cloud Intrusion Detection Model. *International Journal of Advanced Science and Technology*, 71-82.

Gupta, R., & Somani, A. K. (2005). Game theory as a tool to strategize as well as predict nodes behavior in peer-to-peer networks. In *Proceedings of the 11th international conference on parallel and distributed systems* (pp. 244–249). Washington, DC: IEEE Computer Society. Retrieved from doi:doi:10.1109/ICPADS.2005.157 doi:10.1109/ICPADS.2005.157 doi:10.1109/ICPADS.2005.157

Hacigumus, H., Iyer, B., Li, C., & Mehrotra, S. (2004). Efficient Execution of Aggregation Queries over Encrypted Relational Databases. In *Proc. of the 9th International Conference on Database Systems for Advanced Applications (DASFAA'04)*.

Hamlen, Kantarcioglu, Khan, & Thuraisingham. (2010). Security Issues for Cloud Computing. *International Journal of Information Security and Privacy*, 36–48.

Hardin, G. (1968). The Tragedy of the Commons. *Science*, (162): 1243–1248. PMID:5699198

Hardy, G. (2006). New roles for board members on IT. *Governance Journal*, *13*(151), 11–14.

Hardy, K. (1992, Spring). Contingency Planning. *Business Quarterly*, *56*(4), 26–28.

Harnik, D. (2010). *Side Channels in Cloud Services: Deduplication in Cloud Storage.* IEEE.

Harsanyi, J. C. (1967). Games with incomplete information played by bayesian players, parts i, ii, and iii. *Management Science*, *14*(3), 159–182. doi:10.1287/mnsc.14.3.159

HBR (Harvard Business Review). (2011). *Harvard Business Review on Aligning Technology with Strategy.* Boston: Harvard Business School Publishing.

Heberlein, L. (1990). A Network Security Monitor, *Proceedings of the IEEE Computer Society Symposium, Research in Security and Privacy*, (pp. 296-303).

Heinzelman, W. R., Chandrakasan, A., & Balakrishnan, H. (2000, January). Energy-efficient communication protocol for wireless microsensor networks. In *System sciences, 2000.Proceedings of the 33rd annual Hawaii international conference on*. IEEE. doi:10.1109/HICSS.2000.926982

Heinzelman, W. B., Chandrakasan, A. P., & Balakrishnan, H. (2002). An application-specific protocol architecture for wireless microsensor networks. *IEEE Transactions on Wireless Communications*, *1*(4), 660–670. doi:10.1109/TWC.2002.804190

Hillson, D. (2008). Why risk includes opportunity. *The Risk Register Journal of PMI's Risk Management Special Interest Group*, *10*(4), 1–3.

Hoang, T. (2011). *A survey of Mobile Cloud Computing: Architecture, Applications, and Approaches*. Wireless Communications and Mobile Computing.

Horwath, C., Chan, W., Leung, E., & Pili, H. (2012). *Enterprise Risks Management For Cloud Computing*. The Committee of Sponsoring Organizations of the Treadway Commission (COSO).

Hsueh, S. C., Lin, & Lin. (2011). Secure cloud storage for conventional data archive of smart phones. In *Proc. 15th IEEE Int. Symposium on Consumer Electronics*.

Hua, J. S., Huang, D. C., Yen, S. M., & Chena, C. W. (2012). A dynamic game theory approach to solve the free riding problem in the peer-to-peer networks. *Journal of Simulation*, *6*(1), 43–55. doi:10.1057/jos.2011.11

Huang, X., Zhang, M., Kang, & Luo. (2010). MobiCloud: building secure cloud framework for mobile computing and communication. In *Proceeding 5th IEEE International Symposium on Service Oriented System Engineering, SOSE '10*. doi:10.1109/SOSE.2010.20

Hu, H., Wen, Y., Chua, T. S., & Li, X. (2014). Toward Scalable Systems for Big Data Analytics: A Technology Tutorial. *IEEE Access*, *2*, 652–687. doi:10.1109/ACCESS.2014.2332453

Hulme. (2011). *NIST formalizes cloud computing definition, issues security and privacy guidance*. Retrieved from http://www.csoonline.com/article/661620/nistformalizes-cloud-computing-definition-issuessecurity-and-privacy-guidance

IDC. (2015). Retrieved from: https://www.idc.com/prodserv/4Pillars/cloud

IITP. (2013). Cloud computing code of practice version 2. Wellington, New Zealand: Institute of IT Professionals (IITP).

Intel IT Center. (n.d.). *Preparing your Virtualized Data Center for the Cloud.* Intel.

Irazoqui, G., Inci, M. S., Eisenbarth, T., & Sunar, B. (2014). Fine grain Cross-VM Attacks on Xen and VMware are possible!*IEEE Fourth International Conference on Big Data and Cloud Computing (BdCloud),* (pp. 3-5).

ISACA. (2013). COBIT5 for Risk. Rolling Meadows, IL: Information Systems Audit and Control Association (ISACA).

ITU Telecommunication Development Bureau. (2015). *ICT facts and figures.* Retrieved from: https://www.itu.int/en/ITU-D/Statistics/Documents/facts/ICTFacts-Figures2015.pdf

Jansen, W., & Grance, T. (2011). *Guidelines on security and privacy in public cloud computing.* NIST special publication, 800, 144

Jansen, W., & Grance, T. (2011). *NIST Guidelines on Security and Privacy in Public Cloud Computing.* Retrieved from http://csrc.nist.gov/publications/drafts/800-144/DraftSP-800-144_cloud-computing.pdf

Jayaswal, K., Kallakurchi, K., Houde, D., & Shah, D. (2014). *Cloud Computing Black Book.* New Delhi, India: Dreamtech Press.

Jeng, Tseng, Tseng, & Wang. (2010). A Study of CAPTCHA and its Application to User Authentication. *In Proc. of 2nd Intl. Conference on Computational Collective Intelligence: Technologies and Applications.*

Jensen, M., Schwenk, J., Gruschka, N., & Iacono, L. L. (2009). On Technical Security Issues in Cloud Computing. *IEEE International Conference on Cloud Computing,* Bangalore, India. doi:10.1109/CLOUD.2009.60

Jia, W., Zhu, H., Cao, Z., Wei, L., & Lin, X. (2011). SDSM: a secure data service mechanism in mobile cloud computing. In *Proceeding IEEE Conference on Computer Communications Workshops, INFOCOM WKSHPS.*

Jia, W., Zhu, H., Cao, Z., Wei, L., & Lin, X. (2011). SDSM: a secure data service mechanism in mobile cloud computing. In *ProceedingIEEE Conference on Computer Communications Workshops, INFOCOM WKSHPS.* doi:10.1109/INFCOMW.2011.5928784

Jla, W., Zhu, H., Cao, Z., Wei, L., & Lin, X. (2011). SDSM: A secure data service mechanism in mobile cloud computing. In *Proc. IEEE Conference on Computer Communications Workshops, INFOCOM WKSHPS.*

John, H. C. (1994). *Games with incomplete information*. Nobel Lectures.

Julisch, K., & Hall, M. (2010). Security and control in the cloud. Information Security Journal: A Global Perspective, 19(6), 299-309.

Kalpana, P. (2012). Cloud Computing–Wave of the Future. *International Journal of Electronics Communication and Computer Engineering, 3*(3).

Kandori, G., Mailath, M., & Rob, R. (1993). Learning, mutations and long run equilibria in games. *Econometrica, 61*(1), 27–56. doi:10.2307/2951777

Kannan, A., Maguire, G. Q., Sharma, A., & Schoo, P. (2012). Genetic Algorithm based Feature Selection Algorithm for Effective Intrusion Detection in Cloud Networks. *IEEE 12th International Conference on Data Mining Workshops*, (pp. 416 – 423).

Kant, H., & Ruchi, D. (2014). *The Proliferation of Smart Devices on Mobile Cloud Computing. Haroldstr*. Düsseldorf, Germany: LAP Lambert Academic Publishing.

Karakaya, M., Korpeoglu, I., & Ulusoy, O. (2008, February). Counteracting free riding in Peer-to-Peer networks. *Computer Networks, 52*(3), 675–694. doi:10.1016/j.comnet.2007.11.002

Karnwal, T., Sivakumar, T., & Aghila, G. (2012). A comber approach to protect cloud computing against XML DDoS and HTTP DDoS attack. *IEEE Students Conference on Electrical, Electronics and Computer Science (SCEECS)*, (pp. 1 - 5). doi:10.1109/SCEECS.2012.6184829

Kaufman, & Potter. (n.d.). *Monitoring Cloud Computing by Layer, Part 1*. IEEE.

Khalid, O., Khan, M., Khan, S., & Zomaya, A. (2014). *Omni Suggest: A Ubiquitous Cloud based Context Aware Recommendation System for Mobile Social Networks. IEEE Transactions on Services Computing.*

Khalil, M., Khreishah, A., Bouktif, S., & Ahmad, A. (2013). Security Concerns in Cloud Computing. *10th International Conference on Information Technology: New Generations* (pp. 411 – 416).

Khanai, & Kulkarni. (2014). Crypto-Coding as DES-Convolution for Land Mobile Satellite Channel. *International Journal of Computer Applications, 86*(18).

Khanai, R., Kulkarni, G.H., & Torse, D.A. (2014). Neural Crypto-Coding as DES: Turbo over Land Mobile Satellite (LMS) channel. In *Communications and Signal Processing (ICCSP),2014International Conference.*

Kirsch. (2012). *The Future of Authentication.* IEEE.

Krishna, K., & Roger, L. (2012). *Database as a Service (DBaaS) using Enterprise Manager 12c.* Oracle Open World.

Krishnan, R., & Smith, M. (2002). *The economics of peer-to-peer networks.* Heinz Research Showcase, Carnegie Mellon University. Retrieved from http://repository.cmu.edu/heinzworks/52/

Krishnan, R., & Smith, M. D. (2008). The Virtual Commons: Why Free-Riding Can Be Tolerated in File Sharing Networks. In *International Conference on Information Systems.*

Kulkarni & Khannai. (n.d.). Addressing Mobile Cloud Computing Security Issues: A Survey. *IEEE ICCSP 2015 Conference.*

Kumar, R., & Rajalakshmi. (2013). Mobile Cloud Computing Standard approach to protecting and securing of mobile cloud ecosystems. *IEEE International Conference on Computer Sciences and Applications.*

Leavitt, N. (2009). Is Cloud Computing Really Ready for Prime Time? *IEEE Computer.*

Li, H. (2010, October). An energy efficient routing algorithm for heterogeneous wireless sensor networks. In *Computer Application and System Modeling (ICCASM), 2010 International Conference on* (Vol. 3, pp. V3-612). IEEE.

Li, W., Chen, J., & Zhou, B. (2011). Game theory analysis for graded punishment mechanism restraining free-riding in p2p networks. In *Proceedings of the 2011 international symposium on computer science and society* (pp. 262–266). Washington, DC: IEEE Computer Society. doi:doi:10.1109/ISCCS.2011.78 doi:10.1109/ISCCS.2011.78

Lindsey, S., & Raghavendra, C. S. (2002). PEGASIS: Power-efficient gathering in sensor information systems. In *Aerospace conference proceedings, 2002. IEEE* (Vol. 3, pp. 3-1125). IEEE.

LinkedIn. (2012a). An Update On Taking Steps To Protect Our Members. *LinkedIn Blog.* June 7, 2012, Retrieved from: http://blog.linkedin.com/2012/06/09/an-update-on-taking-steps-to-protect-our-members/

LinkedIn. (2012b). LinkedIn sued over hacking incident that exposed six million passwords. *Gigaom.* Retrieved from: http://gigaom.com/2012/06/19/linkedin-will-connect-with-a-federal-judge-after-privacy-breach/

Lo, Huang, & Ku. (2010). A Cooperative Intrusion Detection System Framework for Cloud Computing Networks. *ICPPW '10 Proceedings of the 201039th International Conference on Parallel Processing Workshops.* IEEE Computer Society.

Luca, F., Michele, C., & Mirco, M. (2012). Lecture Notes in Computer Science: Vol. 7672. *Supporting security and consistency for Cloud database.* Cyberspace Safety and Security.

Luo, S. (2011). *Virtualization security for Cloud computing service.* IEEE.

Maciej, B., Gracjan, J., Michał, J., Stanisław, J., Tomasz, J., & Norbert, M. ... Sławomir, Z. (2013). National Data Storage 2: Secure Storage Cloud with Efficient and Easy Data Access. Academic Press.

Mailath, G. J., & Larry, S. (2006). *Repeated games and reputations: long-run relationships.* Oxford University Press. doi:10.1093/acprof:oso/9780195300796.001.0001

Manjeshwar, A., & Agrawal, D. P. (2001, April). TEEN: a routing protocol for enhanced efficiency in wireless sensor networks. In Null (p. 30189a). IEEE. doi:10.1109/IPDPS.2001.925197

Marks, N. (2015). *The myth of IT risk.* Retrieved September 09, 2015, from https://normanmarks.wordpress.com/2015/08/28/the-myth-of-it-risk/

Marler, J. (2011). *Securing the Cloud: Addressing Cloud Computing Security Concerns with Private Cloud.* Rackspace Knowledge Centre. Retrieved from http://www.rackspace.com/knowledge_center/privatecloud/securing-the-cloud-addressing-cloud-computingsecurity-concerns-with-private-cloud

Marwell, G., & Ames, R. (1979). Experiments in the provision of public goods: Resources, interest, group size, and the free-rider problem. *American Journal of Sociology, 84.*

Mastorakis, G., Mavromoustakis, C., & Pallis, E. (2015). *Resource Management of Mobile Cloud Computing Networks and Environments.* Hershey, PA: IGI Global. doi:10.4018/978-1-4666-8225-2

McConnell, M., & Hamilton, B. A. (2002). Information Assurance in the Twenty-First Century. *Security & Privacy, IEEE. Computers & Society,* 16–19.

Mell, P., & Grace, T. (2011). The NIST Definition of Cloud Computing. Gaithersburg, MD: National Institute of Standards and Technology (NIST). doi:doi:10.6028/NIST.SP.800-145 doi:10.6028/NIST.SP.800-145

Mell. (2012). What's Special about Cloud Security?. *IEEE, IT Pro*, 6 – 8.

Menken, I., & Blokdijk, G. (2008). *Virtualization: The complete cornerstone guide to virtualization best practices*. Brisbane, Australia: Emereo Pty Ltd.

Merkle, R. C. (1989). A Certified Digital Signature, Advances in Cryptology - CRYPTO '89. *9th Annual International Cryptology Conference Proceedings*, *435*, 218–238.

Metz, C. (2009). DDoS Attack Rains Down on Amazon Cloud. *The Register*. Retrieved from: http://www.theregister.co.uk/2009/10/05/amazon_bitbucket_outage/

Mingqiang, Z., Hui, H., & Qian, W. (2012). A Graph-based Clustering Algorithm for Anomaly Intrusion Detection. *The 7th International Conference on Computer Science & Education (ICCSE)*, (pp. 1311- 1314).

Moeller. (2013). *Executive's guide to IT Governance: Improving Systems Processes with Service Management*. John Wiley & Sons.

Mohammed, A., & Eric, P. (2011). Using Multi Shares for Ensuring Privacy in Database-as-a-Service. *Proceedings of 44th Hawaii International Conference on System Sciences*.

Moorthy, M., & Sathiyabama, S. (2012). A Study of Intrusion Detection using Data Mining. *IEEE-International Conference On Advances In Engineering, Science And Management (ICAESM)*, (pp. 8-15).

Moreno-Vozmediano, Montero, & Llorente. (n.d.). *Key Challenges in Cloud Computing to Enable the Future Internet of Services*. IEEE. .10.1109/MIC.2012.69

Morris, P. (1994). *Introduction to game theory*. Springer New York. doi:10.1007/978-1-4612-4316-8

Motahari-Nezhad, Bartolini, Graupner, Singhal, & Spence. (2010). IT Support Conversation Manager: A Conversation-Centered Approach and Tool for Managing Best Practice IT Processes. *Proceedings of the 2010 14thIEEE International Enterprise Distributed Object Computing Conference*.

Mrmol, F. G., & Prez, G. M. (2009). Security threats scenarios in trust and reputation models for dis-tributed systems. *Computers & Security*, *28*(7), 545–556. doi:10.1016/j.cose.2009.05.005

Munir. (2015). Security Model for Cloud Database as a Service (DBaaS). *IEEE Proceedings of the International Conference on Cloud Computing Technologies and Applications.*

Nash, J. (1951). Non-cooperative games. *The Annals of Mathematics, 54,* 286–295.

Nithiavathy, R. (2013). Data Integrity and Data Dynamics with Secure Storage Service in Cloud. *Proceedings of the 2013 International Conference on Pattern Recognition, Informatics and Mobile Engineering.* IEEE. doi:10.1109/ICPRIME.2013.6496459

Oberheide, J., Veeraraghavan, K., Cooke, E., & Jahanian, F. (2008). Virtualized in-cloud security services for mobile devices. In *Proceedings of the 1st Workshop on Virtualization in Mobile Computing (MobiVirt).* doi:10.1145/1622103.1629656

Oracle Corporation. (2011). *Database as a Service: Reference Architecture – An Overview.* Author.

Osbourne, M. J. (2003). *An introduction to game theory.* Oxford University Press.

Paper, W. (2010). *Mobile Cloud Computing Solution Brief.* AEPONA.

Parker, D. B. (1998). *Fighting Computer Crime: A new Framework for Protecting Information.* New York: John Wiley & Sons Inc.

Pauley. (2010). Cloud Provider Transparency – An empirical evaluation. *IEEE Computer and Reliability Societies.*

Pavel, L. (2012). *Game theory for control of optical networks, static and dynamic game theory: Foundations and applications.* Springer Science. doi:10.1007/978-0-8176-8322-1

Pearson, S. (2009). Taking account of privacy when designing cloud computing services. *CLOUD '09 Proc. of ICSE Workshop on Software Engineering Challenges of Cloud Computing,* (pp. 44-52). IEEE. doi:10.1109/CLOUD.2009.5071532

Perez, R., van Doorn, L., & Sailer, R. (2008). Virtualization and hardware-based security. *IEEE Security and Privacy, 6*(5), 24–31. doi:10.1109/MSP.2008.135

Philip, J., & Levine, D. K. (2001). Evolution and information in a gift-giving game. *Journal of Economic Theory, 100*(1), 1–21. doi:10.1006/jeth.2001.2823

Portokalidis, G., Homburg, P., Anagnostakis, K., & Bos, H. (2010). Paranoid Android: versatile protection for smartphones. In *Proceedings of the 26thAnnual Computer Security Application Conference (ACSAC).*

Portokalidis, G., Homburg, P., Anagnostakis, K., & Bos, H. (2010). Paranoid Android: versatile protection for smartphones. In *Proceedings of the 26th Annual Computer Security Application Conference (ACSAC)*.

Prabakar Muniyandi, A., Rajeswari, R., & Rajaram, R. (2011). Network Anomaly Detection by Cascading K-Means Clustering and C4.5 Decision Tree algorithm. *International Conference on Communication Technology and System Design*, (pp. 176 – 182).

Pradeep, , Kumar, N., & Shekar, R. S., Reddy, & Krishna, C. (2012, February). Preventive measures for malware in p2p networks. *International Journal of Engineering Research and Applications*, 2(1), 391–400.

Qaisar, S., & Khawaja, K. F. (2012). Cloud Computing: Network/Security Threats and counter measures. *Interdisciplinary Journal of Contemporary Research in Business, 3*(9), 1323 – 1329.

Qiao Yan, Yu, Gong, & Li. (n.d.). Software-Defined Networking (SDN) and Distributed Denial of Service (DDoS) Attacks in Cloud Computing Environments: A Survey, Some Research Issues, and Challenges. *IEEE Communications Surveys & Tutorials*.

Qingji, Z., Shouhuai, X., & Giuseppe, A. (2012). Efficient Query Integrity for Outsourced Dynamic Databases. CCSW'12, Raleigh, NC.

Qing, L., Zhu, Q., & Wang, M. (2006). Design of a distributed energy-efficient clustering algorithm for heterogeneous wireless sensor networks. *Computer Communications*, 29(12), 2230–2237. doi:10.1016/j.comcom.2006.02.017

Rappaport, T. S. (1996). *Wireless communications: principles and practice* (vol. 2). Prentice Hall PTR.

Rashmi, V. D., & Kailas, K. D. (2015). Understanding DDoS Attack & its Effect in Cloud Environment. *Proceedings of 4th International Conference on Advances in Computing, Communication and Control (ICAC3'15)*, (pp 202–210).

Rassan, & AlShaher. (2014). Securing Mobile Cloud Computing using Biometric Authentication (SMCBA). *IEEE International Conference on Computational Science and Computational Intelligence*.

Robert, W. (1971). Computing equilibria of n-person games. *Society for Industrial and Applied Mathematics Journal, 21*(1), 80–87. doi:10.1137/0121011

Rodrigues, J., Lin, K., & Lioret, J. (2013). *Mobile Networks and Cloud Computing Convergence for Progressive Services and Applications*. Hershey, PA: IGI Global.

Rohrmann. (2000). Risk Information and Communication. *The Australasian Journal of Disaster and Trauma Studies, 2.*

Roschke, S., Cheng, F., & Meinel, C. (2009). Intrusion Detection in the Cloud. *Eighth IEEE International Conference on Dependable, Autonomic and Secure Computing*, (pp. 729 – 734).

Roussopoulos, M., Baker, M., & Rosenthal, D. S. H. (2004). 2 P2P or Not 2 P2P? In *Iptps'04 proceedings of the third international conference on peer-to-peer systems* (pp. 1–6).

Rowstron, A., & Druschel, P. (2001). Pastry: Scalable, decentralized object location and routing for large-scale peer-to-peer systems. In In ifip/acm international conference on distributed system platforms (pp. 329–350).

Saad, W., Han, Z., Debbah, M., & Hjrungnes, A. (2009). Coalitional game theory for communication networks: A tutorial. IEEE Signal Processing Magazine, 77–97. doi:doi:10.1109/MSP.2009.000000 doi:10.1109/MSP.2009.000000

Sabahi, F. (2011). *Cloud Computing Security Threats and Responses*. IEEE.

Sahoo, J. (2010). *Virtualization: A Survey on Concepts, Taxonomy and Associated Security Issues*. IEEE.

Saleh, S., Ahmed, M., Ali, B. M., Rasid, M. F. A., & Ismail, A. (2014). A survey on energy awareness mechanisms in routing protocols for wireless sensor networks using optimization methods. *Transactions on Emerging Telecommunications Technologies*, 25(12), 1184–1207. doi:10.1002/ett.2679

Sanaei, Z., Abolfazli, S., Gani, A., & Buyya, R. (2014). Heterogeneity in Mobile Cloud Computing: Taxonomy and Open Challenges. *IEEE Communications Surveys and Tutorials*, 16(1), 369–392. doi:10.1109/SURV.2013.050113.00090

Sathya, G., & Vasanthraj, K. (2013). Network Activity Classification Schema in IDS and Log Audit for Cloud Computing. *International Conference on Information Communication and Embedded Systems (ICICES)*, (pp. 502 – 506). doi:10.1109/ICICES.2013.6508322

Schlarman, S. (2009). IT risk exploration: The IT risk management taxonomy and evolution. *Information Systems Audit and Control Association Journal, 2009*(3), 27-30.

Schulze, H. (2015). *Cloud Security Spotlight Report – 2015, Crowd Research Partners*. Retrieved from: http://go.alertlogic.com/

Segal, S. (2011). *Corporate Value of Enterprise Risk Management: The Next Step in Business Management*. Hoboken, NJ: John Wiley & Sons.

Sen, J. (2014). *Security and Privacy Issues in Cloud Computing. In Architectures and Protocols for Secure Information Technology Infrastructures* (pp. 1–45). IGI Global. doi:10.4018/978-1-4666-4514-1.ch001

Shalan, M. A. (2010). Managing IT Risks in Virtual Enterprise Networks: A Proposed Governance Framework. In S. Panios (Ed.), *Managing Risk in Virtual Enterprise Networks: Implementing Supply Chain Principles* (pp. 115–136). Hershey, PA: IGI Global. doi:10.4018/978-1-61520-607-0.ch006

Shanna, & Garg. (2014). *An Efficient and Secure Data Storage in Mobile Cloud Computing through RSA and Hash Function*. IEEE.

Shawish, A., & Salama, M. (2014). Cloud Computing: Paradigms and Technologies. In F. Xhafa & N. Bessis (Eds.), *Inter-cooperative Collective Intelligence: Techniques and Applications* (pp. 39–67). Berlin, Germany: Springer-Verlag. doi:10.1007/978-3-642-35016-0_2

Shelton, T. (2013). *Business Models for the Social Mobile Cloud: Transform Your Business Using Social Media, Mobile Internet, and Cloud Computing*. Indianapolis, IN: John Wiley & Sons. doi:10.1002/9781118555910

Shih-Fen, C., Daniel, V. M., Reeves, Y., & Michael, P. W. (2004). Notes on equilibria in symmetric games. In *International joint conference on autonomous agents multi agent systems, 6th workshop on game theoretic and decision theoretic agents*.

Shinder, D. (2013). *Selecting a Cloud Provider*. Retrieved September 09, 2015, from http://www.cloudcomputingadmin.com/articles-tutorials/architecture-design/selecting-cloud-provider-part1.html

Shoham, Y., & Leyton-Brown, K. (2009). *Multiagent system: Algorithmic, game theoretic and logic foundation*. New York: Cambridge University Press.

Slaviero, M. (2009). BlackHat presentation demo vids: Amazon, part 4 of 5. *AMI-Bomb*. Retrieved from: http://www.sensepost.com/blog/3797.html

Smaragdakis, G., Matta, I., & Bestavros, A. (2004, August). SEP: A stable election protocol for clustered heterogeneous wireless sensor networks. In *Second international workshop on sensor and actor network protocols and applications (SANPA 2004)* (pp. 1-11).

Snapp, Brentano, Dias, Goan, Heberlein, Ho, ... Mansur. (1991). DIDS (Distributed Intrusion Detection System) – Motivation, Architecture, and An Early Prototype. In *Proceeding of the14th National Computer Security Conference.*

Sosinsky, B. (2011). *Cloud Computing Bible.* Hoboken, NJ: Wiley Publishing, Inc.

Soyata, T. (2015). *Enabling Real-Time Mobile Cloud Computing through Emerging Technologies.* Hershey, PA: IGI Global. doi:10.4018/978-1-4666-8662-5

Stantchev, V., & Stantcheva, L. (2013). Applying IT-Governance Frameworks for SOA and Cloud Governance. In M. D. Lytras, D. Ruan, R. D. Tennyson, P. Ordonez De Pablos, F. J. García Peñalvo, & L. Rusu (Eds.), *Information Systems, E-learning, and Knowledge Management Research* (pp. 398–407). Berlin, Germany: Springer-Verlag. doi:10.1007/978-3-642-35879-1_48

Subramanian, K. (2011). *Private, Public and Hybrid Clouds. Whitepaper.* Trend Micro.

Suo, H. (2013). *Security and Privacy in Mobile Cloud Computing.* IEEE.

Sweeny, J. (1973). An experimental investigation of the free-rider problem. *Social Science Research, 2.*

Szefer, J., & Lee, R. B. (2012). Architectural support for hypervisor-secure virtualization. *The Seventeenth International Conference on Architectural Support for Programming Languages and Operating Systems,* (pp. 437-450).

Takabi, H., Joshi, J. B. D., & Ahn, G.-J. (2010). University of Pittsburgh, Gail – Joon and Ahn Arizona State University, "Security and Privacy Challenges in Cloud Computing Environments. *IEEE Security and Privacy, 8*(6), 24–31. doi:10.1109/MSP.2010.186

Theodore, B., Lawrence, B., & Hal, R. V. (1986). On the private provision of public goods. *Journal of Public Economics,* (29): 25–49.

Turban, E., Leidner, D., McLean, E., & Wetherbe, J. (2008). *Information technology for management: Transforming organizations in the digital economy.* John Wiley and Sons Inc.

Varadharajan, V. (2014). *Security as a Service Model for Cloud Environment. IEEE Transactions on Network and Service Management, 11(1).*

Veijalainen, J. (2007). Autonomy, Heterogeneity, Trust, Security, and Privacy in Mobile P2P Environments. *International Journal of Security and Its Applications, 1*(1), 57–72.

Vice, P. (2015). *Should IT Risks Be Part of Corporate Governance?* Retrieved September 09, 2015, from http://insurance-canada.ca/blog/2015/08/30/should-it-risks-be-part-of-corporate-governance/

Vice, P. (2015). *Taking risk management from the silo across the enterprise.* Retrieved September 09, 2015, from http://www.aciworldwide.com/-/media/files/collateral/aci_taking_risk_mgmt_from_silo_across_enterprise_tl_us_0211_4572.pdf

Vieira, K., Schulter, A., & Westphall, C. (2009). Westphall, Ca. (2009). Intrusion Detection Techniques in Grid and Cloud Computing Environment. *IT Professional, IEEE. Computers & Society, 26.*

Vogt, P., Nentwich, F., Jovanovic, N., Kirda, E., Kruegel, C., & Vigna, G. (n.d.). Cross-Site Scripting Prevention with Dynamic Data Tainting and Static Analysis. *Proceedings of the Network and Distributed System.*

Wang, Cao, Ren, & Lou. (2011). Enabling Secure and Efficient Ranked Keyword Search over Outsourced Cloud Data. *IEEE Transactions on Parallel and Distributed Systems.*10.1109/TPDS.2011.282

Wang, H., Wu, S., Chen, M., & Huazhong, W. W. (2014, March). Secunty ProtectIOn between Users and the Mobile Media Cloud. *IEEE Communications Magazine, 52*(3), 73–79. doi:10.1109/MCOM.2014.6766088

Wang, S. & Wang, X. (2010). In-device spatial cloaking for mobile user privacy assisted by the cloud. In *Proceeding 11th International Conference on Mobile Data Management, MDM '10.*

Wang, S. S., & Chen, Z. P. (2013). LCM: A link-aware clustering mechanism for energy-efficient routing in wireless sensor networks. *Sensors Journal, IEEE, 13*(2), 728–736. doi:10.1109/JSEN.2012.2225423

Wang, S., & Wang, X. (2010). In-device spatial cloaking for mobile user privacy assisted by the cloud. In *Proceeding 11th Interantional Conference on Mobile Data Management.*

Wired. (2012a). How Apple and Amazon Security Flaws Led to My Epic Hacking. *Wired*. Retrieved from: http://www.wired.com/gadgetlab/2012/08/apple-amazon-mat-honan-hacking/all/

Wired. (2012b). Amazon Quietly Closes Security Hole After Journalist's Devastating Hack. *Wired*. Retrieved from: http://www.wired.com/gadgetlab/2012/08/amazon-changes-policy-wont-add-new-credit-cards-to-accounts-over-the-phone/

Xiao, S., & Gong, W. (2010). Mobility can help: protect user identity with dynamic credential. In *Proceeding 11th International Conference on Mobile Data Management, MDM '10*. doi:10.1109/MDM.2010.73

Yang, Wang, Wang, Tan & Yu. (2011). Provable data possession of resource constrained mobile devices in cloud computing. *Journal of Networks*, 1033–1040.

Yang, Wang, Wang, Tan, & Yu. (2011). Provable data possession of resource constrained mobile devices in cloud computing. *Journal of Networks*, 1033–1040.

Yu, Z. (2012). Peer-to-peer multimedia sharing based on social norms. *Signal Processing Image Communication*, *27*(5), 383–400. doi:10.1016/j.image.2012.02.003

Zhang, Juels, Reiter, & Ristenpart. (2012). Cross-VM Side Channels and Their Use to Extract Private Keys. ACM Conference on Computer and Communications Security, (pp. 305-316).

Zhang, K., & Antonopoulos, N. (2013, January). A novel bartering exchange ring based incentive mechanism for peer-to-peer systems. *Future Gener. Comput. Syst.*, *29*(1), 361–369. doi: 10.1016/j.future.2011.06.005

Zhang, L. J., & Zhou. (2009). CCOA: Cloud Computing Open Architecture. *IEEE International Conference on Web Services*. Doi:10.1109/ICWS.2009.144

Zhang, X., Schiffman, J., Gibbs, S., Kunjithapatham, A., & Jeong, S. (2009). Securing elastic applications on mobile devices for cloud computing. In *Proceeding ACM workshop on Cloud computing security, CCSW '09*. doi:10.1145/1655008.1655026

Zhao, B. Q., Lui, J. C. S., & Chiu, D.-M. (2012, April). A mathematical framework for analyzing adaptive incentive protocols in p2p networks. *IEEE/ACM Trans. Netw.*, *20*(2), 367–380. doi: 10.1109/TNET.2011.2161770

Zhou, Q., Cao, X., Chen, S., & Lin, G. (2009, December). A solution to error and loss in wireless network transfer. In *Wireless Networks and Information Systems, 2009. WNIS'09. International Conference on* (pp. 312-315). IEEE. doi:10.1109/WNIS.2009.103

Zissis, D., & Lekkas, D. (2012, March). Addressing cloud computing security issues. *Future Generation Computer Systems, 28*(3), 583–592. doi:10.1016/j.future.2010.12.006

Zonouz, Houmansadr, Barthier, Borisov, & Sanders. (2013). Secloud: A cloud based comprehensive and lightweight security solution for smartphones. *Science Direct journal of Computers and Security, 37*, 215-227.

Zonouz, Houmansadr, Barthier, Borisov, & Sanders. (2013). Secloud: A cloud based comprehensive and lightweight security solution for smartphones. *Science Direct Journal of Computers and Security, 37*, 215-227.

About the Contributors

Kashif Munir received his BSc degree in Mathematics and Physics from Islamia University Bahawalpur, Pakistan in 1999. He received his MSc degree in Information Technology from University Sains Malaysia in 2001. He also obtained another MS degree in Software Engineering from University of Malaya, Malaysia in 2005. He completed his PhD in Informatics from Malaysia University of Science and Technology, Malaysia. His research interests are in the areas of Cloud Computing Security, Software Engineering, and Project Management. He has published journal, conference papers and book chapters. Kashif Munir has been in the field of higher education since 2002. After an initial teaching experience with courses in Stamford College, Malaysia for around four years, he later relocated to Saudi Arabia. He worked with King Fahd University of Petroleum and Minerals, KSA from September 2006 till December 2014. He moved into University of Hafr Al-Batin, KSA in January 2015.

* * *

Hassan El Alami received his Specialized Master in Electronic Engineering and Computer Sciences from the Faculty of Sciences Oujda in 2012; He is currently PhD student at National Institute of Posts and Telecommunications (INPT) in Rabat Morocco. His research interests include Wireless Sensor Networks and Internet of Things. He is an IEEE Student Member.

Nadya El Moussaid received a degree on mathematics and informatics, and then received a specialized master on network and systems from faculty of science of Ibn Zohr University; she is currently a Ph.D. candidate in the same university. Her current research interests include the security of computer systems, system protection and virus analysis by formulation of security properties by combining machine learning algorithms and mobile agents.

Lawan A. Mohammed receives his BSC (ED) degree in Mathematics and Education from Ahmadu Bello University, Zaria, Nigeria. He received his MSc degree in Operational Research from University Putra Malaysia. He also obtained an MSc degree in Computer Science from DeMontfort University, UK. He completed his PhD degree in Computer and Communication Systems Engineering from University Putra Malaysia in 2004. His PhD research area was in the field secure network communication particular in the design of authentication protocol for both wired and wireless network.

Abdellah Najid received his Master degrees in Networking and Communication Systems and PhD thesis in Microwaves and Wireless Networking in 1997 from National Polytechnic Institute of Toulouse (INPT) France. He was working as researcher Engineer at French Institute for Research in Computer Science and Automation (INRIA) Labs from 1998 to 2000. Abdellah NAJID research fields are routing Protocols, wireless networking, Microwave and Antennas design. He is full Professor at National Institute of Posts and Telecommunications (INPT) in Rabat Morocco.

Jasmine K. S. received BSc degree in Mathematics from Mahatma Gandhi University, Kerala in 1991, MSc degree in computer science from Kerala University, Kerala in 1994 and M.Phil degree in Computer science from Bharathidasan University, Tamilnadu in 2005. She has completed her PhD in Computer science from Mother Teresa Women's University, Kodaikanal, Tamilnadu in the year 2011. She is currently working as Associate Professor in the Department of MCA, R. V. College of Engineering, Bangalore. Since from 1995, she is working as a lecturer. During 1998-99, she held a visiting faculty position at Visveswarapura College of science, Bangalore. She has authored 70 research papers in the national and international level conferences and journals. She is also reviewer for various journals and conferences. She has written three book chapters and also authored two books in the international level. Ms. Jasmine is the authorized research guide under Visvesvaraya Technological University, Belgaum and guiding three research scholars. Her research interests include Software reuse, Software performance, Software testing, Data mining, Experimental software engineering, Mobile Computing and Cloud Computing.

Mohammad Ali Shalan is Professional Engineer, with 20 years of international experience in telecommunications, cloud computing, enterprise architecture, project management, risk analysis, audit and governance, graduated with a B.Sc. in Electrical Engineering in 1995 from University of Jordan, and acquired a Master degree in Telecommunication Engineering from the same university in 2005.

Darshan Tank did his B.E. in Information Technology from Lukhdhirji Engineering College, Morbi and M.E. in Computer Engineering from Dharmsinh Desai University, Nadiad. At present He is working as Lecturer in IT department at L E College, Morbi, Gujarat. Currently, he is pursuing PhD in CE/IT Engineering at GTU, Ahmedabad. His areas of interest include cloud storage, mobile computing, mobile cloud computing and wireless networks.

Mohammed Onimisi Yahaya is currently an assistant professor at the College of Computer Science and Engineering, University of Hafr Al Batin. He received the Ph.D. degree in computer science and engineering from King Fahd University of Petroleum and Minerals, Dhahran, Saudi Arabia in 2014. His Research interest includes game theory application in modelling interactions behavior in peer-to-peer networks and application of Machine Learning in various disciplines.

Index

A

algorithm based routing protocols 3, 8, 20, 26

B

base station 1-10, 12-15, 17-23, 26-27
big data 41, 145, 169
Business Transformation 43, 62

C

Client enterprises 43, 55-63
cloud-backed infrastructure. 149
Cloud Computing 29, 32-35, 40-45, 48, 50-51, 53-55, 61-70, 72-75, 79-80, 82, 89-91, 121-124, 126-128, 133-135, 143-154, 156-162, 164-169, 173, 179-180
Cloud Databases 169
Cloud security 64, 68, 73-74, 80, 82, 91, 133, 154, 160, 167
Cloud Service Provider (CSP) 55, 71
cluster head 1, 3-4, 6-9, 12-16, 18-19
clustering algorithm 1-3, 8, 20, 25-27, 41
Code of Conduct 61-63, 71
complex interactions 94, 97, 114
Contracting 53, 62
corporate information 44, 153
cyclic multiplicative group 160, 163

D

Database as a Service 169, 171-173, 178, 180

Database security 169
Data Encryption Standard 131-132
DBaaS 170-175, 179-180
Deployment models 67, 128, 148, 157
disaster recovery 74, 84-85

E

energy efficiency 1, 3, 25, 27, 124
Ethics 43-44, 46, 55-56, 59, 61-63, 71, 117

F

false negative 30, 32, 34

G

Game Theory 92, 94, 97-98, 101-102, 111, 114-115, 117-120
Governance 43-52, 54-55, 62-72, 82, 128, 154, 165, 180

H

human behaviour 94, 114

I

Incentives 92-94, 111, 118
International Data Corporation (IDC), 74
intrusion detection system 29-30, 32, 34-35, 40, 42, 134, 166

L

limited processing power 121-122, 144

M

machine learning 29, 31-32, 34-36, 40
manage database-backed apps 170
mathematical framework 92, 94, 97, 114, 120
Maturity 45, 49, 63
Middle Circle (MC) 43, 46, 53, 55, 63, 72
Mobile 27, 29, 32, 34-36, 40, 43-46, 48, 50-52, 54-55, 58, 61-66, 70, 72, 82, 92-93, 120-129, 133, 144-155, 158, 160-163, 165-169, 171, 178-180
Mobile Cloud Computing (MCC) 43-45, 48, 50-51, 55, 62, 65-66, 72, 121-124, 128, 144-146, 148-154, 160-161, 166-167, 179
Mobile Cloud Computing Provider (MCCP) 55, 72
Mobile Computing 64, 70, 72, 92, 121-123, 144-146, 149, 152, 166-167
Mobile Services 121, 144
multiplicative group 160, 163
MySQL 170

N

network lifetime 1-4, 6-8, 17, 20-21, 23, 25-27, 112, 115
Networks 2-4, 25, 27-29, 32, 34, 41, 51, 59, 65-66, 71, 76, 82-83, 92-97, 108, 111, 115, 118-120, 122-124, 130, 142, 145, 147, 149, 152, 154, 166, 168
nodes 2, 4-7, 12-13, 15, 23, 25, 93, 95-96, 112, 114-115, 118
NoSQL 169

P

payoff function. 94, 111
Peer-to-Peer (P2P) 92-97, 108-120

R

rationality assumption 94, 97, 111
regulatory issues 165
Relational Cloud 173

rich application 149
rich mathematical framework 94, 97, 114
Risk 43-55, 62-76, 80-82, 85-87, 89, 91, 96, 128, 133, 137-138, 151-153
risk analysis 49, 64, 68, 70-71, 73, 86-87
risk assessment 49, 55, 67, 71, 73, 86-87
Risk Governance 43-44, 48-52, 55, 62-63, 70, 72
Risk Management 44-47, 49-51, 55, 63-72, 75, 86, 89
routing protocol 1-2, 7-8, 17, 27

S

Security 29-30, 32, 34-35, 40-42, 52, 56-58, 60-61, 64, 67-68, 70-71, 73-77, 79-83, 86, 88-91, 96, 119-123, 125-131, 133-142, 144-161, 165-171, 173-176, 178-180
security challenges 73-75, 96, 128, 154, 169, 173-174, 179
security management 68, 73, 96, 148, 160, 169
senior executives 47, 52, 63
sensitive data 29-30, 32, 40, 76, 82, 131-132, 152, 156, 158, 164
Service models 32, 148, 154
service providers 44, 55, 59-63, 71, 77, 123, 154, 159, 175
stakeholders 46-52, 55, 62-63, 71-72
storage service 123, 160, 163, 180

T

throughput maximization 1-3, 17, 25-26
Top 10 strategic technologies 149, 165
two-factor Web authentication 132-133

V

vulnerabilities 32-33, 53, 73, 86, 148, 151, 158, 165

W

WSNs 1-8, 15, 20-21, 23, 26-27

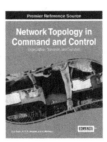

Printed in the United States
By Bookmasters